Paton Thomson, John Stockdale, Isaac Weld, James Storer, Samuel Springsguth

Travels through the States of North America and the Provinces of Upper and Lower Canada during the Years 1795, 1796 and 1797

Vol. 2

Paton Thomson, John Stockdale, Isaac Weld, James Storer, Samuel Springsguth

Travels through the States of North America and the Provinces of Upper and Lower Canada during the Years 1795, 1796 and 1797
Vol. 2

ISBN/EAN: 9783337346010

Printed in Europe, USA, Canada, Australia, Japan

Cover: Foto ©Andreas Hilbeck / pixelio.de

More available books at **www.hansebooks.com**

TRAVELS

THROUGH THE STATES

OF

NORTH AMERICA,

AND THE

PROVINCES OF

UPPER AND LOWER CANADA,

DURING

THE YEARS 1795, 1796, AND 1797.

By ISAAC WELD, Junior.

SECOND EDITION.

ILLUSTRATED AND EMBELLISHED WITH SIXTEEN PLATES.

IN TWO VOLUMES.
VOL. II.

LONDON:
PRINTED FOR JOHN STOCKDALE, PICCADILLY.

1799.

CONTENTS

To VOLUME II.

LETTER XXVIII.

Leave Quebec.—Convenience of travelling between that City and Montreal.—Post Houses.—Calashes.—Drivers.—Canadian Horses very serviceable.—Salutations on arriving at different Post Houses.—Beautiful Prospects from the Road on the Top of the Banks of the St. Lawrence.—Female Peasants.—Style of Farming in Canada.—Considerably improved of late.—Inactivity of Canadians in not clearing more Land.—Their Character contrasted with that of the People of the States.—Arrival at Trois Rivieres.—Description of that Town and its Vicinity.—Visit to the Convent of St. Ursule.—Manufactures of Birch-Bark. — Birch Canoes, how formed. — Leave Trois Rivieres, and reach Montreal - - - - - page 1

CONTENTS.

LETTER XXIX.

The Party make the usual Preparations for ascending the St. Lawrence.—Buffalo Skins.—How used by Travellers.—Difficulty of proceeding to Lake Ontario otherwise than by Water.—Rapids above Montreal.—Village of La Chine.—King's Stores there.—Indian Village on the opposite Side of the River.—Similitude between French Canadians and Indians in Person and Disposition of Mind.—Owing to this the Power of the French over the Indians.— Summary View of the Indians in Lower Canada.—The Party embark in a Bateau at La Chine.—Mode of conducting Bateaux against a strong Current. —Great Exertion requisite—Canadians addicted to smoking.—How they measure Distances.—Description of Lake St. Louis.—Clouds of Insects over Reed Banks.—Party encamps on l'Isle Perot.—Passage of Rapids called Les Cascades—Their tremendous Appearance.—Description of the Village of the Hill of Cedars.—Rapids du Coteau du Lac.—Wonderful Rapidity of the Current.—Party encamps.—Lake St. Francis.—Point au Baudet.—L'Isle aux Raisins.—Island in the River still the Property of the Indians.—

Not

CONTENTS.

Not determined yet whether in the British Territory or that of the States.—Party encamps.—Storm.—Unpleasant Situation of the Party.—Relieved.—Continue the Voyage.—Account of more Rapids.—Canals and Locks at different Places on the River St. Lawrence.—Immense Flights of Pigeons.—Emigration of Squirrels and Bears.—Oswegatchee River and Fort la Galette described.—Advantageous Position of the latter.—Current above this gentle.—Bateaux sail on all Night.—Songs of the Canadians.—Good Ear for Music.—Lake of a Thousand Isles.—Arrival at Kingston on Lake Ontario.—Observations on the Navigation of the St. Lawrence.—The St. Lawrence compared with the Mississippi.—A View of the different Rivers which open a Water Communication between the Great Lakes and the Atlantic.—Great Superiority of the St. Lawrence over all the rest.—Of the Lake Trade. - - page 19

LETTER XXX.

Description of the Town of Kingston.—Formerly called Fort Cadaraqua.—Extensive Trade carried on here.—Nature of it.—Inhabitants very hospitable.

hospitable.—Harbours on Lake Ontario.—Ships of War on that Lake.—Merchant Vessels.—Naval Officers.—Expence of building and keeping up Vessels very great.—Why.— No Iron Mines yet opened in the Country.—Copper may be more easily procured than Iron.—Found in great Quantities on the Borders of Lake Superior.—Embark in a Trading Vessel on Lake Ontario.—Description of that Lake.—A Septennial Change in the Height of the Waters said to be observable—also a Tide that ebbs and flows every two Hours.—Observations on these Phenomena.—Voyage across the Lake similar to a Sea Voyage.---Come in Sight of Niagara Fort.—Land at Mississaguis Point.—Mississaguis Indians.—One of their Chiefs killed in an Affray.—How treated by the British Government.—Their revengeful Disposition.—Mississaguis good Hunters.—How they kill Salmon.—Variety of Fish in the Lakes and Rivers of Canada.—Sea Wolves.—Sea Cows.—Description of the Town of Niagara or Newark.—The present Seat of Government.—Scheme of removing it elsewhere.—Unhealthiness of the Town of Niagara and adjacent Country.—Navy Hall.—Fort of Niagara surrendered pursuant to Treaty.—Description

3

tion

CONTENTS. vii

tion of it.—Defcription of the other Forts furrendered to the People of the United States.— Shewn not to be fo advantageous to them as was expected.—Superior Pofition of the new British Pofts pointed out -   -   -   page 64

LETTER XXXI.

Defcription of the River and Falls of Niagara and the Country bordering upon the navigable Part of the River below the Falls   -   page 108

LETTER XXXII.

Defcription of Fort Chippeway.—Plan in meditation to cut a Canal to avoid the Portage at the Falls of Niagara.—Departure from Chippeway.—Intenfe Heat of the Weather.—Defcription of the Country bordering on Niagara River above the Falls.—Obfervations on the Climate of Upper Canada.—Rattlefnakes common in Upper Canada.—Fort Erie.—Miferable Accommodation there.—Squirrel hunting.—Seneka Indians.—Their Expertnefs at the Ufe of the Blowgun.—Defcription of the Blow-gun.—Excurfion to the Village of the Senekas.—Whole Nation abfent.

absent.—Passage of a dangerous Sand Bar at the Mouth of Buffalo Creek.—Sail from Fort Erie. —Driven back by a Storm.—Anchor under Point Abineau.—Description of the Point.— Curious Sand Hills there.—Bear hunting.— How carried on.—Dogs, what Sort of, used.— Wind changes.—The Vessel suffers from the Storm whilst at Anchor.—Departure from Point Abineau.—General Description of Lake Erie.— Anecdote.—Reach the Islands at the Western End of the Lake.—Anchor there.—Description of the Islands.—Serpents of various Kinds found there.—Rattlesnakes. — Medicinal Uses made of them.—Fabulous Accounts of Serpents.—Departure from the Islands.—Arrival at Malden. —Detroit River - - page 135

LETTER XXXIII.

Description of the District of Malden.—Establishment of a new British Post there.—Island of Bois Blanc.—Difference between the British and Americans respecting the Right of Possession.— Block Houses, how constructed.—Captain E—'s Farm.—Indians.—Description of Detroit River,

CONTENTS.

ver, and the Country bordering upon it.—Town of Detroit.—Head Quarters of the American Army.—Officers of the Western Army.—Unsuccessful Attempt of the Americans to impress upon the Minds of the Indians an Idea of their Consequence.—Of the Country round Detroit.— Doubts concerning our Route back to Philadelphia.—Determine to go by Presqu' Isle.—Departure from Detroit - - page 170

LETTER XXXIV.

Presents delivered to the Indians on the Part of the British Government.—Mode of distributing them.—Reasons why given.—What is the best Method of conciliating the good Will of the Indians.—Little Pains taken by the Americans to keep up a good Understanding with the Indians. —Consequences thereof.—War between the Americans and Indians.—A brief Account of it.— Peace concluded by General Wayne.—Not likely to remain permanent.—Why.—Indian Manner of making Peace described - - page 192

LET-

LETTER XXXV.

A brief Account of the Persons, Manners, Character, Qualifications, mental and corporeal, of the Indians; interspersed with Anecdotes page 224

LETTER XXXVI.

Departure from Malden.—Storm on Lake Erie.— Driven back amongst the Islands.—Shipwreck narrowly avoided.—Voyage across the Lake.— Land at Fort Erie.—Proceed to Buffalo Creek. —Engage Indians to go through the Woods.— Set out on Foot.—Journey through the Woods. —Description of the Country beyond Buffalo Creek.—Vast Plains.—Grand Appearance of the Trees here.—Indian Dogs.—Arrival at the Settlements on Genesee River.—First Settlers.— Their general Character.—Description of the Country bordering on Genesee River.—Fevers common in Autumn.—Proceed on Foot to Bath - - - - - page 296

CONTENTS.

LETTER XXXVII.

Account of Bath.—Of the Neighbourhood.—Singular Method taken to improve it.—Speculators.—Description of one, in a Letter from an American Farmer.—Conhorton Creek.—View of the Navigation from Bath downwards.— Leave Bath for Newtown.— Embark in Canoes.—Stranded in the Night.—Seek for Shelter in a neighbouring House.—Difficulty of procuring Provisions.—Resume our Voyage.—Lochartsburgh.—Description of the eastern Branch of the Susquehannah River.—French Town.—French and Americans ill suited to each other.—Wilkesbarré.—Mountains in the Neighbourhood.— Country thinly settled towards Philadelphia.— Description of the Wind-Gap in the Blue Mountains.—Summary Account of the Moravian Settlement at Bethlehem.—Return to Philadelphia - - - - - - page 332

LETTER XXXVIII.

Leave Philadelphia.—Arrive at New York.— Visit Long Island.—Dreadful Havoc by the Yellow

CONTENTS.

low Fever.—Dutch Inhabitants suspicious of Strangers.— Excellent Farmers.— Number of Inhabitants.—Culture of Corn.—Immense Quantities of Grouse and Deer.—Laws to protect them.—Increase of the same.—Decrease of Beavers.—New York agreeable to Strangers.— Conclusion - - - - - 367

TRAVELS, &c.

LETTER XXVIII.

Leave Quebec.—Convenience of Travelling between that City and Montreal.—Post Houses. —Calashes.— Drivers.— Canadian Horses very serviceable.—Salutations on arriving at different Post Houses.—Beautiful Prospects from the Road on the Top of the Banks of the St. Lawrence.—Female Peasants.—Style of Farming in Canada.—Considerably improved of late.—Inactivity of Canadians in not clearing more Land.—Their Character contrasted with that of the People of the States.—Arrival at Trois Rivieres.—Description of that Town and its Vicinity.—Visit to the Convent of St. Ursule.—Manufactures of Birch-Bark. —Birch Canoes, how formed.—Leave Trois Rivieres, and reach Montreal.

Montreal, August.

HAVING remained in Quebec and the neighbourhood as long as we could, consistently with the plan which we had formed of vifiting the Falls of Niagara, and returning again into the States before the commencement of winter, we fet out for Montreal by land.

In no part of North America can a traveller proceed fo commodioufly as along this road between Quebec and Montreal; a regular line of poft houfes, at convenient diftances from each other, being eftablifhed upon it, where calafhes or carioles, according to the feafon, are always kept in readinefs. Each poft-mafter is obliged to have four calafhes, and the fame number of carioles; and befides thefe, as many more are generally kept at each ftage by perfons called aids-de-pofte, for which the poft-mafter calls when his own happen to be engaged. The poftmafter has the exclufive privilege of furnifhing thefe carriages at every ftage, and, under a penalty, he muft have them ready in a quarter of an hour after they are demanded by a traveller, if it be day-light, and in half an hour fhould it be in the night. The drivers are bound to take you on at the rate of two leagues an hour. The charge for a calafh with a fingle horfe is one fhilling Halifax * currency per league; no gratuity is expected by the driver.

The

---

* According to Halifax currency, which is the eftablifhed currency of Lower Canada, the dollar pafies for five fhillings.

The post calashes are very clumsily built, but upon the whole we found them easy and agreeable carriages; they are certainly far superior to the American stage waggons, in which, if persons wish to travel with comfort, they ought always to set out provided with cushions for their hips and elbows, otherwise they cannot expect but to receive numberless contusions before they get to the end of their journey.

The horses in Canada are mostly small and heavy, but extremely serviceable, as is evident from those employed for the post carriages being in general fat and very brisk on the road, notwithstanding the poor fare and ill usage they receive. They are seldom rubbed down; but as soon as they have performed their journey are turned into a field, and there left until the next traveller arrives, or till they are wanted to perform the work of the farm. This is contrary to the regulations of the post, according to which the horses should be kept in the stable, in perfect readiness for travellers; however, I do not recollect that we were at

---

The silver coins current in Canada are dollars, halves, quarters, eighths, and sixteenths of dollars, pistareens, Spanish coins somewhat less valuable than quarter dollars, and French and English crowns and half crowns. Gold coins pass only as bullion by weight. British and Portugal gold coins are deemed the best; next to them those of Spain, then those of France.

any place detained much beyond the quarter of an hour prescribed, notwithstanding that the people had frequently to send for their horses, more than a mile, to the fields where they were employed. When the horses happened to be at a distance, they were always brought home in a full gallop, in order to avoid complaints; they were yoked in an instant, and the driver set off at the rate of nine or ten miles an hour; a little money, indeed, generally induces them to exceed the established rate; this, however, does not always answer, but play upon their vanity and you may make them go on at what rate you please, for they are the vainest people, perhaps, in the world. Commend their great dexterity in driving, and the excellence of the Canadian horses, and it seldom fails to quicken your pace at least two or three miles an hour; but if you wish to go in a gallop, you need only observe to your companion, so as to be overheard by the driver, that the Canadian calashes are the vilest carriages on earth, and so heavy that you believe the people are afraid the horses would fall down and break their necks if they attempted to make them go as fast as in other countries; above all, praise the carriages and drivers of the United States. A few remarks of this sort at once discompose the tempers

tempers of the drivers, and their paffion is conftantly vented in lafhes on their horfes.

To haften the fpeed of their horfes they have three expreffions, rifing above each other in a regular climax. The firft, "Marche," is pronounced in the ufual tone of voice; "Marche-donc," the fecond, is pronounced more haftily and louder; if the horfe is dull enough not to comprehend this, then the "Marche-donc," accompanied with one of Sterne's magical words, comes out, in the third place, in a fhrill piercing key, and a fmart lafh of the whip follows. From the frequent ufe made by the drivers of thefe words, the calafhes have received the nickname of "marche-doncs."

The firft poft houfe is nine miles from Quebec, which our drivers, of their own accord, managed to reach in one hour. No fooner were we in fight of it, than the poftmafter, his wife in her clofe French cap, and all the family, came running out to receive us. The foremoft driver, a thin fellow of about fix feet high, with a queue bound with eel fkins that reached the whole way down his back, immediately cracked his whip, and having brought his calafh to the door, with a great air he leapt out, bowed refpectfully at a diftance to the hoftefs, then advancing with his hat off, paid her a few compliments, and

kiffed

kissed both her cheeks in turn, which she presented to him with no small condescension. Some minutes are generally spent thus at every post house in mutual congratulations on meeting, before the people ever think of getting a fresh carriage ready.

The road between Quebec and Montreal runs, for the most part, close upon the banks of the River St. Lawrence, through those beautiful little towns and villages seen to so much advantage from the water; and as the traveller passes along, he is entertained with prospects, if possible, superior to those which strike the attention in sailing down the river.

For the first thirty or forty miles in the way from Quebec, the views are in particular extremely grand. The immense River St. Lawrence, more like a lake confined between ranges of mountains than a river, appears at one side rolling under your feet, and as you look down upon it from the top of the lofty banks, the largest merchant vessels scarcely seem bigger than fishing boats; on the other side, steep mountains, skirted with forests, present themselves to the view at a distance, whilst, in the intermediate space, is seen a rich country, beautifully diversified with whitened cottages and glittering spires, with groves of trees and cultivated fields, watered by innumerable little streams: groups of the peasantry,

try, bufied as we paffed along in getting in the harveft, which was not quite over, diffufed an air of cheerfulnefs and gaiety over the fcene, and heightened all its charms.

The female French peafants are in general, whilft young, very pretty, and the neat fimplicity of their drefs in fummer, which confifts moftly of a blue or fcarlet bodice without fleeves, a petticoat of a different colour, and a ftraw hat, makes them appear extremely interefting; like the Indians, however, they lofe their beauty very prematurely, and it is to be attributed much to the fame caufe, namely, their laborious life, and being fo much expofed to the air, the indolent men fuffering them to take a very active part in the management of the farms.

The ftyle of farming amongft the generality of the French Canadians has hitherto been very flovenly; manure has been but rarely ufed; the earth juft lightly turned up with a plough, and without any other preparation the grain fown; more than one half of the fields alfo have been left without any fences whatfoever, expofed to the ravages of cattle. The people are beginning now, however, to be more induftrious, and better farmers, owing to the increafed demand for grain for exportation, and to the advice and encouragement given to them by the Englifh merchants at Quebec and Montreal, who fend agents through the country to the farmers to buy up all the corn they can fpare. The farmers are bound to have their corn ready by a certain day on the banks of the St. Lawrence, and bateaux are then fent by the merchants to receive and convey it to the port where it is to be fhipped,

All the fettlements in Lower Canada lie contiguous to the River St. Lawrence : in no place perhaps do they extend farther back than twelve miles from it, except along the banks of the River St. Jean, the River des Prairies, and fome other navigable ftreams falling into the St. Lawrence. This is owing to the difpofition of the French Canadians, who, like the Germans, are fond of living near each other ; nay more, as long as the farm of the father will admit of a divifion, a fhare of it is given to the fons when they are grown up, and it is only when the farm is exceedingly fmall, or the family numerous, that they ever think of taking up a piece of frefh land from the feignior. In this refpect a wonderful difference appears between their conduct and that of the young people of the United States, particularly of thofe of New England, who, as foon as they are grown up, immediately emigrate, and bury themfelves in the woods, where, perhaps, they are five or fix hundred

hundred mies diftant from every relation upon earth: yet a fpirit of enterprize is not wanting amongft the Canadians; they eagerly come forward, when called upon, to traverfe the immenfe lakes in the weftern regions; they laugh at the dreadful ftorms on thofe prodigious bodies of water; they work with indefatigable perfeverance at the oar and the pole in ftemming the rapid currents of the rivers; nor do they complain, when, on thefe expeditions, they happen to be expofed to the inclemency of the feafons, or to the fevereft pangs of hunger. The fpirit of the Canadian is excited by vanity; he delights in talking to his friends and relatives of the excurfions he has made to thofe diftant regions; and he glories in the perils which he has encountered: his vanity would not be gratified by chopping down trees and tilling the earth; he deems this therefore merely a fecondary purfuit, and he fets about it with reluctance: felf intereft, on the contrary, it is that roufes the citizen of the ftates into action, and accordingly he haftily emigrates to a diftant part of the country, where he thinks land is in the moft rifing ftate, and where he hopes to be able the fooneft to gratify a paffion to which he would readily make a facrifice of every focial tie, and of all that another man would hold dear.

On

On the second day of our journey from Quebec to Montreal we reached Trois Rivieres, lying nearly midway between the two places. This town is situated on the banks of the St. Lawrence, close to the mouth of the River St. Maurice, the largest of upwards of thirty that fall into the St. Lawrence, on the north-west side alone, between Quebec and Montreal. This river, before it unites with the St. Lawrence, is divided into three streams by two large islands, so that to a person sailing past its mouth it appears as if three distinct rivers disembogued at the one spot; from hence it is that the town of Trois Rivieres receives its name.

The St. Maurice is not navigable for large vessels, neither is it for sloops more than a few miles above its mouth. In bateaus and canoes, however, it may be ascended nearly to its source; from whence, if credit is to be given to the accounts of the Indians, the distance is not very great to the head of navigable rivers that fall into Hudson's Bay; at a future day, therefore, if ever the dreary and inhospitable waste through which it passes shall put on a different aspect from what it now wears, and become the abode of human beings instead of wild beasts, the St. Maurice may be esteemed a river of the first importance in a commercial point of view; at present there are a few
scattered

scattered settlements on each side of it, from its mouth as far as the iron works, which are about nine miles distant from Trois Rivieres; beyond that the country is but little known except to Indians.

Trois Rivieres contains about two hundred and fifty or three hundred houses, and ranks as the third town, in point of size, in the provinces. It is one of the oldest settlements in the country, and its founder, it is said, calculated upon its becoming in a short time a city of great extent. It has hitherto, however, increased but very slowly in size, and there is no reason to imagine that it will increase more rapidly in future, at least until the country bordering upon the St. Maurice becomes settled, a period that may be very distant. The bank of iron ore in the neighbourhood, by the manufacture of which it was expected that the town would suddenly become opulent, is now nearly exhausted; nor do we find that this bank has ever furnished more ore than was sufficient to keep one small forge and one small foundry employed at intervals. The fur trade also, from which so much benefit was expected, is now almost wholly centered at Quebec and Montreal; it is merely the small quantity of furs brought down the St. Maurice, and some of the northern rivers that fall into the St. Lawrence, nearer to the town of Trois Rivieres than to Quebec or Montreal, that is shipped there. These furs are laden on board the Montreal ships, which stop opposite to the town as they go down the river.

The country in the vicinity of Trois Rivieres has been represented by some French travellers as wonderfully fertile, and as one of the most agreeable parts of Canada; but it is totally the reverse. It is a level barren tract, and so sandy, that in walking along many of the streets of the town, and the roads in the neighbourhood, you sink into the sand at every step above the ankles. The sand is of a whitish colour, and very loose. The air also swarms with musquitoes, a certain proof of the low damp situation of the place. In none of the other inhabited parts of Canada, except in the neighbourhood of Lake St. Charles, were we ever annoyed with these troublesome insects. In Quebec, indeed, and Montreal, they are scarcely ever seen.

The streets in Trois Rivieres are narrow, and the houses in general small and indifferent; many of them are built of wood. There are two churches in the town, the one an English episcopalian, the other a large Roman catholic parish church, formerly served by the Recollets, or Franciscan friars, but the order is now extinct in Trois Rivieres. The old monastery of the order, a large stone building,
at

at prefent lies quite deferted; and many of the houfes in the neighbourhood being alfo uninhabited, that part of the town wherein it is fituated has a very dull gloomy afpect. The college or monaftery of the Jefuits, alfo a large old building of ftone in the fame neighbourhood, has been converted into a gaol.

The only religious order at prefent exifting in the town is that of St. Urfule, the fifterhood of which is as numerous as the convent will well permit. It was founded by M. de St. Vallier, bifhop of Quebec, in the year 1677. It is a fpacious building, fituated near that formerly belonging to the Recollets; and annexed to it, under the fame roof, there is an hofpital attended by the nuns. We were introduced to the chaplain of the order, a poor French emigrant curé, an interefting and apparently a moft amiable man, and under his guidance we received permiffion to vifit the convent.

The firft part we entered was the chapel, the doors of which open to the ftreet under a porch. It is very lofty, but the area of it is fmall. The altar, which is grand, and richly ornamented, ftands nearly oppofite to the entrance, and on each fide of it is a lattice, the one communicating with an apartment allotted for fick nuns, the other with the cœur of the chapel. On ringing a fmall bell, a

curtain

curtain at the infide of this laſt lattice was withdrawn, and an apartment diſcovered, ſomewhat larger than the chapel, ſurrounded with pews, and furniſhed with an altar, at the foot of which ſat two of the fiſterhood, with books in their hands, at their meditations. The fair Urſuline, who came to the lattice, ſeemed to be one of thoſe unfortunate females that had at laſt begun to feel all the horrors of confinement, and to lament the raſhneſs of that vow which had ſecluded her for ever from the world, and from the participation of thoſe innocent pleaſures, which, for the beſt and wiſeſt of purpoſes, the beneficent Ruler of the univerſe meant that his creatures ſhould enjoy. As ſhe withdrew the curtain, ſhe caſt a momentary glance through the grating, that imparted more than could be expreſſed by the moſt eloquent words; then retiring in ſilence, ſeated herſelf on a bench in a diſtant part of the cœur. The melancholy and ſorrow pourtrayed in the features of her lovely countenance intereſted the heart in her behalf, and it was impoſſible to behold her without partaking of that dejection which hung over her ſoul, and without deprecating at the ſame time the cruelty of the cuſtom which allows, and the miſtaken zeal of a religion that encourages, an artleſs and inexperienced young creature to renounce a world, of which

which she was destined, perhaps, to be a happy and useful member, for an unprofitable life of solitude, and unremitted penance for sins never committed!

The hospital, which lies contiguous to the chapel, consists of two large apartments, wherein are about twelve or fourteen beds. The apartments are airy, and the beds neat and well appointed. Each bed is dedicated to a particular saint, and over the foot of it is an invocation to the tutelary saint, in large characters, as, " St. Jaques priez pour moi." " St. Jean priez pour moi," &c. The patients are attended by a certain number of the sister-hood appointed for that purpose. An old priest, who appeared to be near his death, was the only person in the hospital when we passed through it; he was seated in an easy chair by the bed-side, and surrounded by a number of the sisters, who paid him the most assiduous attention.

The dress of the Ursulines consists of a black stuff gown; a handkerchief of white linen tied by a running string close round the throat, and hanging down over the breast and shoulders, being rounded at the corners; a head-piece of white linen, which covers half the forehead, the temples, and ears, and is fastened to the handkerchief; a black gauze veil, which conceals half the face only when down,

down, and flows loofely over the fhoulders; and a large plain filver crofs fufpended from the breaft. The drefs is very unbecoming, the hair being totally concealed, and the fhape of the face completely difguifed by the clofe white head-piece.

From the hofpital we were conducted through a long paffage to an agreeable light parlour, the windows of which opened into the gardens of the convent. This was the apartment of the " Superieure," who foon made her appearance, accompanied by a number of the lay fifters. The converfation of the old lady and her protegées was lively and agreeable; a thoufand queftions were afked us refpecting the former part of our tour, and our future deftination; and they seemed by no means difpleafed at having a few ftrangers of a different fex from their own within the walls of the convent. Many apologies were made, becaufe they could not take us through the " interieure," as there was an ordinance againft admitting any vifiters into it without leave from the bifhop; they regretted exceedingly that we had not obtained this leave before we left Quebec. After fome time was fpent in converfation, a great variety of fancy works, the fabrication of the fifterhood, was brought down for our infpection, fome of which it is always expected that ftrangers will

will purchafe, for the order is but poor. We felected a few of the articles which appeared moft curious, and having received them packed up in the neateft manner in little boxes kept for the purpofe, and promifed to preferve them in memory of the fair Urfulines, that handed them to us, we bade adieu to the fuperieure, and returned to our lodgings.

It is for their very curious bark work that the fifters of this convent are particularly diftinguifhed. The bark of the birch tree is what they ufe, and with it they make pocket-books, work-bafkets, drefling-boxes, &c. &c. which they embroider with elk hair died of the moft brilliant colours. They alfo make models of the Indian canoes, and various warlike implements ufed by the Indians.

Nearly all the birch bark canoes in ufe on the St. Lawrence and Utawa Rivers, and on the nearer lakes, are manufactured at Three Rivers, and in the neighbourhood, by Indians. The birch tree is found in great plenty near the town; but it is from the more northern part of the country, where the tree attains a very large fize, that the principal part of the bark is procured that canoes are made with. The bark refembles in fome degree that of the cork tree, but it is of a clofer grain, and alfo much more pliable, for it admits of being rolled up the fame as a piece of cloth. The

Indians of this part of the country always carry large rolls of it in their canoes when they go on a hunting party, for the purpofe of making temporary huts. The bark is fpread on fmall poles over their heads, and faftened with ftrips of elm bark, which is remarkably tough, to ftakes, fo as to form walls on the fides.

The canoes are made with birch bark, as follows: The ribs, confifting of thick tough rods, are firft bound together; then the birch bark is fowed on in as large pieces as poffible, and a thick coat of pitch is laid over the feams between the different pieces. To prevent the bark being injured by the cargo, and to make the canoe ftronger, its infide is lined with two layers of thin pieces of pine, laid in a contrary direction to each other. A canoe made in this manner is fo light that two men could eafily carry one on their fhoulders capable of containing fix people.

The birch canoes made at Three Rivers are put together with the utmoft neatnefs, and on the water they appear very beautiful. They are made from a fize fufficient to hold one man only, to a fize large enough for upwards of twenty. It is wonderful to fee with what velocity a few fkilful men with paddles can take one of thefe canoes of a fize fuitable to their number. In a few minutes they would leave the beft moulded keel boat, conducted by by a similar number of men with oars, far behind. None but experienced persons ought ever to attempt to navigate birch canoes, for they are so light that they are apt to be overset by the least improper movement of the persons in them.

The day after that on which we quitted Trois Rivieres, we reached Montreal once more. The villages between the two places are very numerous, and the face of the country around them is pleasing, so that the eye of the traveller is constantly entertained as he passes on; but there is nothing in this part of the country particularly deserving of mention.

LETTER XXIX.

The Party make the usual Preparations for ascending the St. Lawrence.—Buffalo Skins.—How used by Travellers.—Difficulty of proceeding to Lake Ontario otherwise than by Water.—Rapids above Montreal.—Village of La Chine.—King's Stores there.—Indian Village on the opposite side of the River.—Similitude between French Canadians and Indians in Person and Disposition of Mind.—Owing to this the Power of the French over the Indians.

dians.—*Summary View of the Indians in Lower Canada.—The Party embark in a Bateau at La Chine.—Mode of conducting Bateaux against a strong Current.—Great Exertion requisite—Canadians addicted to smoking. —How they measure Distances.—Description of Lake St. Louis.—Clouds of Insects over Reed Banks.—Party encamps on l'Isle Perot.—Passage of Rapids called Les Cascades—Their tremendous Appearance.—Description of the Village of the Hill of Cedars.—Rapids du Coteau du Lac—Wonderful Rapidity of the Current.—Party encamps.—Lake St. Francis.—Point au Baudet.—L'Isle aux Raisins.—Islands in the River still the Property of the Indians.—Not determined yet whether in the British Territory or that of the States.—Party encamps.—Storm.—Unpleasant Situation of the Party.—Relieved.—Continue the Voyage.—Account of more Rapids.—Canals and Locks at different Places on the River St. Lawrence.—Immense Flights of Pigeons.—Emigration of Squirrels and Bears. —Oswegatchee River and Fort la Galette described.—Advantageous Position of the latter.—Current above this gentle.—Bateaux sail on all Night.—Songs of the Canadians. —Good Ear for Music.—Lake of a Thousand Isles.—Arrival at Kingston on Lake Ontario.—Observations on the Navigation of the*

the St. Lawrence.—The St. Lawrence compared with the Mississipi.—A View of the different Rivers which open a Water Communication between the Great Lakes and the Atlantic.—Great Superiority of the St. Lawrence over all the rest.—Of the Lake Trade.

Kingston, September.

ON arriving at Montreal, our first concern was to provide a large travelling tent, and some camp equipage, buffalo skins*, a store of dried provisions, kegs of brandy and wine, &c. &c. and, in short, to make every usual and necessary preparation for proceeding up the River St. Lawrence. A few days afterwards, we took our passage for Kingston, on board a bateau, which, together with twelve others, the commissary was sending thither for the purpose of bringing down to Quebec the can-

---

* In the western parts of Lower Canada, and throughout Upper Canada, where it is customary for travellers to carry their own bedding with them, these skins are very generally made use of for the purpose of sleeping upon. For upwards of two months we scarcely ever had any other bed than one of the skins spread on the floor and a blanket to each person. The skins are dressed by the Indians with the hair on, and they are rendered by a certain process as pliable as cloth. When the buffalo is killed in the beginning of the winter, at which time he is fenced against the cold, the hair resembles very much that of a black bear; it is then long, straight, and of a blackish colour; but when the animal is killed in the summer, the hair is short and curly, and of a light brown colour, owing to its being scorched by the rays of the sun.

non and ordnance ſtores that had been taken from the different military poſts on the lakes, preparatory to their being delivered up to the United States.

On the north-weſt ſide of the St. Lawrence, except for about fifty miles or thereabouts, are roads, and alſo ſcattered ſettlements, at no great diſtance from each other, the whole way between Montreal and Kingſton, which is ſituated at the eaſtern extremity of Lake Ontario; but no one ever thinks of going thither by land, on account of the numberleſs inconveniencies ſuch a journey would be attended with; indeed, the difficulty of getting horſes acroſs the many deep and rapid rivers falling into the St. Lawrence, would in itſelf be ſufficient to deter travellers from proceeding by land to Kingſton, ſuppoſing even that there were none other to encounter. A water conveyance is by far the moſt eligible, and except only between Quebec and Montreal, it is the conveyance univerſally made uſe of in every part of the country, that is, when people wiſh merely to follow the courſe of the rivers, in the neighbourhood of which alone there are any ſettlements.

The rapids in the St. Lawrence are ſo very ſtrong juſt above Montreal, that the bateaux are never laden at the town, but ſuffered to proceed empty as far as the village of La Chine,

Chine, which ſtands on the iſland of Montreal, about nine miles higher up. The goods are ſent, from Montreal, thither in carts.

La Chine is built on a fine gravelly beach, at the head of a little bay at the lower end of Lake St. Louis, which is a broad part of the river St. Lawrence. A ſmart current ſets down the lake, and owing to it there is generally a conſiderable curl on the ſurface of the water, even cloſe to the ſhore, which, with the appearance of the boats and canoes upon it in motion, gives the place a very lively air. The ſituation of the village is indeed extremely agreeable, and from ſome of the houſes there are moſt charming views of the lake, and of the country at the oppoſite ſide of it. There are very extenſive ſtorehouſes belonging to the King, and alſo to the merchants of Montreal. In the former the preſents for the Indians are depoſited as ſoon as they arrive from England; and prior to their being ſent up the country they are inſpected by the commanding officer of the garriſon of Montreal and a committee of merchants, who are bound to make a faithful report to government, whether the preſents are agreeable to the contract, and as good as could be obtained for the price that is paid for them.

In ſight of La Chine, on the oppoſite ſide of the St. Lawrence, ſtands the village of the

Cache-

Cachenonaga Indians, whom I have already had occasion to mention. The village contains about fifty log houses and a Roman catholic church, built in the Canadian style, and ornamented within with pictures, lamps, &c. in such a manner as to attract the eye as forcibly as possible. The outward shew, and numerous ceremonies of the Roman catholic religion, are particularly suited to the capacities of the Indians, and as but very little restraint is imposed upon them by the missionaries, more of them become converts to that religion than to any other. The worship of the Holy Virgin meets in a very peculiar manner with the approbation of the squaws, and they sing her praises with the most profound devotion.

In this and all the other Indian villages situated in the improved parts of Lower Canada, a great mixture of the blood of whites with that of the aborigines is observable in the persons of the inhabitants; there are also considerable numbers of the French Canadians living in these villages, who have married Indian wives, and have been adopted into the different nations with whom they reside. Many of the French Canadians bear such a close resemblance to the Indians, owing to their dark complexions, black eyes, and long black hair, that when attired in the same habits it is only a person intimately acquainted with the features

of

of the Indians that could diftinguifh the one race of men from the other. The difpofitions of the two people alfo accord together in a very ftriking manner; both are averfe to a fettled life, and to regular habits of induftry; both are fond of roving about, and procuring fuftenance by hunting rather than by cultivating the earth; nature feems to have implanted in their hearts a reciprocal affection for each other; they affociate together, and live on the moft amicable terms; and to this one circumftance more than to any other caufe is to be attributed that wonderful afcendancy which the French were ever known to have over the Indians, whilft they had poffeffion of Canada. It is very remarkable indeed, that in the upper country, notwithftanding that prefents to fuch a very large amount are diftributed amongft the Indians through the hands of the Englifh inhabitants, and that their natural rights are as much refpected by them as they poffibly can be, yet an Indian, even at this day, will always go to the houfe of a poor French farmer in preference to that of an Englifhman.

The numbers of the Cachenonaga nation, in the village near La Chine, are eftimated at one hundred and fifty perfons. The other Indian villages, in the civilized parts of Lower Canada, are, one of the Canafadogas, fituated near the mouth of the Utawas River; one of the

Little

Little Algonquins, near Trois Rivieres; one of the Aberachies, near Trois Rivieres, at the oppofite fide of the river; and one of the Hurons, near Quebec; but none of thefe villages are as large as that of the Cachenonagas. The numbers of the Indians in the lower province have diminifhed very faft of late years, as they have done in every other part of the continent, where thofe of the white inhabitants have increafed; in the whole lower province, at prefent, it is thought that there are not more than twelve hundred of them. Many of thefe Indians are continually loitering about the large towns, in expectation of getting fpirits or bread, which they are extremely fond of, from the inhabitants. No lefs than two hundred, that had come a great diftance in canoes, from the lower parts of the river St. Lawrence, were encamped on Point Levi when we vifited Quebec. Thefe Indians, fqualid and filthy in the extreme, and going about the ftreets every day in large parties, begging, prefented a moft melancholy picture of human nature; and indeed, if a traveller never faw any of the North American Indians, but the moft decent of thofe who are in the habit of frequenting the large towns of Lower Canada, he would not be led to entertain an opinion greatly in their favour. The farther you afcend up the country, and confequently the nearer you fee the Indians

Indians to what they were in their original ſtate, before their manners were corrupted by intercourſe with the whites, the more do you find in their character and conduct deſerving of admiration.

It was on the 28th day of Auguſt that we reached La Chine; the next day the "brigade," as it was called, of bateaux was ready, and in the afternoon we ſet out on our voyage. Three men are found ſufficient to conduct an empty bateau of about two tons burthen up the St. Lawrence, but if the bateau be laden more are generally allowed. They aſcend the ſtream by means of poles, oars, and ſails. Where the current is very ſtrong, they make uſe of the former, keeping as cloſe as poſſible to the ſhore, in order to avoid the current, and to have the advantage of ſhallow water to pole in. The men ſet their poles altogether at the ſame moment, and all work at the ſame ſide of the bateau; the ſteerſman, however, ſhifts his pole occaſionally from ſide to ſide, in order to keep the veſſel in an even direction. The poles commonly uſed are about eight feet in length, extremely light, and headed with iron. On coming to a deep bay or inlet, the men abandon the poles, take to their oars, and ſtrike if poſſible directly acroſs the mouth of the bay; but in many places the current proves ſo ſtrong that it is abſolutely impoſſible to ſtem it by

means

means of oars, and they are obliged to pole entirely round the bays. Whenever the wind is favourable they set their sail; but it is only at the upper end of the river, beyond the rapids, or on the lakes or broad parts of it, where the current is not swift, that the sail by itself is sufficient to impel them forward.

The exertion it requires to counteract the force of the stream by means of poles and oars is so great, that the men are obliged to stop very frequently to take breath. The places at which they stop are regularly ascertained; some of them, where the current is very rapid, are not more than half a mile distant one from the other; others one or two, but none of them more than four miles apart. Each of these places the boatmen, who are almost all French Canadians, denominate " une pipe," because they are allowed to stop at it and fill their pipes. A French Canadian is scarcely ever without a pipe in his mouth, whether working at the oar or plough; whether on foot, or on horseback; indeed, so much addicted are the people to smoking, that by the burning of the tobacco in their pipes they commonly ascertain the distance from one place to another. Such a place, they say, is three pipes off, that is, it is so far off that you may smoke three pipes full of tobacco whilst you go thither. A pipe, in the most general acceptation

ceptation of the word, seemed to be about three quarters of an English mile.

Lake St. Louis, commencing, or rather terminating, at La Chine, for that village stands at the lower end of it, is about twelve miles in length and four in breadth. At its uppermost extremity it receives a large branch of the Utawas River, and also the south-west branch of the River St. Lawrence, which by some geographers is called the River Cadaraqui, and by others the River Iroquois; but in the country, generally speaking, the whole of that river, running from Lake Ontario to the Gulph of St. Lawrence, goes simply under the name of the St. Lawrence.

At the upper end of Lake St. Louis the water is very shallow, owing to the banks of mud and sand washed up by the two rivers. These very extensive banks, are entirely covered with reeds, so that when a vessel sails over them she appears at a little distance to be absolutely sailing over dry land. As we passed along this part of the lake we were enveloped with clouds of little insects, different from any I ever saw before or afterwards in the country; but they are common, it is said, on various parts of the River St. Lawrence. Their size was somewhat larger than that of the gnat; their colour a pure white; and so delicately were they formed, that by the slightest touch

touch they were deftroyed and reduced to powder. They were particularly attracted by any white object, and having once alighted were not to be driven away but by force. The leaves of a book, which I happened to have in my hand, were in a few feconds fo thickly covered by them that it was impoffible to difcern a fingle letter, and no fooner was one fwarm of them brufhed off than a frefh one immediately alighted. Thefe infects have very broad wings in proportion to their fize, and fly heavily, fo that it is only when the air is remarkably calm that they can venture to make their appearance.

About funfet on this, the firft evening of our voyage, we reached the ifland of Perot, fituated at the mouth of the Utawas River. This ifland is about fourteen miles in circumference; its foil is fertile, and it is well cultivated. There are two confiderable villages near its center, but towards Point St. Claire, at its lower extremity, the fettlements are but very few. We landed at the point, and pitched our tent in a meadow which ftood bordering upon the water. Here the bateaux were drawn up, and having been properly fecured, the different crews, amounting in all to upwards of fifty men, divided themfelves into fmall parties, and kindled fires along the fhore, in order to cook their provifions for the fucceeding

ceeding day, and to keep themselves warm during the night. These men, who are engaged in conducting bateaux in Canada, are, as I have before observed, a very hardy race: when the weather is fair, they sleep on the grass at night, without any other covering than a short blanket, scarcely reaching down to their knees; during wet weather a sail or a blanket to the weather side, spread on poles stuck into the ground in an inclined direction, is all the shelter they deem necessary. On setting out each man is furnished with a certain allowance of salted pork, biscuit, pease, and brandy; the pease and biscuit they boil with some of the pork into porridge, and a large vessel full of it, is generally kept at the head of the bateau, for the use of the crew when they stop in the course of the day. This porridge, or else cold fat salted pork, with cucumbers, constitutes the principal part of their food. The cucumber is a fruit that the lower classes of the French Canadians are extremely fond of; they use it however in a very indifferent state, as they never pull it until it has attained a large size, and is become yellow and seedy. Cucumbers thus mellow, chopped into small pieces without being peeled, and afterwards mixed with sour cream, is one of their favourite dishes.

At

At day break on the second morning of our voyage, we quitted the island of Perot, and crossed the Utawas River, in order to gain the mouth of the south-west branch of the St. Lawrence. A tremendous scene is here presented to the view; each river comes rushing down into the lake, over immense rocks, with an impetuosity which, seemingly, nothing can resist. The waves are as high as what are commonly met with in the British Channel during a smart breeze, and the breakers so numerous and dangerous, that one would imagine a bateau could not possibly live in the midst of them; and indeed, unless it were navigated by men intimately acquainted with the place, and very expert at the same time, there would be evident danger of its being filled with water. Several times, as we passed through the breakers, the water dashed over the sides of our bateau. Tremendous and dangerous, however, as the rapids are at this spot, they are much less so than some of those met with higher up the River St. Lawrence.

The water of the Utawas River is remarkably clear, and of a bright greenish colour; that of the St. Lawrence, on the contrary, is muddy, owing to its passing over deep beds of marl for some miles before it enters into Lake St. Louis. For a considerable way down the lake

lake the waters of the two rivers may be plainly diftinguifhed from each other.

The Rapids immediately at the mouth of the fouth-weft branch of the St. Lawrence are called "Les Cafcades," or, "Le Saut de "Trou." In laden bateaux it is no arduous tafk to fhoot down them, but it is impoffible to mount againft the ftream even in fuch as are empty. In order to avoid the laborious tafk therefore of carrying them along the fhore paft the rapids, as ufed formerly to be done, a canal with a double lock has been made here at a great expence. This canal extends but a very little way, not more than fifty yards perhaps. Beyond this there is a fucceffion of other rapids, the firft of which, called "Le Saut de Buiffon' on account of the clofenefs of the woods along the fhores on each fide, is fo ftrong, that in order to pafs it, it is neceffary to lighten the bateaux very confiderably. If the cargoes are large, they are wholly taken out at once, and fent forward in carts to the diftance of a mile and a half, paft all the rapids. The men are always obliged here to get out of the bateaux, and haul them along with ropes, it being wholly impracticable to counteract the force of the current by means of poles alone.

The paffage of thefe rapids is fo very tedious, that we here quitted the bateaux, took our guns

guns in hand, and proceeded on foot to "Le Coteau des Cedres," the Hill of Cedars, about nine miles higher up the river. In going thither you soon lose sight of the few straggling houses at the cascades, and enter the recesses of a remarkably thick wood, whose solemn gloom, together with the loud roaring of the waters at a distance, and the wild appearance of every object around you, inspire the mind with a sort of pleasing horror. As you approach "Le Coteau des Cedres," the country assumes a softer aspect; cultivated fields and neat cottages once more appear in view, and the river, instead of being agitated by tremendous rapids, is here seen gliding on with an even current between its lofty banks.

The village of the Hill of Cedars contains about thirty houses, amongst which we were agreeably surprised to find a remarkably neat and excellent tavern, kept by an English woman. We remained here until three in the afternoon, when we again set off on foot, partly for the pleasure of beholding, from the top of the steep banks, the many noble and beautiful prospects laid open before us, and partly for the pleasure of stopping occasionally to chat with the lively French girls, that, during this delicious season of the year, sat spinning in groups at the doors of the cottages. About five o'clock the bateaux overtook us; but

but after proceeding in them for about two miles, we again landed to efcape the tedious procefs of afcending frefh rapids. Thefe are called the rapids " du Coteau du Lac St. François;" they are feveral miles in length, and though not the moft dangerous, are yet the moft tremendous to appearance of any in the whole river, the white breakers being diftinctly vifible at the diftance of four miles; fome travellers have gone fo far as to reprefent them as even more terrible to the beholder than the falls of Niagara, but this is a very exaggerated account. Boats are here carried down with the ftream at the rate of fourteen or fifteen miles an hour, according to the beft information I could procure on the fubject, though the Canadian boatmen and others declare that they are carried down at the rate of twenty miles in the hour. At fome of the rapids, higher up the river, the current is confiderably fwifter than at this place.

In defcending thefe rapids they pafs through the breakers in the middle of the river, but in going up they keep clofe in to the fhore, on the north-weft fide, and being here fheltered by a numerous clufter of iflands, which break the force of the current, and having the benefit of a fhort canal and locks, they get paft the rapids with lefs difficulty even than they pafs the cafcades. One of the iflands here,

farther

farther removed from the fhore than the reft, is called Prifoners Ifland, having been allotted for the refidence of fome of the American prifoners during the laft war. There were fome buildings on the ifland at that time, but it has been quite deferted fince, on account of the great difficulty of getting to it through the ftrong rapids. During the war, an officer, who had compelled fome of the Canadians, notwithftanding their remonftrances, to make an attempt to reach the ifland at an improper feafon, perifhed, with a great number of men, in going thither. Of the whole party one alone efcaped with his life. The St. Lawrence is here about two miles wide.

This evening, the fecond of our voyage, the bateaux were drawn up for the night at the bottom of " Le Coteau du Lac," the Hill of the Lake, and we pitched our tent on the margin of a wood, at a little diftance from the river. The next morning we proceeded again on foot for about two miles, when we came to a tavern, where we waited the arrival of the bateaux. The people of this houfe were Englifh. From hence upwards there are but few French to be met with.

We were detained here nearly half the day in endeavouring to procure a frefh man, one of the conductor's crew having been feized with an intermittent fever. At laft a man from

from a neighbouring fettlement made his appearance, and we proceeded on our voyage. We now entered Lake St. François, which is about twenty-five miles in length, and five in breadth; but the wind being unfavourable, we were prevented from proceeding farther upon it than Point au Baudet, at which place the boundary line commences, that feparates the upper from the lower province. When the wind comes from the fouth-weft, the immenfe body of water in the lake is impelled directly towards this point, and a furge breaks in upon the beach, as tremendous as is feen on the fea-fhore. There was one folitary houfe here, which proved to be a tavern, and afforded us a well-dreft fupper of venifon, and decent accommodation for the night.

The next day the wind was not more favourable; but as it was confiderably abated, we were enabled to profecute our voyage, coafting along the fhores of the lake. This was a moft laborious and tedious bufinefs, on account of the numerous bays and inlets, which the wind was not fufficiently abated to fuffer us to crofs at their mouths: notwithftanding all the difficulties, however, we had to contend with, we advanced nearly twenty-five miles in the courfe of the day.

At the head of Lake St. François, we landed on a fmall ifland, called "Ifle aux Raifins," on account of the number of wild vines growing upon it. The bateaux men gathered great quantities of the grapes, wherewith the trees were loaded, and alfo an abundance of plumbs, which they devoured with great avidity. Neither of the fruits, however, were very tempting to perfons whofe palates had been accuftomed to the tafte of garden fruits. The grapes were four, and not larger than peas; and as for the plumbs, though much larger in fize, yet their tafte did not differ materially from that of floes.

Beyond L'Ifle aux Raifins, in the narrow part of the river, there are feveral other iflands, the largeft of which called L'ifle St. Regis, is near ten miles in length. All thefe iflands ftill continue in the poffeffion of the Indians, and many of them, being fituated as nearly as poffible in the middle of the river, which here divides the Britifh territory from that of the United States, it yet remains to be determined of what territory they form a part. It is fincerely to be defired that this matter may be adjufted amicably in due time. A ferious altercation has already taken place about an ifland fimilarly fituated in Detroit River, that will be more particularly mentioned hereafter. The Indians not only retain poffeffion of thefe different iflands, but likewife of the whole of the fouth-eaft fhore, of the St. Lawrence,

Lawrence, fituated within the bounds of the United States; they likewife have confiderable ftrips of land on the oppofite fhore, within the Britifh dominions, bordering upon the river; thefe they have referved to themfelves for hunting. The Iroquois Indians have a village upon the Ifle of St. Regis, and another alfo upon the main land, on the fouth-eaft fhore; as we paffed it, feveral of the inhabitants put off in canoes, and exchanged unripe heads * of Indian corn with the men for bread; they alfo brought with them fome very fine wild ducks and fifh, which they difpofed of to us on very moderate terms.

On the fourth night of our voyage we encamped, as ufual, on the main land oppofite the ifland of St. Regis; and the excellent viands we had procured from the Indians having been cooked, we fet down to fupper before a large fire, materials for which are never wanting in this woody country. The night was uncommonly ferene, and we were induced to remain until a late hour in front of our tent, talking of the various occurrences in the courfe of the day; but we had fcarcely retired to reft, when the fky became overcaft,

---

* The heads of Indian corn, before they become hard, are efteemed a great delicacy; the moft approved method of dreffing, is to parboil, and afterwards roaft them.

a dread-

a dreadful storm arose, and by day-break the next morning we found ourselves, and every thing belonging to us, drenched with rain. Our situation now was by no means agreeable; torrents still came pouring down; neither our tent nor the woods afforded us any shelter, and the wind being very strong, and as adverse as it could blow, there was no prospect of our being enabled speedily to get into better quarters. In this state we had remained for a considerable time, when one of the party, who had been rambling about in order to discover what sort of a neighbourhood we were in, returned with the pleasing intelligence that there was a house at no great distance, and that the owner had politely invited us to it. It was the house of an old provincial officer, who had received a grant of land in this part of the country for his past services. We gladly proceeded to it, and met with a most cordial welcome from the captain and his fair daughters, who had provided a plenteous breakfast, and spared no pains to make their habitation, during our stay, as pleasing to us as possible. We felt great satisfaction at the idea, that it would be in our power to spend the remainder of the day with these worthy and hospitable people; but alas, we had all formed an erroneous opinion of the weather; the wind suddenly veered about; the sun broke through the thick clouds; the conductor

ductor gave the parting order; and in a few minutes we found ourselves once more seated in our bateau.

From hence upwards, for the distance of forty miles, the current of the river is extremely strong, and numberless rapids are to be encountered, which, though not so tremendous to appearance as those at the Cascades, and "Le Coteau du Lac," are yet both more dangerous and more difficult to pass. The great danger, however, consists in going down them; it arises from the shallowness of the water and the great number of sharp rocks, in the midst of which the vessels are hurried along with such impetuosity, that if they unfortunately get into a wrong channel, nothing can save them from being dashed to pieces; but so intimately are the people usually employed on this river acquainted with the different channels, that an accident of the sort is scarcely ever heard of. "Le Long Saut," the Long Fall or Rapid, situated about thirty miles above Lake St. Francis, is the most dangerous of any one in the river, and so difficult a matter is it to pass it, that it requires no less than six men on shore to haul a single bateau against the current. There is a third canal with locks at this place, in order to avoid a point, which it would be wholly impracticable to weather in the ordinary way. These different canals and locks have

have been made at the expence of government, and the profits arifing from the tolls paid by every bateau that paffes through them are placed in the public treafury. At thefe rapids, and at feveral of the others, there are very extenfive flour and faw mills.

On the fifth night we arrived at a fmall farm houfe, at the top of the " Long Saut," wet from head to foot, in confequence of our having been obliged to walk paft the rapids through woods and bufhes ftill dripping after the heavy rain that had fallen in the morning. The woods in this neighbourhood are far more majeftic than on any other part of the St. Lawrence; the pines in particular are uncommonly tall, and feem to wave their tops in the very clouds. In Canada, pines grow on the richeft foils; but in the United States they grow moftly on poor ground: a tract of land covered folely with pines is there generally denominated " a pine barren," on account of its great poverty.

During a confiderable part of the next day, we alfo proceeded on foot, in order to efcape the tedious paffage up the " Rapide Plat," and fome of the other dangerous rapids in this part of the river. As we paffed along, we had excellent diverfion in fhooting pigeons, feveral large flights of which we met with in the woods. The wild pigeons of Canada are not unlike

WILD PIGEONS.

unlike the common English wood pigeons, except that they are of a much smaller size: their flesh is very well flavoured. During particular years, these birds come down from the northern regions in flights that it is marvellous to tell of. A gentleman of the town of Niagara assured me, that once as he was embarking there on board ship for Toranto, a flight of them was observed coming from that quarter; that as he sailed over Lake Ontario to Toronto, forty miles distant from Niagara, pigeons were seen flying over head the whole way in a contrary direction to that in which the ship proceeded; and that on arriving at the place of his destination, the birds were still observed coming down from the north in as large bodies as had been noticed at any one time during the whole voyage; supposing, therefore, that the pigeons moved no faster than the vessel, the flight, according to this gentleman's account, must at least have extended eighty miles. Many persons may think this story surpassing belief; for my own part, however, I do not hesitate to give credit to it, knowing, as I do, the respectability of the gentleman who related it, and the accuracy of his observation. When these birds appear in such great numbers, they often light on the borders of rivers and lakes, and in the neighbourhood of farm houses, at which time they
are

are so unwary that a man with a short stick might easily knock them down by hundreds. It is not oftener than once in seven or eight years, perhaps, that such large flocks of these birds are seen in the country. The years in which they appear are denominated " pigeon " years."

There are also " bear years" and " squirrel " years." This was both a bear and a squirrel year. The former, like the pigeons, came down from the northern regions, and were most numerous in the neighbourhood of lakes Ontario and Erie, and along the upper parts of the River St. Lawrence. On arriving at the borders of these lakes, or of the river, if the opposite shore was in sight, they generally took to the water, and endeavoured to reach it by swimming. Prodigious numbers of them were killed in crossing the St. Lawrence by the Indians, who had hunting encampments, at short distances from each other, the whole way along the banks of the river, from the island of St. Regis to Lake Ontario. One bear, of a very large size, boldly entered the river in the face of our bateaux, and was killed by some of our men whilst swimming from the main land to one of the islands. In the woods it is very rare that bears will venture to attack a man; but several instances that had recently occurred were mentioned to us, where they

had

had attacked a single man in a canoe whilst swimming, and so very strong are they in the water, that the men thus set upon, being unarmed, escape narrowly with their lives.

The squirrels, this year, contrary to the bears, migrated from the south, from the territory of the United States. Like the bears, they took to the water on arriving at it, but as if conscious of their inability to cross a very wide piece of water, they bent their course towards Niagara River, above the falls, and at its narrowest and most tranquil part crossed over into the British territory. It was calculated, that upwards of fifty thousand of them crossed the river in the course of two or three days, and such great depredations did they commit on arriving at the settlements on the opposite side, that in one part of the country the farmers deemed themselves very fortunate where they got in as much as one third of their crops of corn. These squirrels were all of the black kind, said to be peculiar to the continent of America; they are in shape similar to the common grey squirrel, and weigh from about one to two pounds and a half each. Some writers have asserted, that these animals cannot swim, but that when they come to a river, in migrating, each one provides itself with a piece of wood or bark, upon which, when a favourable wind offers, they embark, spread their bushy

tails

tails to catch the wind, and are thus wafted over to the oppofite fide. Whether thefe animals do or do not crofs in this manner fometimes, I cannot take upon me to fay; but I can fafely affirm, that they do not always crofs fo, as I have frequently fhot them in the water whilft fwimming: no animals fwim better, and when purfued, I have feen them eagerly take to the water. Whilft fwimming, their tail is ufeful to them by way of rudder, and they ufe it with great dexterity; owing to its being fo light and bufhy, the greater part of it floats upon the water, and thus helps to fupport the animal. The migration of any of thefe animals in fuch large numbers is faid to be an infallible fign of a fevere winter*.

On the fixth evening of our voyage we ftopped nearly oppofite to Point aux Iroquois, fo named from a French family having been cruelly maffacred there by the Iroquois Indians in the early ages of the colony. The ground being ftill extremely wet here, in confequence of the heavy rain of the preceding day, we did not much relifh the thoughts of paffing the night in our tent; yet there feemed to be no alternative, as the only houfe in fight was crowded with people, and not capable of affording

---

* In the prefent inftance it certainly was fo, for the enfuing winter proved to be the fevereft that had been known in North America for feveral years.

ing us any accommodations. Luckily, however, as we were searching about for the driest spot to pitch our tent upon, one of the party espied a barn at a little distance, belonging to the man of the adjoining house, of whom we procured the key; it was well 'stored with straw, and having mounted to the top of the mow, we laid ourselves down to rest, and slept soundly there till awakened in the morning by the crowing of some cocks, that were perched on the beams above our head.

At an early hour we pursued our voyage, and before noon passed the last rapid, about three miles below the mouth of Ofwegatchee River, the most considerable of those within the territory of the United States, which fall into the St. Lawrence. It consists of three branches, that unite together about fifteen miles above its mouth, the most western of which issues from a lake twenty miles in length and eight in breadth. Another of the branches issues from a small lake or pond, only about four miles distant from the western branch of Hudson's River, that flows past New York. Both the Hudson and Ofwegatchee are said to be capable of being made navigable for light bateaux as far as this spot, where they approach within so short a distance of each other, except only at a few places, so that the portages will be but very trifling. This however

ever is a mere conjecture, for Ofwegatchee River is but very imperfectly known, the country it paffes through being quite uninhabited; but fhould it be found, at a future period, that thefe rivers are indeed capable of being rendered navigable fo far up the country, it will probably be through this channel that the chief part of the trade that there may happen to be between New York and the country bordering upon Lake Ontario will be carried on. It is at prefent carried on between that city and the lake by means of Hudfon River, as far as Albany, and from thence by means of the Mohawks River, Wood Creek, Lake Oneida, and Ofwego River, which falls into Lake Ontario. The harbour at the mouth of Ofwego River is very bad on account of the fand banks; none but flat bottomed veffels can approach with fafety nearer to it than two miles; nor is there any good harbour on the fouth fide of Lake Ontario in the neighbourhood of any large rivers. Sharp built veffels, however, of a confiderable fize, can approach with fafety to the mouth of Ofwegatchee River. The Seneca, a Britifh veffel of war of twenty-fix guns, ufed formerly to ply conftantly between Fort de la Galette, fituated at the mouth of that river, and the fort at Niagara; and the Britifh fur fhips on the lakes ufed alfo, at that time,

time, to difcharge the cargoes there, brought down from the upper country. As therefore the harbour at the mouth of Ofwegatchee is fo much better than that at the mouth of Ofwego River, and as they are nearly an equal diftance from New York, there is reafon to fuppofe, that if the river navigation fhould prove equally good, the trade between the lakes and New York will be for the moft part, if not wholly, carried on by means of Ofwegatchee rather than of Ofwego River. With a fair wind, the paffage from Ofwegatchee River to Niagara is accomplifhed in two days; a voyage only one day longer than that from Ofwego to Niagara with a fair wind.

Fort de la Galette was erected by the French, and though not built till long after Fort Cataraguis or Frontignac, now Kingfton, yet they efteemed it by far the moft important military poft on the St. Lawrence, in the upper country, as it was impoffible for any boat or veffel to pafs up or down that river without being obferved, whereas they might eafily efcape unfeen behind the many iflands oppofite to Kingfton. Since the clofe of the American war, Fort de la Galette has been difmantled, as it was within the territory of the United States: nor would any advantage have arifen from its retention; for it was never of any importance to us but as a trading poft, and as fuch Kingfton, which is within our own territory, is far more eligibly fituated in every point of view; it has a more fafe and commodious harbour, and the fur fhips coming down from Niagara, by ftopping there, are faved a voyage of fixty miles up and down the St. Lawrence, which was oftentimes found to be more tedious than the voyage from Niagara to Kingfton.

In the neighbourhood of La Galette, on the Ofwegatchee River, there is a village of the Ofwegatchee Indians, whofe numbers are eftimated at one hundred warriors.

The current of the St. Lawrence, from Ofwegatchee upwards, is much more gentle than in any other part between Montreal and Lake Ontario, except only where the river is confiderably dilated, as at lakes St. Louis and St. François; however, notwithftanding its being fo gentle, we did not advance more than twenty-five miles in the courfe of the day, owing to the numerous ftops that we made, more from motives of pleafure than neceffity. The evening was uncommonly fine, and towards fun-fet a brifk gale fpringing up, the conductor judged it advifable to take advantage of it, and to continue the voyage all night, in order to make up for the time we had loft during the day. We accordingly proceeded, but

but towards midnight the wind died away; this circumftance, however, did not alter the determination of the conductor. The men were ordered to the oars, and notwithftanding that they had laboured hard during the preceding day, and had had no reft, yet they were kept clofely at work until day-break, except for one hour, during which they were allowed to ftop to cook their provifions. Where there is a gentle current, as in this part of the river, the Canadians will work at the oar for many hours without intermiffion; they feemed to think it no hardfhip to be kept employed in this inftance the whole night; on the contrary, they plied as vigoroufly as if they had but juft fet out, finging merrily the whole time. The French Canadians have in general a good ear for mufic, and fing duets with tolerable accuracy. They have one very favourite duet amongft them, called the "rowing duet," which as they fing they mark time to with each ftroke of the oar; indeed, when rowing in fmooth water, they mark the time of moft of the airs they fing in the fame manner.

About eight o'clock the next, and eighth morning of our voyage, we entered the laft lake before you come to that of Ontario, called the Lake of a Thoufand Iflands, on account of the multiplicity of them which it contains.

Many

Many of thefe iflands are fcarcely larger than a bateau, and none of them, except fuch as are fituated at the upper and lower extremities of the lake, appeared to me to contain more than fifteen Englifh acres each. They are all covered with wood, even to the very fmalleft. The trees on thefe laft are ftunted in their growth, but the larger iflands produce as fine timber as is to be found on the main fhores of the lake. Many of thefe iflands are fituated fo clofely together, that it would be eafy to throw a pebble from one to the other, notwithftanding which circumftance, the paffage between them is perfectly fafe and commodious for bateaux, and between fome of them that are even thus clofe to each other, is water fufficient for a frigate. The water is uncommonly clear, as it is in every part of the river, from Lake St. Francis upwards: between that lake and the Utawas River downwards it is difcoloured, as I have before obferved, by paffing over beds of marl. The fhores of all thefe iflands under our notice are rocky; moft of them rife very boldly, and fome exhibit perpendicular maffes of rock towards the water upwards of twenty feet high. The fcenery prefented to view in failing between thefe iflands is beautiful in the higheft degree. Sometimes, after paffing through a narrow ftrait, you find yourfelf in a bafon, land locked on every fide, that appears to have no communication with the lake, except by the paffage through which you entered; you are looking about, perhaps, for an outlet to enable you to proceed, thinking at laft to fee fome little channel which will juft admit your bateau, when on a fudden an expanded fheet of water opens upon you, whofe boundary is the horizon alone; again in a few minutes you find yourfelf land locked, and again a fpacious paffage as fuddenly prefents itfelf; at other times, when in the middle of one of thefe bafons, between a clufter of iflands, a dozen different channels, like fo many noble rivers, meet the eye, perhaps equally unexpectedly, and on each fide the iflands appear regularly retiring till they fink from the fight in the diftance. Every minute, during the paffage of this lake, the profpect varies. The numerous Indian hunting encampments on the different iflands, with the fmoke of their fires rifing up between the trees, added confiderably to the beauty of the fcenery as we paffed it. The Lake of a Thoufand Iflands is twenty-five miles in length, and about fix in breadth. From its upper end to Kingfton, at which place we arrived early in the evening, the diftance is fifteen miles.

The length of time required to afcend the River St. Lawrence, from Montreal to Kingfton, ston, is commonly found to be about seven days. If the wind should be strong and very favourable, the passage may be performed in a less time; but should it, on the contrary, be adverse, and blow very strong, the passage will be protracted somewhat longer; an adverse or favourable wind, however, seldom makes a difference of more than three days in the length of the passage upwards, as in each case it is necessary to work the bateaux along by means of poles for the greater part of the way. The passage downwards is performed in two or three days, according to the wind. The current is so strong, that a contrary wind seldom lengthens the passage in that direction more than a day.

The Mississippi is the only river in North America, which, for grandeur and commodiousness of navigation, comes in competition with the St. Lawrence, or with that river which runs from Lake Ontario to the ocean. If, however, we consider that immense body of water that flows from Lake Winnipeg through the Lake of the Woods, Lake Superior, &c. down to the sea, as one entire stream, and of course as a continuation of the St. Lawrence, it must be allowed to be a very superior river to the Mississippi in every point of view; and we may certainly consider it as one stream, with as much reason as we look upon

upon that as one river which flows from Lake Ontario to the sea; for before it meets the ocean it passes through four large lakes, not indeed to be compared with those of Erie or Superior, in size, but they are independent lakes notwithstanding, as much as any of the others. The Mississippi is principally to be admired for the evenness of its current, and the prodigious length of way it is navigable, without any interruption, for bateaux of a very large burthen; but in many respects it is a very inferior river to the St. Lawrence, properly so called. The Mississippi at its mouth is not twenty miles broad, and the navigation is there so obstructed by banks or bars, that a vessel drawing more than twelve feet water cannot ascend it without very imminent danger. These bars at its mouth or mouths, for it is divided by several islands, are formed by large quantities of trees that come drifting down from the upper country, and when once stopped by any obstacle, are quickly cemented together by the mud, deposited between the branches by the waters of the river, which are uncommonly foul and muddy. Fresh bars are formed, or the old bars are enlarged every year, and it is said, that unless some steps are taken to prevent the lodgments of the trees annually brought down at the time of the inundation, the navigation may in a few years be still more obstructed

ſtructed than it is at preſent. It is notorious, that ſince the river was firſt diſcovered, ſeveral iſlands and points have been formed near its mouth, and the different channels have undergone very material alterations for the worſe, as to their courſes and depths. The River St. Lawrence, however, on the contrary, is no leſs than ninety miles wide at its mouth, and it is navigable for ſhips of the line as far as Quebec, a diſtance of four hundred miles from the ſea. The channel alſo, inſtead of having been impaired by time, is found to be conſiderably better now than when the river was firſt diſcovered; and there is reaſon to imagine that it will improve ſtill more in proceſs of time, as the clear water that flows from Lake Ontario comes down with ſuch impetuoſity, during the floods in the ſpring of the year, as frequently to remove banks of gravel and looſe ſtones in the river, and thus to deepen its bed. The channel on the north ſide of the iſland of Orleans, immediately below Quebec, which, according to the account of Le P. de Charlevoix, was not ſufficiently deep in the year 1720 to admit a ſhallop of a ſmall ſize, except at the time of high tides, is at preſent found to be deep enough for the largeſt veſſels, and is the channel moſt generally uſed.

The

NAVIGATION. 57

The following table shews for what vessels the St. Lawrence is navigable in different places; and also points out the various breadths of the river from its mouth upwards:

Names of Places.	Distances in miles ascending.	Breadth in miles.
At its mouth	—	90
At Cape Cat	140	30
At Saguenay River	120	18
At the lower extremity of the Isle of Orleans	110	15*
At the bason between the Isle of Orleans and Quebec	30	5†
From Quebec to Lake St. Pierre	90	
Lake St. Pierre	30	14
To La Valterie	10	1
To Montreal	30	2 to 4‡

* This island is 25 miles in length and 6 in breadth, the river on each side is about 2 miles wide.

† Thus far, 400 miles from its mouth, it is navigable for ships of the line with safety.

‡ To this place, 560 miles, it is navigable with perfect safety for ships drawing 14 feet water. Vessels of a much larger draught have proceeded many miles above Quebec, but the channel is very intricate and dangerous.

Names of Places.	Distances in miles ascending.	Breadth in miles.
To Lake St. Louis	6	— 3/4
Lake St. Louis	12	4
To Lake St. Francis	25	1/2 to 2
Lake St. Francis	20	5
To the Lake of a Thousand Isles	90	1/4 to 1
Lake of a Thousand Isles	25	6
To Kingston, on Lake Ontario	15	2 1/4 to 6
	743	

During the whole of its course the St. Lawrence is navigable for bateaux of two tons burthen, except merely at the rapids above Montreal, at the Fall of the Thicket, and at the Long Fall, where, as has been already pointed out, it is necessary to lighten the bateaux, if heavily laden. At each of these places, however, it is possible to construct canals, so as to prevent the trouble of unlading any part of the cargoes of the bateaux, and at a future day, when the country becomes rich, such canals no doubt will be made.

Although the lakes are not immediately connected with the Atlantic Ocean by any other river than the St. Lawrence, yet there are

are several streams that fall into the Atlantic, so nearly connected with others flowing into the lakes, that by their means trade may be carried on between the ocean and the lakes. The principal channels for trade between the ocean and the lakes are four in number; the first, along the Mississippi and the Ohio, and thence up the Wabash, Miami, Mushingun, or the Alleghany rivers, from the head of which there are portages of from one to eighteen miles to rivers that fall into Lake Erie; secondly, along the Patowmac River, which flows past Washington, and from thence along Cheat River, the Monongahela and Alleghany rivers and French Creek to Presqu' Isle on Lake Erie; thirdly, along Hudson's River, which falls into the Atlantic at New York, and afterwards along the Mohawk River, Wood Creek, Lake Oneida, and Oswego River, which last falls into Lake Ontario; fourthly, along the St. Lawrence.

The following is a statement of the entire length of each of these channels or routes, and of the lengths of the portages in each, reckoning from the highest seaport on each river that will receive vessels of a suitable size for crossing the Atlantic to Lake Erie, which is the most central of the lakes to the four ports:

From

	Length of Way in Miles.	Length of the Portages.
From Montreal	440	22
From Wafhington	450	80*
From New York	500	30
From New Orleans	1,800	1 to 18†

* When the navigation is opened, this will be reduced, it is faid, to 50 miles.

† According to the route followed from the Ohio to the Lake.

From this ftatement it not only appears evident that the St. Lawrence opens a fhorter paffage to the lakes than any of the other rivers, but alfo that the portages are fhorter than in any of the other routes; the portages are alfo fewer, and goods may be tranfported in the fame boats the whole way from Montreal to the lakes; whereas in conveying goods thither either from Wafhington or New York, it is neceffary to employ different boats and men on each different river, or elfe to tranfport the boats themfelves on carriages over the portages from one river to another. It is always an object of importance to avoid a portage, as by every change in the mode of conveyance the expence of carriage is increafed, and there is an additional rifk of pillage from the goods paffing through the hands of a greater number

number of people. Independent of thefe confiderations, the St. Lawrence will, on another account, be found a more commodious channel than any other for the carrying on of trade between the ocean and the lakes. Conftantly fupplied from that immenfe refervoir of water, Lake Ontario, it is never fo low, even in the drieft feafon, as not to be fufficiently deep to float laden bateaux. The fmall ftreams, on the contrary, which connect Hudfon's River, the Patowmac, and the Miffiffippi with the lakes, are frequently fo dried up in fummer time, that it is fcarcely poffible to pafs along them in canoes. For upwards of four months in the fummer of 1796, the Mohawk River was fo low, that it was totally impracticable to tranfport merchandize along it during the greater part of its courfe, and the traders in the back country, after waiting for a length of time for the goods they wanted, were under the neceffity at laft of having them forwarded by land carriage. The navigation of this river, it is faid, becomes worfe every year, and unlefs feveral long canals are cut, there will be an end to the water communication between New York and Lake Ontario by that route. The Alleghany River and French Creek, which connect the Patowmac with Lake Erie, are equally affected by droughts; indeed it is only during floods, occafioned by the melting of the

fnow,

snow, or by heavy falls of rain, that goods can be transported with ease either by the one route or the other.

By far the greater part of the trade to the lakes is at present centered at Montreal; for the British merchants not only can convey their goods from thence to the lakes for one third less than what it costs to convey the same goods thither from New York, but they can likewise afford to sell them, in the first instance, considerably cheaper than the merchants of the United States. The duties paid on the importation into Canada of refined sugar, spirits, wine, and coffee, are considerably less than those paid on the importation of the same commodities into the United States; and all British hardware, and dry goods in general, are admitted duty free into Canada, whereas, in the United States, they are chargeable, on importation from Europe, with a duty of fifteen per cent. on the value. To attempt to levy duties on foreign manufactures sent into the states from Canada would be an idle attempt, as from the great extent of their frontier, and its contiguity to Canada, it would at all times be an easy matter to send the goods clandestinely into them, in order to avoid the duties.

The trade carried on from Montreal to the lakes is at present very considerable, and increasing every year. Already are there extensive

five settlements on the British side of Lake Ontario, at Niagara, at Toronto, at the Bay of Canti, and at Kingston, which contain nearly twenty thousand inhabitants; and on the opposite shore, the people of the states are pushing forward their settlements with the utmost vigour. On Lake Erie, and along Detroit River also, the settlements are increasing with astonishing rapidity, both on the British and on the opposite side.

The importance of the back country trade, and the trade to the lakes is in fact the back country trade, has already been demonstrated; and it has been shewn, that every sea-port town in the United States has increased in size in proportion to the quantum it enjoyed of this trade; and that those towns most conveniently situated for carrying it on, were those that had the greatest share of it; as, therefore, the shores of the lake increase in population, and of course as the demand for European manufactures increases amongst the inhabitants, we may expect to see Montreal, which of all the sea-ports in North America is the most conveniently situated for supplying them with such manufactures, increase proportionably in size; and as the extent of back country it is connected with, by means of water, is as great, and also as fertile as that with which any of the large towns of the
United

United States are connected, it is not improbable but that Montreal at a future day will rival in wealth and in size the greatest of the cities on the continent of North America.

LETTER XXX.

Description of the Town of Kingston.—Formerly called Fort Cadaraqua.— Extensive Trade carried on here.—Nature of it.—Inhabitants very hospitable.—Harbours on Lake Ontario.—Ships of War on that Lake.—Merchant Vessels.—Naval Officers.—Expence of building and keeping up Vessels very great.—Why.—No Iron Mines yet opened in the Country.—Copper may be more easily procured than Iron.—Found in great Quantities on the Borders of Lake Superior.—Embark in a Trading Vessel on Lake Ontario.—Description of that Lake.—A Septennial Change in the Height of the Waters said to be observable—also a Tide that ebbs and flows every Two Hours.—Observations on these Phenomena.—Voyage across the Lake similar to a Sea Voyage.—Come in Sight of Niagara Fort.—Land at Mississaguis Point.—Mississaguis Indians.—One of their Chiefs killed in

an

an Affray.—How treated by the British Government.—Their revengeful Disposition.—Mississaguis good Hunters.—How they kill Salmon.—Variety of Fish in the Lakes and Rivers of Canada.—Sea Wolves.—Sea Cows.—Description of the Town of Niagara or Newark.—The present Seat of Government.—Scheme of removing it elsewhere.—Unhealthiness of the Town of Niagara and adjacent Country.—Navy Hats.—Fort of Niagara surrendered pursuant to Treaty.—Description of it.—Description of the other Forts surrendered to the People of the United States.—Shewn not to be so advantageous to them as was expected.—Superior Position of the new British Posts pointed out.

Niagara, September.

KINGSTON is situated at the mouth of a deep bay, at the north eastern extremity of Lake Ontario. It contains a fort and barracks, an English episcopalian church, and about one hundred houses, the most of which last were built, and are now inhabited by persons who emigrated from the United States at the close of the American war. Some few of the houses are built of stone and brick, but by far the greater part of them are of wood. The fort is of stone, and consists of a square with four bastions. It was erected by M.

le Comte de Frontinac, as early as the year 1672, and was for a time called after him; but infenfibly it loft his name, and received inftead of it that of Cadaraqui, the name of a creek which falls into the bay. This name remained common to the fort and to the town until a few years ago, when it was changed to that of Kingfton. From fixty to one hundred men are ufually quartered in the barracks.

Kingfton is a place of very confiderable trade, and it is confequently increafing moft rapidly in fize. All the goods brought up the St. Lawrence for the fupply of the upper country are here depofited in ftores, preparatory to their being fhipped on board veffels fuitable to the navigation of the lake; and the furs from the various pofts on the nearer lakes are here likewife collected together, in order to be laden on board bateaux, and fent down the St. Lawrence. Some furs are brought in immediately to the town by the Indians, who hunt in the neighbouring country, and along the upper parts of the St. Lawrence, but the quantity is not large. The principal merchants refident at Kingfton are partners of old eftablifhed houfes at Montreal and Quebec. A ftranger, efpecially if a Britifh fubject, is fure to meet with a moft hofpitable and friendly reception from them, as he paffes through the place.

During

During the autumn the inhabitants of Kingston suffer very much from intermittent fevers, owing to the town being situated on a low spot of ground, contiguous to an extensive morafs.

The bay adjoining to Kingston affords good anchorage, and is the fafeft and moft commodious harbour on all Lake Ontario. The bay of Great Sodus, on the fouth fide of the lake, and that of Toronto, fituated on the north fide of the lake, nearly in the fame meridian with Niagara, are faid to be the next beft to that of Kingston; but the entrance into each of them is obftructed by fand banks, which in rough weather cannot be croffed without imminent danger in veffels drawing more than five or fix feet water. On the borders of the bay at Kingston there is a King's dock yard, and another which is private property. Moft of the Britifh veffels of burthen on Lake Ontario have been built at thefe yards. Belonging to his Majefty there were on Lake Ontario, when we croffed it, three veffels of about two hundred tons each, carrying from eight to twelve guns, befides feveral gun boats; the laft, however, were not in commiffion, but laid up in Niagara River; and in confequence of the ratification of the treaty of amity and commerce between the United States and his Britannic Majefty, orders were

issued

iffued, fhortly after we left Kingfton, for laying up the other veffels of war, one alone excepted*. For one King's fhip there would be ample employment on the lake, in conveying to the upper country the prefents for the Indians and the ftores for the troops, and in tranfporting the troops acrofs the lake when they changed quarters. Every military officer at the outpofts enjoys the privilege of having a certain bulk, according to his rank, carried for him in the King's veffels, free of all charges. The naval officers, if their veffels be not otherwife engaged, are allowed to carry a cargo of merchandize when they fail from one port to another, the freight of which is their perquifite; they likewife have the liberty, and are conftantly in the practice, of carrying paffengers acrofs the lake at an eftablifhed price. The commodore of the King's veffels on Lake Ontario is a French Canadian, and fo likewife are moft of the officers under him. Their uniform is blue and white, with large yellow buttons, ftamped with the figure of a beaver, over which is infcribed the word, " Canada." The naval officers are under the controul of the military officer commandant, at every poft where

---

* Subfequent orders, [it was faid, were iffued, during the fummer of 1797, to have one or more of thefe veffels put again in commiffion.

their

their veffels happen to touch; and they cannot leave their veffels to go up into the country at any time without his permiffion.

Several decked merchant veffels, fchooners, and floops, of from fifty to two hundred tons each, and alfo numberlefs large failing bateaux, are kept employed on Lake Ontario. No veffels are deemed proper for the navigation of thefe lakes but complete fea boats, or elfe flat bottomed veffels, fuch as canoes and bateaux, that can fafely run afhore on an emergency At prefent the people of the United States have no other veffels than bateaux on the lake, and whether they will deem it proper to have larger veffels, as their harbours are all fo indifferent, remains yet to be determined. The large Britifh veffels ply moftly between Kingfton and Niagara, and but very rarely touch at any other place.

The expence of building, and equipping veffels on Lake Ontario, is very confiderable; and it is ftill greater on the more diftant lakes, as the larger part of the iron implements, and all the cordage wanted for that purpofe, are imported from Great Britain, through the medium of the lower province. There can be no doubt, however, but that when the country is become more populous, an ample fupply of thefe neceffary articles will be readily procured on the fpot; for the foil of the upper province is well adapted to the growth of hemp, and iron ore has been difcovered in many parts of the country. Hemp already begins to be cultivated in fmall quantities; but it has hitherto been the policy of government to direct the attention of the people to agriculture, rather than to any other purfuit, fo that none of the iron mines, which, together with all other mines that are, or that may hereafter be difcovered, are the exclufive property of the crown, have yet been opened. The people of the United States, however, alive to every profpect of gain, have already fent perfons to look for iron ore in that part of their territory fituated conveniently to the lakes. Thefe perfons have been very fuccefsful in their fearches; and as works will undoubtedly be eftablifhed fpeedily by them in this quarter for the manufacture of iron, and as they will be able to afford it on much better terms than that which is brought all the way from Lower Canada, it is probable that government will encourage the opening of mines in our own dominions, rather than fuffer the people of the States to enjoy fuch a very lucrative branch of trade as they muft neceffarily have, if the fame policy is perfifted in which has hitherto been purfued.

Copper, in the more remote parts of Upper Canada, is found in much greater abundance than

than iron, and as it may be extracted from the earth with considerably less trouble than any of the iron ore that has yet been discovered, there is reason to imagine, that at a future day it will be much more used than iron for every purpose to which it can be applied. On the borders of a river, which falls into the southwest side of Lake Superior, virgin copper is found in the greatest abundance; and on most of the islands on the eastern side it is also found. In the possession of a gentleman at Niagara I saw a lump of virgin copper of several ounces weight, apparently as pure as if it had passed through fire, which I was informed had been struck off with a chisel from a piece equally pure, growing on one of these islands, which must at least have weighed forty pounds. Rich veins of copper are visible in almost all the rocks on these islands towards the shore; and copper ore, resembling copperas, is likewise found in deep beds near the water: in a few hours bateaux might here be filled with ore, and in less than three days conveyed to the Straits of St. Mary, after passing which the ore might be laden on board large vessels, and conveyed by water without any further interruption as far as Niagara River. The portage at the Straits of St. Mary may be passed in a few hours, and with a fair wind large vessels, proper for traversing

Lakes Huron and Erie, may come down to the eastern extremity of the latter lake in six days.

Not only the building and fitting out of vessels on the lakes is attended with considerable expence, but the cost of keeping them up is likewise found to be very great, for they wear out much sooner than vessels employed commonly on the ocean; which circumstance, according to the opinion of the naval gentlemen on the lakes, is owing to the freshness of the water; added to this, no sailors are to be hired but at very high wages, and it is found necessary to retain them at full pay during the five months of the year that the vessels are laid up on account of the ice, as men cannot be procured at a moment's notice. The sailors, with a few exceptions only, are procured from sea ports, as it is absolutely necessary on these lakes, the navigation of which is more dangerous than that of the ocean, to have able and experienced seamen. Lake Ontario itself is never frozen out of sight of land, but its rivers and harbours are regularly blocked up by the ice.

The day after that on which we reached Kingston, we took our passage for Niagara on board a schooner of one hundred and eighty tons burthen, which was waiting at the merchant's wharf for a fair wind. The established

blished price of the passage across the lake in the cabin is two guineas, and in the steerage one guinea, for each person: this is by no means dear, considering that the captain, for the money, keeps a table for each respective set of passengers. The cabin table on board this vessel was really well served, and there was abundance of port and sherry wine, and of every sort of spirits, for the use of the cabin passengers. The freight of goods across the lake is dearer in proportion, being thirty-six shillings British per ton, which is nearly as much as was paid for the transportation of a ton of goods across the Atlantic previous to the present war; it cannot, however, be deemed exorbitant, when the expence of building and keeping the vessels in repair, and the high wages of the sailors, &c. are taken into consideration.

On the 7th of September, in the afternoon, the wind became favourable for crossing the lake; notice was in consequence immediately sent round to the passengers, who were dispersed in different parts of the town, to get ready; all of them hurried on board; the vessel was unmoored, and in a few minutes she was wafted out into the lake by a light breeze. For the first mile and a half, in going from Kingston, the prospect is much confined, on account of the many large islands
on

on the left hand fide; but on weathering a point on one of the iflands, at the end of that diftance, an extenfive view of the lake fuddenly opens, which on a ftill clear evening, when the fun is finking behind the lofty woods that adorn the fhores, is extremely grand and beautiful.

Lake Ontario is the moft eafterly of the four large lakes through which the boundary line paffes, that feparates the United States from the province of Upper Canada. It is two hundred and twenty miles in length, from eaft to weft, and feventy miles wide in the broadeft part, and, according to calculation, contains about 2,390,000 acres. This lake is lefs fubject to ftorms than any of the others, and its waters in general, confidering their great expanfe, are wonderfully tranquil. During the firft evening of our voyage there was not the leaft curl even on their furface, they were merely agitated by a gentle fwell; and during the fubfequent part of the voyage, the waves were at no time fo high as to occafion the flighteft ficknefs amongft any of the paffengers. The depth of the water in the lake is very great; in fome parts it is unfathomable. On looking over the fide of a veffel, the water, owing to its great depth, appears to be of a blackifh colour, but it is neverthelefs very clear, and any white fubftance thrown overboard

board may be difcerned at the depth of feveral fathoms from the furface; it is, however, by no means fo clear and tranfparent as the water of fome of the other lakes. Mr. Carver, fpeaking of Lake Superior, fays, " When it was
" calm, and the fun fhone bright, I could fit
" in my canoe, where the depth was upwards
" of fix fathoms, and plainly fee huge piles
" of ftone at the bottom, of different fhapes,
" fome of which appeared as if they had been
" hewn; the water was at this time as pure
" and tranfparent as air, and my canoe feemed
" as if it hung fufpended in that element. It
" was impoffible to look attentively through
" this limpid medium, at the rocks below,
" without finding, before many minutes were
" elapfed, your head fwim, and your eyes no
" longer able to behold the dazzling fcene."

The water of Lake Ontario is very well tafted, and is that which is conftantly ufed on board the veffels that traverfe it.

It is very confidently afferted, not only by the Indians, but alfo by great numbers of the white people who live on the fhores of Lake Ontario, that the waters of this lake rife and fall alternately every feventh year; others, on the contrary, deny that fuch a fluctuation does take place; and indeed it differs fo materially from any that has been obferved in large bodies of water in other parts of the globe, that for

my

my own part I am fomewhat tempted to believe it is merely an imaginary change; neverthelefs, when it is confidered, that according to the belief of the oldeft inhabitants of the country, fuch a periodical ebbing and flowing of the waters of the lake takes place, and that it has never been clearly proved to the contrary, we are bound to fufpend our opinions on the fubject. A gentleman, whofe habitation was fituated clofe upon the borders of the lake, not far from Kingfton, and who, from the nature of his profeffion, had more time to attend to fuch fubjects than the generality of the people of the country, told me, that he had obferved the ftate of the lake attentively for nearly fourteen years that he had refided on the borders of it, and that he was of opinion the waters did not ebb and flow periodically; yet he acknowledged this very remarkable fact, that feveral of the oldeft white inhabitants in his neighbourhood declared, previoufly to the rifing of the lake, that the year 1795 would be the high year; and that in the fummer of that year, the lake actually did rife to a very uncommon height. He faid, however, that he had reafon to think the rifing of the lake on this occafion was wholly owing to fortuitous circumftances, and not to any regular eftablifhed law of nature; and he conceived, that if the lake had not rifen as it had done, yet the people

people would have fancied, neverthelefs, that it was in reality higher than ufual, as he fuppofed they had fancied it to be on former occafions. He was induced to form this opinion, he faid, from the following circumftance: When the lake had rifen to fuch an unufual height in the year 1795, he examined feveral of the oldeft people on the fubject, and queftioned them particularly as to the comparative height of the waters on this and former occafions. They all declared that the waters were not higher than they ufually were at the time of their periodical rifing; and they affirmed, that they had themfelves feen them equally high before. Now a grove of trees, which ftood adjoining to this gentleman's garden, and muft at leaft have been of thirty years growth, was entirely deftroyed this year by the waters of the lake, that flowed amongft the trees; had the lake, therefore, ever rifen fo high before, this grove would have been then deftroyed. This circumftance certainly militated ftrongly againft the evidence which the people gave as to the height of the waters; but it only proved that the waters had rifen on this occafion higher than they had done for thirty years preceding; it did not prove that they had not, during that term, rifen periodically above their ordinary level.

What

What Mr. Carver relates concerning this fubject, rather tends to confirm the opinion that the waters of the lake do rife. " I had " like," he fays, " to have omitted a very ex- " traordinary circumftance relative to thefe " ftraits ;" the Straits of Michillimakinac, between lakes Michigan and Huron. " According to obfervations made by the French, " whilft they were in poffeffion of the fort " there, although there is no diurnal flood or " ebb to be perceived in thefe waters, yet from " an exact attention to their ftate, a periodical " alteration in them has been difcovered. It " was obferved, that they arofe by gradual but " almoft imperceptible degrees, till they had " reached the height of three feet; this was " accomplifhed in feven years and a half; and " in the fame fpace of time they as gently de- " creafed, till they had reached their former " fituation; fo that in fifteen years they had " completed this inexplicable revolution. At " the time I was there, the truth of thefe ob- " fervations could not be confirmed by the " Englifh, as they had then been only a few " years in poffeffion of the fort; but they all " agreed that fome alterations in the limits " of the ftraits was apparent." It is to be lamented that fucceeding years have not thrown more light on the fubject; for fince the fort has been in our poffeffion, perfons competent to determine the truth of obfervations of fuch a nature, have never ftaid a fufficient length of time there to have had it in their power to do fo.

A long feries of minute obfervations are neceffary to determine pofitively whether the waters of the lake do or do not rife and fall periodically. It is well known, for inftance, that in wet feafons the waters rife much above their ordinary level, and that in very dry feafons they fink confiderably below it; a clofe attention, therefore, ought to be paid to the quantity of rain that falls, and to evaporation; and it ought to be afcertained in what degree the height of the lake is altered thereby; otherwife, if the lake happened to be higher or lower than ufual on the feventh year, it would be impoffible to fay with accuracy whether it were owing to the ftate of the weather, or to certain laws of nature that we are yet unacquainted with. At the fame time, great attention ought to be paid to the ftate of the winds, as well in refpect to their direction as to their velocity, for the height of the waters of all the lakes is materially affected thereby. At Fort Erie, fituated at the eaftern extremity of the lake of the fame name, I once obferved the waters to fall full three feet in the courfe of a few hours, upon a fudden change of the wind from the weftward, in which direction

rection it had blown for many days, to the eastward. Moreover, thefe obfervations ought not only to be made at one place on the borders of any one of the lakes, but they ought to be made at feveral different places at the fame time; for the waters have encroached, owing to fome unknown caufes, confiderably and gradually upon the fhores in fome places, and receded in others. Between the ftone houfe, in the fort at Niagara, and the lake, for inftance, there is not at prefent a greater fpace than ten yards, or thereabouts; though when firft built there was an extenfive garden between them. A water battery alfo, erected fince the commencement of the prefent war, at the bottom of the bank, beyond the walls of the fort, was fapped away by the water in the courfe of two feafons, and now fcarcely any veftige of it remains. At a future day, when the country becomes more populous and more wealthy, perfons will no doubt be found who will have leifure for making the obfervations neceffary for determining whether the lakes do or do not undergo a periodical change, but at prefent the inhabitants on the borders of them are too much engaged in commercial and agricultural purfuits to attend to matters of mere fpeculation, which, however they might amufe the philofopher, could be productive of no folid advantages to the generality of the inhabitants of the country.

It is believed by many perfons that the waters of Lake Ontario not only rife and fall periodically every feventh year, but that they are likewife influenced by a tide, which ebbs and flows frequently in the courfe of twenty-four hours. On board the veffel in which I croffed the lake there were feveral gentlemen of the country, who confidently affured me, that a regular tide was obfervable at the Bay of Canti; that in order to fatisfy themfelves on the fubject, they had ftood for feveral hours together, on more than one occafion, at a mill at the head of the bay, and that they had obferved the waters to ebb and flow regularly every four hours, rifing to the height of fourteen inches. There can be no doubt, however, but that the frequent ebbing and flowing of the water at this place muft be caufed by the wind; for no fuch regular fluctuation is obfervable at Niagara, at Kingfton, or on the open fhores of the lake; and owing to the formation of the Bay of Canti, the height of the water muft neceffarily vary there with every flight change of the wind. The Bay of Canti is a long crooked inlet, that grows narrower at the upper end, like a funnel; not only, therefore, a change of wind up or down the bay would make a difference in the height of the water at the uppermoft extremity of it; but owing to the waters being concentrated there at one point, they would be seen to rise or fall, if impelled even in the same direction, whether up or down the bay, more or less forcibly at one time of the day than at another. Now it is very seldom that the wind, at any part of the day or night, would be found to blow precisely with the same force, for a given space of two hours, that it had blown for the preceding space of two hours; an appearance like a tide must therefore be seen almost constantly at the head of this bay whenever there was a breeze. I could not learn that the fluctuation had ever been observed during a perfect calm: were the waters, however, influenced by a regular tide, during a calm the tide would be most readily seen.

To return to the voyage. A few hours after we quitted Kingston, on the 7th of September, the wind died away, and during the whole night the vessel made but little way; early on the morning of the 8th, however, a fresh breeze sprang up, and before noon we lost sight of the land. Our voyage now differed in no wise from one across the ocean; the vessel was steered by the compass, the log regularly heaved, the way marked down in the log book, and an exact account kept of the procedures on board. We continued sailing, out of sight of land, until the evening of the 9th, when we had a view of the blue hills in the neighbourhood

bourhood of Toronto, on the northern side of the lake, but they soon disappeared. Except at this place, the shores of the lake are flat and sandy, owing to which circumstance it is, that in traversing the lake you are generally carried out of sight of land in a very few hours.

At day break on the 10th the fort and town of Niagara appeared under the lee bow, and the wind being favourable, we had every prospect before us of getting up to the town in a few hours; but scarcely had we reached the bar, at the mouth of Niagara River, when the wind suddenly shifted, and after endeavouring in vain to cross it by means of tacking, we were under the necessity of casting anchor at the distance of about two miles from the fort. The fort is seen to great advantage from the water; but the town being built parallel to the river, and no part of it visible to a spectator on the lake, except the few shabby houses at the nearest end, it makes but a very poor appearance. Having breakfasted, and exchanged our *habits de voyage*, for such as it was proper to appear in at the capital of Upper Canada, and at the center of the beau monde of the province, the schooner's yawl was launched, and we were landed, together with such of the passengers as were disposed to go on shore, at Mississaguis Point, from whence there is an agreeable walk of one mile, partly through woods, to the town of Niagara.

This point takes its name from the Miffiffaguis Indians, great numbers of whom are generally encamped upon it. The Miffiffaguis tribe inhabits the fhores of Lake Ontario, and it is one of the moſt numerous of this part of the country. The men are in general very ſtout, and they are eſteemed moſt excellent hunters and fiſhers; but leſs warlike, it is ſaid, than any of the neighbouring nations. They are of a much darker complexion than any other Indians I ever met with; ſome of them being nearly as black as negroes. They are extremely dirty and ſlovenly in their appearance, and the women are ſtill more ſo than the men; ſuch indeed is the odour exhaled in a warm day from the rancid greaſe and fiſh oil with which the latter daub their hair, necks, and faces profuſely, that it is offenſive in the higheſt degree to approach within ſome yards of them. On arriving at Niagara, we found great numbers of theſe Indians diſperſed in knots, in different parts of the town, in great concern for the loſs of a favourite and experienced chief. This man, whoſe name was Wompakanon, had been killed, it appeared, by a white man, in a fray which happened at Toronto, near to which place is the principal village of the Miffiffaguis nation. The remaining chiefs immediately aſſembled their warriors, and marched down to Niagara, to make

make a formal complaint to the British government. To appease their resentment, the commanding officer of the garrison distributed presents amongst them to a large amount, and amongst other things they were allowed no small portion of rum and provisions, upon which the tribe feasted, according to custom, the day before we reached the town; but the rum being all consumed, they seemed to feel severely for the loss of poor Wompakanon. Fear of exciting the anger of the British government would prevent them from taking revenge openly on this occasion; but I was informed by a gentleman in the Indian department, intimately acquainted with the dispositions of the Indians, that as nothing but blood is deemed sufficient in their opinion to atone for the death of a favourite chief, they would certainly kill some white man, perhaps one perfectly innocent, when a favourable and secret opportunity offered for so doing, though it should be twenty years afterwards.

The Mississaguis keep the inhabitants of Kingston, of Niagara, and of the different towns on the lake, well supplied with fish and game, the value of which is estimated by bottles of rum and loaves of bread. A gentleman, with whom we dined at Kingston, entertained us with a most excellent haunch of venison of a very large size, and a salmon weighing

weighing at least fifteen pounds, which he had purchased from one of these Indians for a bottle of rum and a loaf of bread *, and upon enquiry I found that the Indian thought himself extremely well paid, and was highly pleased with having made such a good bargain.

The Indians catch salmon and other large fish in the following manner. Two men go together in a canoe at night; the one sits in the stern and paddles, and the other stands with a spear over a flambeau placed in the head of the canoe. The fish, attracted by the light, come in numbers around the canoe, and the spearsman then takes the opportunity of striking them. They are very expert at this business, seldom missing their aim.

Lake Ontario, and all the rivers which fall into it, abound with excellent salmon, and many different kinds of sea-fish, which come up the River St. Lawrence; it also abounds with such a great variety of fresh water fish, that it is supposed there are many sorts in it which have never yet been named. In almost every part of the River St. Lawrence, fish is found in the greatest abundance; and it is the opinion of many persons, that if the fisheries were properly attended to, particularly the

* Both together probably not worth more than half a dollar.

salmon

salmon fishery, the country would be even more enriched thereby than by the fur trade. Sea wolves and sea cows, amphibious animals, weighing from one to two thousand pounds each, are said to have been found in Lake Ontario: of the truth of this, however, there is some doubt; but certain it is, that in sailing across that lake animals of an immense size are frequently seen playing on the surface of the water. Of the large fishes, the sturgeon is the one most commonly met with, and it is not only found in Lake Ontario, but also in the other lakes that have no immediate communication with the sea. The sturgeon caught in the lakes is valuable for its oil, but it is not a well flavoured fish; indeed, the sturgeon found north of James River in Virginia is in general very indifferent, and seldom or never eaten.

Niagara River runs nearly in a due south direction, and falls into Lake Ontario on the southern shore, about thirty miles to the eastward of the western extremity of the lake. It is about three hundred yards wide at its mouth, and is by far the largest body of water flowing into Lake Ontario. On the eastern side of the river is situated the fort, now in the possession of the people of the States, and on the opposite or British side the town, most generally known by the name of Niagara, notwithstanding

ſtanding that it has been named Newark by the legiſlature. The original name of the town was Niagara, it was afterwards called Lenox, then Naſſau, and afterwards Newark. It is to be lamented that the Indian names, ſo grand and ſonorous, ſhould ever have been changed for others. Newark, Kingſton, York, are poor ſubſtitutes for the original names of theſe reſpective places, Niagara, Cadaragui, Toronto. The town of Niagara hitherto has been, and is ſtill the capital of the province of Upper Canada; orders, however, had been iſſued, before our arrival there, for the removal of the ſeat of government from thence to Toronto, which was deemed a more eligible ſpot for the meeting of the legiſlative bodies, as being farther removed from the frontiers of the United States. This projected change is by no means reliſhed by the people at large, as Niagara is a much more convenient place of reſort to moſt of them than Toronto; and as the governor who propoſed the meaſure has been removed, it is imagined that it will not be put in execution. The removal of the ſeat of government from Niagara to Toronto, according to the plan laid down, was only to have been a preparatory ſtep to another alteration: a new city, to have been named London, was to have been built on the river formerly called La Trenche, but ſince called the Thames, a river a river running into Lake St. Clair; and here the feat of government was ultimately to have been fixed. The fpot marked out for the fcite of the city poffeffes many local advantages. It is fituated in a healthy fertile country, on a fine navigable river, in a central part of the province, from whence the water communication is extenfive in every direction. A few fettlements have already been made on the banks of the river, and the tide of emigration is fetting in ftrongly towards that quarter; at a future day, therefore, it is by no means improbable but that this fpot may be deemed an eligible one for the capital of the country; but to remove the feat of government immediately to a place little better than a wildernefs, and fo far from the populous parts of the province, would be a meafure fraught with numberlefs inconveniencies to the public, and productive apparently of no effential advantages whatfoever.

The town of Niagara contains about feventy houfes, a court houfe, gaol, and a building intended for the accommodation of the legiflative bodies. The houfes, with a few exceptions, are built of wood; thofe next the lake are rather poor, but at the upper end of the town there are feveral very excellent dwellings, inhabited by the principal officers of government. Moft of the gentlemen in official

cial stations in Upper Canada are Englishmen of education, a circumstance which must render the society of the capital agreeable, let it be fixed where it will. Few places in North America can boast of a more rapid rise than the little town of Niagara, nearly every one of its houses having been built within the last five years: it is still advancing most rapidly in size, owing to the increase of the back country trade along the shores of the upper lakes, which is all carried on through the place, and also owing to the wonderful emigrations, into the neighbourhood, of people from the States. The motives which lead the citizens of the United States to emigrate to the British dominions have already been explained. So sudden and so great has the influx of people, into the town of Niagara and its vicinity, been, that town lots, horses, provisions, and every necessary of life have risen, within the last three years, nearly fifty per cent. in value.

The banks of the River Niagara are steep and lofty, and on the top, at each side of the river, are extensive plains. The town stands on the summit of the western bank, about fifty yards from the water's edge. It commands a fine view of the lake and distant shores, and its situation is in every respect pleasing to the eye. From its standing on a spot of ground so much elevated above the level

level of the water, one would imagine that it muſt alſo be a remarkably healthy place, but it is, in fact, lamentably the reverſe. On arriving at the town, we were obliged to call at no leſs than four different taverns, before we could procure accommodations, the people at the firſt places we ſtopped at being ſo ſeverely afflicted with the ague, that they could not receive us; and on enquiring, it appeared that there was not a ſingle houſe in the whole town but where one or more of the inhabitants were labouring under his perplexing diſorder; in ſome of the houſes entire families were laid up, and at the fort on the oppoſite ſide of the river, the whole of the new garriſon, except a corporal and nine men, was diſqualified for doing duty. Each individual of our party could not but entertain very ſerious apprehenſions for his own health, on arriving at a place where ſickneſs was ſo general, but we were aſſured that the danger of catching the diſorder was now over; that all thoſe who were ill at preſent, had been confined many weeks before; and that for a fortnight paſt not a ſingle perſon had been attacked, who had not been ill in the preceding part of the ſeaſon. As a precaution, however, each one of the party took faſting, in the morning, a glaſs of brandy, in which was infuſed a teaſpoonfull of Peruvian bark. This

mixture

mixture is deemed, in the country, one of the moſt certain preventatives againſt the diſorder, and few that take it, in time, regularly, and avoid the evening dews, ſuffer from it.

Not only the town of Niagara and its vicinity are unhealthy places, but almoſt every part of Upper Canada, and of the territory of the States bordering upon the lakes, is likewiſe unhealthy. The ſickly ſeaſon commences about the middle of July, and terminates about the firſt week of September, as ſoon as the nights become cold. Intermittent fevers are the moſt common diſorders; but in ſome parts of the country the inhabitants ſuffer from continual fevers, of which there are different kinds, peculiar to certain diſtricts. In the country, for inſtance, bordering upon the Geneſee River, which falls into Lake Ontario on the ſouthern ſide, a fever is common amongſt the inhabitants of a malignant nature, vulgarly called the Geneſee fever, of which many die annually: and in that bordering upon the Miami River, which falls into Lake Erie, within the north-weſtern territory of the United States, a fever of a different kind, again, is common. It does not appear that the exact nature of theſe different fevers has ever been accurately aſcertained. In the back parts of North America, in general, medical men are rarely to be met with, and

indeed

indeed if they were, the settlements are so far removed from each other, that they could be of little service.

It is very remarkable, that notwithstanding that medical assistance is so rarely to be had in case of sickness in the back country, yet the Americans, when they are about to change their place of abode, seldom or ever consider whether the part of the country to which they are going is healthy or otherwise, at least they are scarcely ever influenced in their choice of a place of residence either by its healthiness or unhealthiness. If the lands in one part of the country are superior to those in another in fertility; if they are in the neighbourhood of a navigable river, or situated conveniently to a good market; if they are cheap, and rising in value, thither the American will gladly emigrate, let the climate be ever so unfriendly to the human system. Not a year passes over, but what numbers of people leave the beautiful and healthy banks of the Susquehannah River for the Genesee country, where nine out of every ten of the inhabitants are regularly seized, during the autumn, with malignant fevers; but the lands bordering upon the Susquehannah are in general poor, whereas those in the Genesee country are in many places so rich, that until reduced by successive crops of Indian corn, wheat, to use the

common

common phrafe, " will run wholly to ftraw:" where it has been fown in the firft inftance, the ftalks have frequently been found fourteen or fifteen feet in length, two thirds of them lying on the ground.

On the margin of Niagara River, about three quarters of a mile from the town, ftands a building called Navy Hall, erected for the accommodation of the naval officers on the lake during the winter feafon, when their veffels are laid up. Oppofite to it there is a fpacious wharf to protect the vefiels from the ice during the winter, and alfo to facilitate the landing of merchandize when the navigation is open. All cargoes brought up the lake, that are deftined for Niagara, are landed here. Adjoining the wharf are very extenfive ftores belonging to the crown, and alfo to private perfons. Navy Hall is now occupied by the troops; the fort on the oppofite fide of the river, where they were formerly ftationed, having been delivered up purfuant to the late treaty between his Majefty and the United States. The troops, however, are only to remain at the hall until a blockhoufe is erected on the top of the banks for their accommodation; this building is in a ftate of forwardnefs, and the engineer hopes to have it finifhed in a few months.

The fort of Niagara ftands immediately at the

the mouth of the river, on a point of land, one fide of which is wafhed by the river and the other by the lake. Towards the water it is ftockaded; and behind the ftockade, on the river fide, a large mound of earth rifes up, at the top of which are embrafures for guns; on the land fide it is fecured by feveral batteries and redoubts, and by parallel lines of fafcines. At the gates, and in various different parts, there are ftrong blockhoufes; and facing the lake, within the ftockade, ftands a large fortified ftone houfe. The fort and outworks occupy about five acres of ground; and a garrifon of five hundred men, and at leaft from thirty to forty pieces of ordnance, would be neceffary to defend it properly. The federal garrifon, however, confifts only of fifty men; and the whole of the cannon in the place amounts merely to four fmall field pieces, planted at the four corners of the fort. This fort was founded by the French, and conftituted one link of that extenfive chain of pofts which they eftablifhed along the lakes and the weftern waters. It was begun by the building of the ftone houfe, after a folemn promife had been obtained from the Indians that the artificers fhould not be interrupted whilft they were going on with the work. The Indians readily made this promife, as, according to their notion, it would have been in-

hofpitable

hofpitable and unfriendly in the extreme not to have permitted a few traders to build a houfe within their territory to protect them againft the inclemency of the feafons: but they were greatly aftonifhed when one fo totally different from any that they had ever feen before, and from any that they had an idea of, was completed; they began to fufpect that the ftrangers had plans in meditation unfavourable to their interefts, and they wifhed to difpoffefs them of their new manfion, but it was too late. In the hall of the houfe a well had been funk to keep it fupplied with water; the houfe was plentifully ftored with provifions in cafe of a fiege; and the doors being once clofed, the tenants remained perfectly indifferent about every hoftile attack the Indians could make againft it. Fortifications to ftrengthen the houfe were gradually erected; and by the year 1759 the place was fo ftrong as to refift, for fome time, the forces under the command of Sir William Johnfton. Great additions were made to the works after the fort fell into the hands of the Britifh. The ftone houfe is a very fpacious building, and is now, as it was formerly, appropriated for the accommodation of the principal officers of the garrifon. In the rear of the houfe is a large apartment, commanding a magnificent view of the lake and of the diftant hills at Toronto,
which

FORT OF NIAGARA. 97

which formerly was the officers mefs room, and a pattern of neatnefs. The officers of the federal garrifon, however, confider it more convenient to mefs in one of the kitchens, and this beautiful room has been fuffered to go to ruin; indeed every part of the fort now exhibits a picture of flovenlinefs and neglect; and the appearance of the foldiers is equally devoid of neatnefs with that of their quarters. Though it was on Sunday morning that we vifited the fort, on which day it is ufual even for the men of the garrifons in the States to appear better dreffed than on other days, yet the greater part of the men were as dirty as if they had been at work in the trenches for a week without intermiffion: their grifly beards demonftrated that a razor had not approached their chins for many days; their hair, to appearance, had not been combed for the fame length of time; their linen was filthy, their guns rufty, and their clothes ragged. That the clothes and accoutrements of the men fhould not be better is not to be wondered at, confidering how very badly the weftern army of the States is appointed in every refpect; but it is ftrange that the officers fhould not attend more than they do to the cleanlinefs of their men. Their garrifons on the frontiers have uniformly fuffered more from ficknefs than thofe of the Britifh; and it is to be attributed,

VOL. II.   H   I fhould

I should imagine, in a great measure to their filthiness; for the men are as stout and hardy, apparently, as any in the world. The western army of the States has been most shamefully appointed from the very outset. I heard General Wayne, then the commander in chief, declare at Philadelphia, that a short time after they had begun their march, more than one third of his men were attacked in the woods, at the same period, with a dysentery; that the surgeons had not even been furnished with a medicine chest; and that nothing could have saved the greater part of the troops from death, had not one of the young surgeons fortunately discovered, after many different things had been tried in vain, that the bark of the root of a particular sort of yellow poplar tree was a powerful antidote to the disorder. Many times also, he said, his army had been on the point of suffering from famine in their own country, owing to the carelessness of their commissaries. So badly indeed had the army been supplied, even latterly, with provisions, that when notice was sent to the federal general by the British officers, that they had received orders to deliver up their respective posts pursuant to the treaty, and that they were prepared to do so whenever he was ready to take possession of them, an answer was returned, that unless the British officers could

supply

supply his army with a confiderable quantity of provifions on arriving at the lakes, he could not attempt to march for many weeks. The federal army was generoufly fupplied with fifty barrels of pork, as much as the Britifh could poffibly fpare; notwithftanding which, it did not make its appearance till a confiderable time after the day appointed for the delivery of the pofts. The federal army is compofed almoft wholly of Irifhmen and Germans, that were brought over as redemptioners, and enlifted as foon as they landed, before they had an opportunity of learning what great wages were given to labourers in the States. The natives of the country are too fond of making money to reft fatisfied with the pay of a common foldier.

The American prints, until the late treaty of amity was ratified, teemed with the moft grofs abufe of the Britifh government, for retaining poffeffion of Niagara Fort, and the other military pofts on the lakes, after the independence of the States had been acknowledged, and peace concluded. It was never taken into confideration, that if the Britifh government had thought proper to have withdrawn its troops from the pofts at once, immediately after the definitive treaty was figned, the works would in all probability have been deftroyed by the Indians, within whofe territories they were situated, long before the people of the States could have taken possession of them; for no part of their army was within hundreds of miles of the posts, and the country through which they must have past in getting to them was a mere wilderness; but if the army had gained the posts, the states were in no condition, immediately after the war, to have kept in them such large bodies of the military as would have been absolutely necessary for their defence whilst at enmity with the Indians, and it is by no means improbable, but that the posts might have been soon abandoned. The retention of them, therefore, to the present day, was, in fact, a circumstance highly beneficial to the interests of the States, notwithstanding that such an outcry was raised against the British on that account, inasmuch as the Americans now find themselves possessed of extensive fortifications on the frontiers, in perfect repair, without having been at the expence of building them, or maintaining troops in them for the space of ten years, during which period no equivalent advantages could have been derived from their possession. It is not to be supposed, however, that the British government meant to confer a favour on her late colonies by retaining the posts; it was well known that the people of the new states would be eager, sooner or later, to get

possession

possession of forts situated within their boundary line, and occupied by strangers; and as there were particular parts of the definitive treaty which some of the states did not seem very ready to comply with, the posts were detained as a security for its due ratification on the part of the States. In the late treaty of amity and commerce, these differences were finally accommodated to the satisfaction of Great Britain, and the posts were consequently delivered up. On the surrender of them very handsome compliments were paid, in the public papers throughout the States, to the British officers, for the polite and friendly manner in which they gave them up. The gardens of the officers were all left in full bearing, and high preservation; and all the little conveniences were spared, which could contribute to the comforts of the federal troops.

The generality of the people of the States were big with the idea, that the possession of these places would be attended with the most important and immediate advantages; and in particular they were fully persuaded, that they would thereby at once become masters of the trade to the lakes, and of three-fourths at least of the fur trade, which, they said, had hitherto been so unjustly monopolized by the British merchants, to their great prejudice. They have now got possession of them, and perceive the futility of all these notions.

The posts surrendered are four in number; namely, Fort Oswego, at the mouth of Oswego River, which falls into Lake Ontario, on the south side; Fort Niagara, at the mouth of Niagara River; Fort Detroit, on the western bank of Detroit River; and Fort Michillimachinack, at the straits of the same name, between Lake Michigan and Lake Huron. From Oswego, the first of these, we derived no benefit whatever. The neighbouring country, for miles round, was a mere forest; it was inhabited by but few Indians, and these few carried their furs to Cadaragui or Kingston, where they got a better price for them than at Oswego, as there were many traders there, and of course some competition amongst them; at the same time, the river, at the mouth of which this fort stands, was always open to the people of the States, and along it a small trade was carried on by them between New York and Lake Ontario, which was in no wise ever interrupted by the troops at the fort. By the surrender of this place, therefore, they have gained nothing but what they enjoyed before and the British government is saved the expence of keeping up a useless garrison of fifty men.

The quantity of furs collected at Niagara is considerable, and the neighbourhood being populous, it is a place of no small trade; but the

the town, in which this trade is carried on, being on the British side of the line, the few merchants that lived within the limits of the fort immediately crossed over to the other side, as soon as it was rumoured that the fort was to be given up. By the possession of a solitary fort, therefore, the people of the States have not gained the smallest portion of this part of the lake trade; nor is it probable that any of them will find it their interest to settle as merchants near the fort; for the British merchants, on the opposite side, as has already been shewn, can afford to sell their goods, brought up the St. Lawrence, on much lower terms than what goods brought from New York can be sold at; and as for the collecting of furs, it is not to be imagined that the Indians, who bear such a rooted hatred to the people of the States, who are attached to the British, and who are not a people ready to forsake their old friends, will carry their furs over to their enemies, and give up their connections with the men with whom they have been in the habit of dealing, and who can afford to pay them so much better than the traders on the opposite side of the water.

Detroit, of all the places which have been given up, is the most important; for it is a town, containing at least twelve hundred inhabitants. Since its surrender, however, a new town has been laid out on the oppofite bank of the river, eighteen miles lower down, and hither many of the traders have removed. The majority of them ſtay at Detroit; but few or none have become citizens of the States in confequence, nor is it likely that they will, at leaſt for fome time. In the late treaty, a particular provifion for them was made; they were to be allowed to remain there for one year, without being called on to declare their fentiments, and if at the end of that period they chofe to remain Britiſh fubjects, they were not to be molefted * in any manner, but fuffered to carry on their trade as formerly in the fulleft extent; the portion of the fur trade, which we fhall lofe by the furrender of this place, will therefore be very inconfiderable.

The fourth poſt, Michillimachinack, is a fmall ſtockaded fort, fituated on an iſland.

---

* This part of the late treaty has by no means been ſtrictly obferved on the part of the States. The officers of the federal army, without aſking permiſſion, and contrary to the defire of feveral of the remaining Britiſh inhabitants, appropriated to their own ufe feveral of the houfes and ſtores of thofe who had removed to the new town, and declared their determination of not becoming citizens of the States; and many of the inhabitants had been called on to ferve in the militia, and to perform duties, from which, as Britiſh fubjects, they were exempted by the articles in the treaty in their favour. When we were at Detroit, the Britiſh inhabitants met together, and drew up a memorial on the fubject, reciting their grievances, which was committed to our care, and accordingly prefented to the Britiſh miniſter at Philadelphia.

The

The agents of the North-weſt Company of merchants at Montreal, and a few independent traders, reſided within the limits of the fort, and bartered goods there for furs brought in by different tribes of Indians, who are the ſole inhabitants of the neighbouring country. On evacuating this place, another poſt was immediately eſtabliſhed, at no great diſtance, on the Iſland of St. Joſeph, in the Straits of St. Mary, between lakes Superior and Huron, and a ſmall garriſon left there, which has ſince been augmented to upwards of fifty men. Several traders, citizens of the States, have eſtabliſhed themſelves at Michillimakinac; but as the Britiſh traders have fixed their new poſt ſo cloſe to the old one, it is nearly certain that the Indians will continue to trade with their old friends in preference, for the reaſons before mentioned.

From this ſtatement it appears evident, that the people of the States can only acquire by their new poſſeſſion a ſmall part of one branch of the fur trade, namely, of that which is carried on on one of the nearer lakes. The furs brought down from the diſtant regions in the north-weſt to the grand portage, and from thence in canoes to Montreal along the Utawa River, are what conſtitute by far the principal part, both as to quantity and value, of thoſe exported from Montreal; to talk, therefore, of their acquiring poſſeſſion of three-
fourths

fourths of the fur trade by the furrender of the pofts on the lakes is abfurd in the extreme; neither is it likely that they will acquire any confiderable fhare of the lake trade in general, which, as I have already pointed out, can be carried on by the Britifh merchants from Montreal and Quebec, by means of the St. Lawrence, with fuch fuperior advantage.

It is worthy of remark, that as military pofts, all thofe lately eftablifhed by the Britifh are far fuperior, in point of fituation, to thofe delivered up. The ground on which the new block houfe is building, on the Britifh fide of Niagara River, is nine feet higher than the top of the ftone houfe in the American fort, and it commands every part of the fort. The chief ftrength of the old fort is on the land fide; towards the water the works are very weak, and the whole might be battered down by a fingle twelve pounder judicioufly planted on the Britifh fide of the river. At prefent it is not propofed to erect any other works on the Britifh fide of the river than the block houfe; but fhould a fort be conftructed hereafter, it will be placed on Miffiffaguis Point, a ftill more advantageous fituation than that on which the block houfe ftands, as it completely commands the entrance into the river.

The new poft on Detroit River commands the channel much more effectually than the

old

old fort in the town of Detroit; veſſels cannot go up or down the river without paſſing within a very few yards of it. It is remarkable, indeed, that the French, when they firſt penetrated into this part of the country, fixed upon the ſpot choſen for this new fort, in preference to that where Detroit ſtands, and they had abſolutely begun their fort and town, when the whole party was unhappily cut off by the Indians.

The iſland of St. Joſeph, in the third place, is a more eligible ſituation for a Britiſh military poſt than Michillimakinac, inaſmuch as it commands the entrance of Lake Superior, whereas Michillimakinac only commands the entrance into Lake Michigan, which is wholly within the territory of the United States.

It is ſincerely to be hoped, however, that Great Britain and the United States may continue friends, and that we never may have occaſion to view thoſe poſts on the frontiers in any other light than as convenient places for carrying on commerce.

LETTER XXXI.

Description of the River and Falls of Niagara and the Country bordering upon the Navigable Part of the River below the Falls.

Fort Chippeway, September.

AT the diſtance of eighteen miles from the town of Niagara or Newark, are thoſe remarkable Falls in Niagara River, which may juſtly be ranked amongſt the greateſt natural curioſities in the known world. The road leading from Lake Ontario to Lake Erie runs within a few hundred yards of them. This road, which is within the Britiſh dominions, is carried along the top of the lofty ſteep banks of the river; for a conſiderable way it runs cloſe to their very edge, and in paſſing along it the eye of the traveller is entertained with a variety of the moſt grand and beautiful proſpects. The river, inſtead of growing narrow as you proceed upwards, widens conſiderably: at the end of nine or ten miles it expands to the breadth of a mile, and here it aſſumes much the appearance of a lake; it is encloſed, ſeemingly on all ſides, by high hills, and the current, owing to the great depth of the water, is ſo gentle as to be ſcarcely perceptible from the top of the banks. It continues thus broad

for

NIAGARA FALLS. 109

for a mile or two, when on a sudden the waters are contracted between the high hills on each side. From hence up to the falls the current is exceedingly irregular and rapid. At the upper end of this broad part of the river, and nearly at the foot of the banks, is situated a small village, that has been called Queens-town, but which, in the adjacent country, is best known by the name of "The Landing." The lake merchant vessels can proceed up to this village with perfect safety, and they commonly do so, to deposit, in the stores there, such goods as are intended to be sent higher up the country, and to receive in return the furs, &c. that have been collected at the various posts on lakes Huron and Erie, and sent thither to be conveyed down to Kingston, across Lake Ontario. The portage from this place to the nearest navigable part of Niagara River, above the Falls, is nine miles in length.

About half way up the banks, at the distance of a few hundred yards from Queenstown, there is a very extensive range of wooden barracks, which, when viewed a little way off, appears to great advantage; these barracks are now quite unoccupied, and it is not probable that they will ever be used until the climate improves: the first troops that were lodged in them sickened in a very few days after their arrival; many of the men died, and had not

those

thofe that remained alive been removed, purſuant to the advice of the phyſicians, to other quarters, the whole regiment might poſſibly have periſhed.

From the town of Niagara to Queenſtown, the country in the neighbourhood of the river is very level; but here it puts on a different afpect; a confuſed range of hills, covered with oaks of an immenſe ſize, ſuddenly riſes up before you, and the road that winds up the ſide of them is ſo ſteep and rugged that it is abſolutely neceſſary for the traveller to leave his carriage, if he ſhould be in one, and proceed to the top on foot. Beyond theſe hills you again come to an unbroken level country; but the ſoil here differs materially from that on the oppoſite ſide; it conſiſts of a rich dark earth intermixed with clay, and abounding with ſtones; whereas, on the ſide next Lake Ontario, the ſoil is of a yellowiſh caſt, in ſome places inclining to gravel and in others to ſand.

From the brow of one of the hills in this ridge, which overhangs the little village of Queenſtown, the eye of the traveller is gratified with one of the fineſt proſpects that can be imagined in nature: you ſtand amidſt a clump of large oaks, a little to the left of the road, and looking downwards, perceive, through the branches of the trees with which the hill is
clothed

clothed from the summit to the base, the tops of the houses of Queenstown, and in front of the village, the ships moored in the river; the ships are at least two hundred feet below you, and their masts appear like slender reeds peeping up amidst the thick foliage of the trees. Carrying your eye forward, you may trace the river in all its windings, and finally see it disembogue into Lake Ontario, between the town and the fort: the lake itself terminates your view in this direction, except merely at one part of the horizon, where you just get a glimpse of the blue hills of Toronto. The shore of the river, on the right hand, remains in its natural state, covered with one continued forest; but on the opposite side the country is interspersed with cultivated fields and neat farm houses down to the water's edge. The country beyond the hills is much less cleared than that which lies towards the town of Niagara, on the navigable part of the river.

From the sudden change of the face of the country in the neighbourhood of Queenstown, and the equally sudden change in the river with respect to its breadth, depth, and current, conjectures have been formed, that the great falls of the river must originally have been situated at the spot where the waters are so abruptly contracted between the hills; and

indeed

indeed it is highly probable that this was the cafe, for it is a fact well afcertained, that the falls have receded very confiderably fince they were firft vifited by Europeans, and that they are ftill receding every year; but of this I fhall have occafion to fpeak more particularly prefently.

It was at an early hour of the day that we left the town of Niagara or Newark, accompanied by the attorney general and an officer of the Britifh engineers, in order to vifit thefe ftupendous Falls. Every ftep that we advanced toward them, our expectations rofe to a higher pitch; our eyes were continually on the look out for the column of white mift which hovers over them; and an hundred times, I believe, did we ftop our carriage in hopes of hearing their thundering found: neither, however, was the mift to be feen, nor the found to be heard, when we came to the foot of the hills; nor after having croffed over them, were our eyes or ears more gratified. This occafioned no inconfiderable difappointment, and we could not but exprefs our doubts to each other, that the wondrous accounts we had fo frequently heard of the Falls were without foundation, and calculated merely to impofe on the minds of credulous people that inhabited a diftant part of the world. Thefe doubts were nearly confirmed, when we found that, after

having

having approached within half a mile of the place, the mist was but just discernible, and that the sound even then was not to be heard; yet it is nevertheless strictly true, that the tremendous noise of the Falls may be distinctly heard, at times, at the distance of forty miles; and the cloud formed from the spray may be even seen still farther off *; but it is only when the air is very clear, and there is a fine blue sky, which however are very common occurrences in this country, that the cloud can be seen at such a great distance. The hearing of the sound of the falls afar off also depends upon the state of the atmosphere; it is observed, that the sound can be heard at the greatest distance, just before a heavy fall of rain, and when the wind is in a favourable point to

* We ourselves, some time afterwards, beheld the cloud with the naked eye, at no less a distance than fifty-four miles, when sailing on Lake Erie, on board one of the king's ships. The day on which we saw it was uncommonly clear and calm, and we were seated on the poop of the vessel, admiring the bold scenery of the southern shore of the lake, when the commander, who had been aloft to make some observations, came to us, and pointing to a small white cloud in the horizon, told us, that that was the cloud overhanging Niagara. At first it appeared to us that this must have been a mere conjecture, but on minute observation it was evident that the commander's information was just. All the other light clouds in a few minutes, flitted away to another part of the horizon, whereas this one remained steadily fixed in the same spot; and on looking at it through a glass, it was plain to see that the shape of the cloud varied every instant, owing to the continued rising of the mist from the cataract beneath.

Vol. II.   I   convey

convey the sound toward the listener : the day on which we first approached the falls was thick and cloudy.

On that part of the road leading to Lake Erie which draws nearest to the falls, there is a small village, consisting of about half a dozen straggling houses: here we alighted, and having disposed of our horses, and made a slight repast, in order to prepare us for the fatigue we had to go through, we crossed over some fields towards a deep hollow place surrounded with large trees, from the bottom of which issued thick volumes of whitish mist, that had much the appearance of smoke rising from large heaps of burning weeds. Having come to the edge of this hollow place, we descended a steep bank of about fifty yards, and then walking for some distance over a wet marshy piece of ground, covered with thick bushes, at last came to the Table Rock, so called from the remarkable flatness of its surface, and its bearing some similitude to a table. This rock is situated a little to the front of the great fall, above the top of which it is elevated about forty feet. The view from it is truly sublime; but before I attempt to give any idea of the nature of this view, it will be necessary to take a more general survey of the river and falls.

Niagara River issues from the eastern extremity

tremity of Lake Erie, and after a courfe of thirty-fix miles difcharges itfelf into Lake Ontario, as has already been mentioned. For the firft few miles from Lake Erie, the breadth of the river is about three hundred yards, and it is deep enough for veffels drawing nine or ten feet water; but the current is fo extremely rapid and irregular, and the channel fo intricate, on account of the numberlefs large rocks in different places, that no other veffels than bateaux ever attempt to pafs along it. As you proceed downward the river widens, no rocks are to be feen either along the fhores or in the channel, and the waters glide fmoothly along, though the current continues very ftrong. The river runs thus evenly, and is navigable with fafety for bateaux as far as Fort Chippeway, which is about three miles above the falls; but here the bed of it again becomes rocky, and the waters are violently agitated by paffing down fucceffive rapids, fo much fo indeed, that were a boat by any chance to be carried but a little way beyond Chippeway, where people ufually ftop, nothing could fave it from being dafhed to pieces long before it came to the falls. With fuch aftonifhing impetuofity do the waves break on the rocks in thefe rapids, that the mere fight of them from the top of the banks is fufficient to make you fhudder. I muft in this place, however,

however, observe, that it is only on each side of the river that the waters are so much troubled; in the middle of it, though the current is also there uncommonly swift, yet the breakers are not so dangerous but boats may pass down, if dexterously managed, to an island which divides the river at the very falls. To go down to this island it is necessary to set off at some distance above Chippeway, where the current is even, and to keep exactly in the middle of the river the whole way thither; if the boats were suffered to get out of their course ever so little, either to the right or left, it would be impossible to stem the current, and bring them again into it; they would be irresistibly carried towards the falls, and destruction must inevitably follow. In returning from the island there is still more difficulty and danger than in going to it. Notwithstanding these circumstances, numbers of persons have the foolhardiness to proceed to this island, merely for the sake of beholding the falls from the opposite side of it, or for the sake of having in their power to say that they had been upon it.

The river forces its way amidst the rocks with redoubled impetuosity, as it approaches towards the falls; at last coming to the brink of the tremendous precipice, it tumbles headlong to the bottom, without meeting with any

any interruption from rocks in its defcent. Juft at the precipice the river takes a confiderable bend to the right, and the line of the falls, inftead of extending from bank to bank in the fhorteft direction, runs obliquely acrofs. The width of the falls is confiderably greater than the width of the river, admeafured fome way below the precipice; but the annexed plan will enable you to form a better idea of their pofition than any written defcription whatfoever. For its great accuracy I cannot vouch, as it was done merely from the eye; fuch as it is, however, I have fent it to you, conceiving it better that you fhould have a plan fomewhat imperfect than no plan at all. On looking it over you will fee that the river does not rufh down the precipice in one unbroken fheet, but that it is divided by iflands into three diftinct collateral falls. The moft ftupendous of thefe is that on the north weftern or Britifh fide of the river, commonly called the Great, or Horfe-fhoe Fall, from its bearing fome refemblance to the fhape of a horfe fhoe. The height of this is only one hundred and forty-two feet, whereas the others are each one hundred and fixty feet high; but to its inferior height it is indebted principally for its grandeur; the precipice, and of courfe the bed of the river above it, being fo much lower at the one

I 3   fide

side than at the other, by far the greater part of the water of the river finds its way to the low side, and rushes down with greater velocity at that side than it does at the other, as the rapids above the precipice are strongest there. It is from the center of the Horseshoe Fall that arises that prodigious cloud of mist which may be seen so far off. The extent of the Horse-shoe Fall can only be ascertained by the eye; the general opinion of those who have most frequently viewed it is, that it is not less than six hundred yards in circumference. The island which separates it from the next fall is supposed to be about three hundred and fifty yards wide; the second fall is about five yards wide; the next island about thirty yards; and the third, commonly called the Fort Schloper Fall, from being situated towards the side of the river on which that fort stands, is judged to admeasure at least as much as the large island. The whole extent of the precipice, therefore, including the islands, is, according to this computation, thirteen hundred and thirty-five yards. This is certainly not an exaggerated statement. Some have supposed, that the line of the falls altogether exceeds an English mile. The quantity of water carried down the falls is prodigious. It will be found to amount to 670,255 tons per minute, though calculated
simply

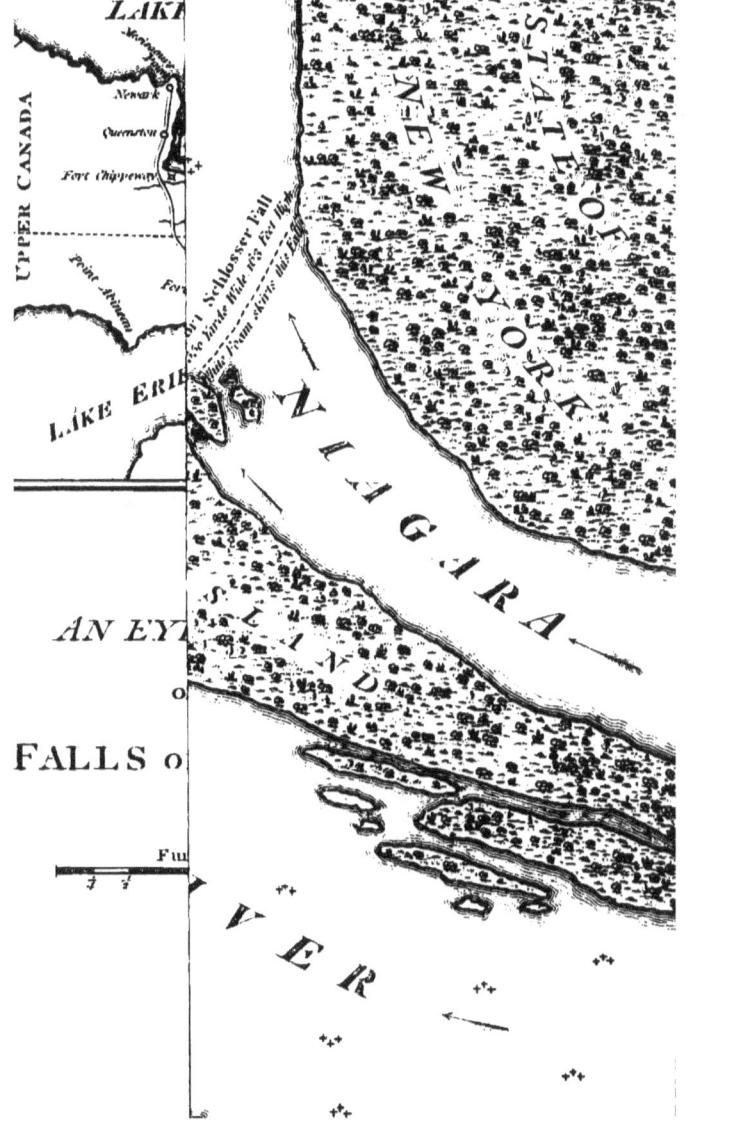

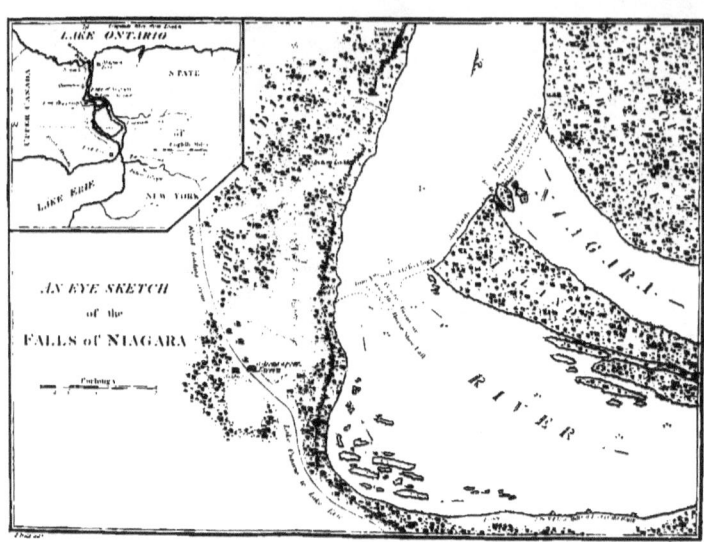

TABLE ROCK.

simply from the following data, which ought to be correct, as coming from an experienced commander of one of the King's ships on Lake Erie, well acquainted in every respect with that body of water, viz. that where Lake Erie, towards its eastern extremity, is two miles and a half wide, the water is six feet deep, and the current runs at the rate of two knots in an hour; but Niagara River, between this part of Lake Erie and the falls, receives the waters of several large creeks, the quantity carried down the falls must therefore be greater than the foregoing computation makes it to be; if we say that six hundred and seventy-two thousand tons of water are precipitated down the falls every minute, the quantity will not probably be much overrated.

To return now to the Table Rock, situated on the British side of the river, and on the verge of the Horse-shoe Fall. Here the spectator has an unobstructed view of the tremendous rapids above the falls, and of the circumjacent shores, covered with thick woods; of the Horse-shoe Fall, some yards below him; of the Fort Schloper Fall, at a distance to the left; and of the frightful gulph beneath, into which, if he has but courage to approach to the exposed edge of the rock, he may look down perpendicularly. The astonishment excited in the mind of the spectator by the vastness of the different objects which he contemplates from hence is great indeed, and few persons, on coming here for the first time, can for some minutes collect themselves sufficiently to be able to form any tolerable conception of the stupendous scene before them. It is impossible for the eye to embrace the whole of it at once; it must gradually make itself acquainted, in the first place, with the component parts of the scene, each one of which is in itself an object of wonder; and such a length of time does this operation require, that many of those who have had an opportunity of contemplating the scene at their leisure, for years together, have thought that every time they have beheld it, each part has appeared more wonderful and more sublime, and that it has only been at the time of their last visit that they have been able to discover all the grandeur of the cataract.

Having spent a considerable time on the Table Rock, we returned to the fields the same way by which we had descended, pursuant to the direction of the officer of engineers accompanying us, who was intimately acquainted with every part of the cataract, and of the adjoining ground, and was, perhaps, the best guide that could be procured in the whole country. It would be possible to pursue your way along the edge of the cliff, from the Table Rock,

Rock, a confiderable way downwards; but the
bufhes are fo exceedingly thick, and the ground
fo rugged, that the tafk would be arduous in
the extreme.

The next fpot from which we furveyed
the falls, was from the part of the cliff nearly
oppofite to that end of the Fort Schloper Fall, which lies next to the ifland. You
ftand here, on the edge of the cliff, behind fome
bufhes, the tops of which have been cut down
in order to open the view. From hence you
have a better profpect of the whole cataract,
and are enabled to form a more correct idea
of the pofition of the precipice, than from any
one other place. The profpect from hence
is more beautiful, but I think lefs grand than
from any other fpot. The officer who fo politely directed our movements on this occafion
was fo ftruck with the view from this fpot,
that he once had a wooden houfe conftructed,
and drawn down here by oxen, in which he
lived until he had finifhed feveral different
drawings of the cataract: one of thefe we were
gratified with the fight of, which exhibited a
view of the cataract in the depth of winter,
when in a moft curious and wonderful ftate.
The ice at this feafon of the year accumu-
lates at the bottom of the cataract in immenfe
mounds, and huge icicles, like the pillars of a
maffy building, hang pendent in many places
from the top of the precipice, reaching nearly
to the bottom.

Having

Having left this place, we returned once more through the woods bordering upon the precipice to the open fields, and then directed our courfe by a circuitous path, about one mile in length, to a part of the cliff where it is poffible to defcend to the bottom of the cataract. The river, for many miles below the precipice, is bounded on each fide by steep, and in moft parts perpendicular, cliffs, formed of earth and rocks, and it is impoffible to defcend to the bottom of them, except at two places, where large maffes of earth and rocks have crumbled down, and ladders have been placed from one break to another, for the accommodation of paffengers. The firft of thefe places which you come to in walking along the river, from the Horfe-fhoe Fall downwards, is called the " Indian Ladder," the ladders having been conftructed there by the Indians. Thefe ladders, as they are called, of which there are feveral, one below the other, confift fimply of long pine trees, with notches cut in their fides, for the paffenger to reft his feet on. The trees, even when firft placed there, would vibrate as you ftepped upon them, owing to their being fo long and flender; age has rendered them ftill lefs firm, and they now certainly cannot be deemed fafe, though many perfons are ftill in the habit of defcending by their means. We did not attempt to get to

NIAGARA

the bottom of the cliff by this route, but proceeded to the other place, which is lower down
the river, called Mrs. Simcoe's Ladder, the ladders having been originally placed there for
the accommodation of the lady of the late governor. This route is much more frequented
than the other; the ladders, properly so called,
are strong, and firmly placed, and none of them,
owing to the frequent breaks in the cliff,
are required to be of such a great length
but what even a lady might pass up or down
them without fear of danger. To descend over
the rugged rocks, however, the whole way
down to the bottom of the cliff, is certainly
no trifling undertaking, and few ladies, I believe, could be found of sufficient strength of
body to encounter the fatigue of such an expedition.

On arriving at the bottom of the cliff, you
find yourself in the midst of huge piles of
mishapen rocks, with great masses of earth and
rocks projecting from the side of the cliff, and
overgrown with pines and cedars hanging over
your head, apparently ready to crumble down
and crush you to atoms. Many of the large
trees grow with their heads downwards, being
suspended by their roots, which had taken
such a firm hold in the ground at the top of
the cliff, that when part of it gave way the
trees did not fall altogether. The river before
you

you here is somewhat more than a quarter of a mile wide; and on the opposite side of it, a little to the right, the Fort Schloper Fall is seen to great advantage; what you see of the Horse-shoe Fall also appears in a very favourable point of view; the projecting cliff conceals nearly one half of it. The Fort Schloper Fall is skirted at bottom by milk white foam, which ascends in thick volumes from the rocks; but it is not seen to rise above the fall like a cloud of smoke, as is the case at the Horse-shoe Fall; nevertheless the spray is so considerable, that it descends on the opposite side of the river, at the foot of Simcoe's Ladder, like rain.

Having reached the margin of the river, we proceeded towards the Great Fall, along the strand, which for a considerable part of the way thither consists of horizontal beds of limestone rock, covered with gravel, except, indeed, where great piles of stones have fallen from the sides of the cliff. These horizontal beds of rock, in some places, extend very far into the river, forming points which break the force of the current, and occasion strong eddies along particular parts of the shore. Here great numbers of the bodies of fishes, squirrels, foxes, and various other animals, that, unable to stem the current of the river above the falls, have been carried down them,

and

and consequently killed, are washed up. The shore is likewise found strewed with trees, and large pieces of timber, that have been swept away from the saw mills above the falls, and carried down the precipice. The timber is generally terribly shattered, and the carcases of all the large animals, particularly of the large fishes, are found very much bruised. A dreadful stench arises from the quantity of putrid matter lying on the shore, and numberless birds of prey, attracted by it, are always seen hovering about the place.

Amongst the numerous stories current in the country, relating to this wonderful cataract, there is one that records the hapless fate of a poor Indian, which I select, as the truth of it is unquestionable. The unfortunate hero of this tale, intoxicated, it seems, with spirits, had laid himself down to sleep in the bottom of his canoe, which was fastened to the beach at the distance of some miles above the falls. His squaw sat on the shore to watch him. Whilst they were in this situation, a sailor from one of the ships of war on the neighbouring lakes happened to pass by; he was struck with the charms of the squaw, and instantly determined upon enjoying them. The faithful creature, however, unwilling to gratify his desires, hastened to the canoe to arouse her husband; but before she could effect her purpose,

pose, the sailor cut the cord by which the canoe was fastened, and set it adrift. It quickly floated away with the stream from the fatal spot, and ere many minutes elapsed, was carried down into the midst of the rapids. Here it was distinctly seen by several persons that were standing on the adjacent shore, whose attention had been caught by the singularity of the appearance of a canoe in such a part of the river. The violent motion of the waves soon awoke the Indian; he started up, looked wildly around, and perceiving his danger, instantly seized his paddle, and made the most surprising exertions to save himself; but finding in a little time that all his efforts would be of no avail in stemming the impetuosity of the current, he with great composure put aside his paddle, wrapt himself up in his blanket, and again laid himself down in the bottom of the canoe. In a few seconds he was hurried down the precipice; but neither he nor his canoe were ever seen more. It is supposed that not more than one third of the different things that happen to be carried down the falls reappear at bottom.

From the foot of Simcoe's Ladder you may walk along the strand for some distance without inconvenience; but as you approach the Horse-shoe Fall, the way becomes more and more rugged. In some places, where the cliff
has

has crumbled down, huge mounds of earth, rocks, and trees, reaching to the water's edge, oppose your course; it seems impossible to pass them; and, indeed, without a guide, a stranger would never find his way to the opposite side; for to get there it is necessary to mount nearly to their top, and then to crawl on your hands and knees through long dark holes, where passages are left open between the torn up rocks and trees. After passing these mounds, you have to climb from rock to rock close under the cliff, for there is but little space here between the cliff and the river, and these rocks are so slippery, owing to the continual moisture from the spray, which descends very heavily, that without the utmost precaution it is scarcely possible to escape a fall. At the distance of a quarter of a mile from the Great Fall we were as wet, owing to the spray, as if each of us had been thrown into the river.

There is nothing whatsoever to prevent you from passing to the very foot of the Great Fall; and you might even proceed behind the prodigious sheet of water that comes pouring down from the top of the precipice, for the water falls from the edge of a projecting rock; and, moreover, caverns of a very considerable size have been hollowed out of the rocks at the bottom of the precipice, owing to the violent

ebullition

ebullition of the water, which extend some way underneath the bed of the upper part of the river. I advanced within about six yards of the edge of the sheet of water, just far enough to peep into the caverns behind it; but here my breath was nearly taken away by the violent whirlwind that always rages at the bottom of the cataract, occasioned by the concussion of such a vast body of water against the rocks. I confess I had no inclination at the time to go farther; nor, indeed, any of us afterwards attempted to explore the dreary confines of these caverns, where death seemed to await him that should be daring enough to enter their threatening jaws. No words can convey an adequate idea of the awful grandeur of the scene at this place. Your senses are appalled by the sight of the immense body of water that comes pouring down so closely to you from the top of the stupendous precipice, and by the thundering sound of the billows dashing against the rocky sides of the caverns below; you tremble with reverential fear, when you consider that a blast of the whirlwind might sweep you from off the slippery rocks on which you stand, and precipitate you into the dreadful gulph beneath, from whence all the power of man could not extricate you; you feel what an insignificant being you are in the creation, and your mind is forcibly impressed with an awful

idea

idea of the power of that mighty Being who commanded the waters to flow.

Since the Falls of Niagara were firſt diſcovered they have receded very confiderably, owing to the difrupture of the rocks which form the precipice. The rocks at bottom are firſt loofened by the conſtant action of the water upon them; they are afterwards carried away, and thoſe at top being thus undermined, are foon broken by the weight of the water ruſhing over them: even within the memory of many of the prefent inhabitants of the country, the falls have receded feveral yards. The commodore of the King's veſſels on Lake Erie, who had been employed on that lake for upwards of thirty years, informed me, that when he firſt came into the country it was a common practice for young men to go to the iſland in the middle of the falls; that after dining there, they ufed frequently to dare each other to walk into the river towards certain large rocks in the midſt of the rapids, not far from the edge of the falls; and fometimes to proceed through the water, even beyond thefe rocks. No fuch rocks are to be feen at prefent; and were a man to advance two yards into the river from the iſland, he would be inevitably fwept away by the torrent. It has been conjectured, as I before mentioned, that the Falls of Niagara were originally fituated at Queenftown; and indeed the more pains you take to examine the courfe of the river from the prefent falls downward, the more reafon is there to imagine that fuch a conjecture is well founded. From the precipice nearly down to Queenftown, the bed of the river is ftrewed with large rocks, and the banks are broken and rugged; circumftances which plainly denote that fome great difruption has taken place along this part of the river; and we need be at no lofs to account for it, as there are evident marks of the action of water upon the fides of the banks, and confiderably above their prefent bafes. Now the river has never been known to rife near thefe marks during the greateft floods; it is plain, therefore, that its bed muft have been once much more elevated than it is at prefent. Below Queenftown, however, there are no traces on the banks to lead us to imagine that the level of the water was ever much higher there than it is now. The fudden increafe of the depth of the river juft below the hills at Queenftown, and its fudden expanfion there at the fame time, feem to indicate that the waters muft for a great length of time have fallen from the top of the hills, and thus have formed that extenfive deep bafin below the village. In the river, a mile or two above

Queen-

Queenstown, there is a tremendous whirlpool, owing to a deep hole in the bed; this hole was probably also formed by the waters falling for a great length of time on the same spot, in consequence of the rocks which composed the then precipice having remained firmer than those at any other place did. Tradition tells us, that the great fall, instead of having been in the form of a horse shoe, once projected in the middle. For a century past, however, it has remained nearly in the present form; and as the ebullition of the water at the bottom of the cataract is so much greater at the center of this fall than in any other part, and as the water consequently acts with more force there in undermining the precipice than at any other part, it is not unlikely that it may remain nearly in the same form for ages to come.

At the bottom of the Horse-shoe Fall is found a kind of white concrete substance, by the people of the country, called spray. Some persons have supposed that it is formed from the earthy particles of the water, which descending, owing to their great specific gravity, quicker than the other particles, adhere to the rocks, and are there formed into a mass. This concrete substance has precisely the appearance of petrified froth; and it is remarkable, that it is found adhering to those rocks against which the greatest quantities of the froth

froth, that floats upon the water, is washed by the eddies.

We did not think of ascending the cliff till the evening was far advanced, and had it been possible to have found our way up in the dark, I verily believe we should have remained at the bottom of it until midnight. Just as we left the foot of the great fall the sun broke through the clouds, and one of the most beautiful and perfect rainbows that ever I beheld was exhibited in the spray that arose from the fall. It is only at evening and morning that the rainbow is seen in perfection; for the banks of the river, and the steep precipice, shade the sun from the spray at the bottom of the fall in the middle of the day.

At a great distance from the foot of the ladder we halted, and one of the party was dispatched to fetch a bottle of brandy and a pair of goblets, which had been deposited under some stones on the margin of the river, in our way to the great fall, whither it would have been highly inconvenient to have carried them. Wet from head to foot, and greatly fatigued, there certainly was not one amongst us that appeared, at the moment, desirous of getting the brandy, in order to pour out a libation to the tutelary deities of the cataract; nor indeed was there much reason to apprehend that our piety would have shone forth more conspicuously after-

wards;

wards; however it was not put to the teft; for the meffenger returned in a few minutes with the woeful intelligence that the brandy and goblets had been ftolen. We were at no great lofs in gueffing who the thieves were. Perched on the rocks, at a little diftance from us, fat a pair of the river nymphs, not " nymphs with fedged crowns and ever " harmlefs looks ;" not " temperate nymphs," but a pair of fquat fturdy old wenches, that with clofe bonnets and tucked up petticoats had crawled down the cliff, and were bufied with long rods in angling for fifh. Their noify clack plainly indicated that they had been well pleafed with the brandy, and that we ought not to entertain any hopes of recovering the fpoil; we e'en flaked our thirft, therefore, with a draught from the wholefome flood, and having done fo, boldly pufhed forward, and before it was quite dark regained the habitations from whence we had ftarted.

On returning we found a well-fpread table laid out for us in the porch of the houfe, and having gratified the keen appetite which the fatigue we had encountered had excited, our friendly guides, having previoufly given us inftructions for examining the falls more particularly, fet off by moonlight for Niagara, and we repaired to Fort Chippeway, three miles above the falls, which place we made our
head-

head-quarters while we remained in the neighbourhood, becaufe there was a tolerable tavern, and no houfe in the village near the falls, where ficknefs was not prevalent.

The Falls of Niagara are much lefs difficult of accefs now than they were fome years ago. Charlevoix, who vifited them in the year 1720, tells us, that they were only to be viewed from one fpot; and that from thence the fpectator had only a fide profpect of them. Had he been able to have defcended to the bottom, he would have had ocular demonftration of the exiftence of caverns underneath the precipice, which he fuppofed to be the cafe from the hollow found of the falling of the waters; from the number of carcafes wafhed up there on different parts of the ftrand, and would alfo have been convinced of the truth of a circum-ftance which he totally difbelieved, namely, that fifh were oftentimes unable to ftem the rapid current above the falls, and were con-fequently carried down the precipice.

The moft favourable feafon for vifiting the falls is about the middle of September, the time when we faw them; for then the woods are feen in all their glory, beautifully variegat-ed with the rich tints of autumn; and the fpectator is not then annoyed with vermin. In the fummer feafon you meet with rattle-fnakes at every ftep, and mufquitoes fwarm fo thickly

thickly in the air, that to ufe a common phrafe of the country, " you might cut them with " a knife." The cold nights in the beginning of September effectually banifh thefe noxious animals.

LETTER XXXII.

Defcription of Fort Chippeway.—Plan in meditation to cut a Canal to avoid the Portage at the Falls of Niagara.—Departure from Chippeway.—Intenfe Heat of the Weather.—Defcription of the Country bordering on Niagara River above the Falls.—Obfervations on the Climate of Upper Canada.—Rattlefnakes common in Upper Canada.—Fort Erie.—Miferable Accommodation there.—Squirrel hunting. —Seneka Indians.—Their Expertnefs at the Ufe of the Blow-gun.—Defcription of the Blow-gun.—Excurfion to the Village of the Senekas.—Whole Nation abfent.—Paffage of a dangerous Sand Bar at the Mouth of Buffalo Creek.—Sail from Fort Erie.—Driven back by a Storm.—Anchor under Point Abineau.—Defcription of the Point.—Curious Sand Hills there.—Bear hunting.—How carried on.—Dogs, what Sort of, ufed.—Wind changes

changes.—The Veſſel ſuffers from the Storm whilſt at Anchor.—Departure from Point Abineau.—General Deſcription of Lake Erie. —Anecdote.—Reach the Iſlands at the Weſtern End of the Lake.—Anchor there.—Deſcription of the Iſlands.—Serpents of various Kinds found there.—Rattleſnakes.—Medicinal Uſes made of them.—Fabulous Accounts of Serpents.—Departure from the Iſlands.—Arrival at Malden.—Detroit River.

Malden, October.

FORT CHIPPEWAY, from whence my laſt letter was dated, is a ſmall ſtockaded fort, ſituated on the borders of a creek of the ſame name, about two hundred yards diſtant from Niagara River. Had it been built immediately on the latter ſtream, its ſituation would have been much more convenient; for the water of the creek is ſo bad that it cannot be drank, and the garriſon is obliged to draw water daily from the river. The fort, which occupies about one rood of ground only, conſiſts of a ſmall block houſe, incloſed by a ſtockade of cedar poſts about twelve feet high, which is merely ſufficient to defend the garriſon againſt muſquet ſhot. Adjoining to the fort there are about ſeven or eight farm houſes, and ſome large ſtone houſes, where goods are depoſited preparatory to their being conveyed up the

the river in bateaux, or acrofs the portage in carts, to Queenftown. It is faid that it would be practicable to cut a canal from hence to Queenftown, by means of which the troublefome and expenfive procefs of unlading the bateaux and tranfporting the goods in carts along the portage would be avoided. Such a canal will in all probability be undertaken one day or other; but whenever that fhall be the cafe, there is reafon to think that it will be cut on the New York fide of the river for two reafons; firft, becaufe the ground on that fide is much more favourable for fuch an undertaking; and, fecondly, becaufe the ftate of New York is much more populous, and far better enabled to advance the large fums of money that would be requifite for cutting a canal through fuch rugged ground as borders upon the river, than the province of Upper Canada either is at prefent, or appears likely to be.

About fifteen men, under the command of a lieutenant, are ufually quartered at Fort Chippeway, who are moftly employed in conducting, in bateaux from thence to Fort Erie, the ftores for the troops in the upper country, and the prefents for the Indians.

After we had gratified our curiofity in regard to the wonderous objects in the neighbourhood, at leaft as far as our time would permit, we were obligingly furnifhed with a

bateau

bateau by the officer at Fort Chippeway, to whom we carried letters, to convey us to Fort Erie. My companions embarked in it with our baggage, when the morning appointed for our departure arrived; but defirous of taking one more look at the Falls, I ftaid behind, determining to follow them on foot in the courfe of the day; I accordingly walked down to the falls from Fort Chippeway after breakfaft, fpent an hour or two there, returned to the fort, and having ftopped a fhort time to reft myfelf after the fatigues of climbing the fteeps about the falls, I fet out for Fort Erie, fifteen miles diftant from Chippeway, accompanied by my faithful fervant Edward, who has indeed been a treafure to me fince I have been in America. The day was by no means favourable for a pedeftrian expedition; it was intenfely hot, and we had not proceeded far before we found the neceffity of taking off our jackets, waiftcoats, and cravats, and carrying them in a bundle on our backs. Several parties of Indians that I met going down the river in canoes were ftark naked.

The banks of Niagara River, between Chippeway and Fort Erie, are very low, and covered, for the moft part, with fhrubs, under whofe fhade, upon the gravelly beach of the river, the weary traveller finds an agreeable refting place. For the firft few miles from Chippeway

Chippeway there are scarcely any houses to be seen; but about half way between that place and Fort Erie they are thickly scattered along the banks of the river. The houses in this neighbourhood were remarkably well built, and appeared to be kept in a state of great neatness; most of them were sheathed with boards, and painted white. The lands adjoining them are rich, and were well cultivated. The crops of Indian corn were still standing here, which had a most luxuriant aspect; in many of the fields there did not appear to be a stem less than eight feet in height. Between the rows they sow gourds, squashes, and melons, of which last every sort attains to a state of great perfection in the open air throughout the inhabited parts of the two provinces. Peaches in this part of the country likewise come to perfection in the open air, but in Lower Canada, the summers are too short to permit them to ripen sufficiently. The winters here are very severe whilst they last, but it is seldom that the snow lies longer than three months on the ground. The summers are intensely hot, Fahrenheit's thermometer often rising to 96°, and sometimes above 100°.

As I passed along to Fort Erie I killed a great many large snakes of different sorts that I found basking in the sun. Amongst them I did

I did not find any rattlesnakes: these reptiles, however, are very commonly met with here; and at the distance of twenty or thirty miles from the river, up the country, it is said that they are so numerous as to render the surveying of land a matter of very great danger. It is a circumstance strongly in favour of Lower Canada, that the rattlesnake is not found there; it is seldom found, indeed, to the northward of the forty-fifth parallel of north latitude.

Fort Erie stands at the eastern extremity of Lake Erie; it is a small stockaded fort, somewhat similar to that at Chippeway; and adjoining it are extensive stores as at Chippeway, and about half a dozen miserable little dwellings. On arriving there I had no difficulty in discovering my companions; I found them lodged in a small log-house, which contained but the one room, and just sitting down to a supper, they had procured through the assistance of a gentleman in the Indian department, who accompanied them from Chippeway. This habitation was the property of an old woman, who in her younger days had followed the drum, and now gained her livelihood by accommodating, to the best of her power, such travellers as passed by Fort Erie. A sorry habitation it was; the crazy door was ready to drop off the hinges, and in all the three

three windows of it not one pane of glafs was there, a young gentleman from Detroit having amufed himfelf, whilft detained in the place by contrary winds, fome little time before our arrival, with fhooting arrows through them. It was not likely that thefe windows would be fpeedily repaired, for no glazier was to be met with nearer than Newark, thirty-fix miles diftant. Here, as we lay folded in our fkins on the floor, the rain beat in upon us, and the wind whiftled about our ears; but this was not the worft. In the morning we found it a difficult matter to get wherewith to fatisfy our hunger; dinner was more difficult to be had than breakfaft, fupper than dinner; there feemed to be a greater fcarcity of provifions alfo the fecond day than there was on the firft. At laft, fearing that we fhould be famifhed if we remained longer under the care of old mother Palmer, we embarked at once on board the veffel of war in which we intended to crofs the lake, where although fometimes tofled about by the raging contrary winds, yet we had comfortable births, and fared plenteoufly every day.

Ships lie oppofite to Fort Erie, at the diftance of about one hundred yards from the fhore; they are there expofed to all the violence of the wefterly winds, but the anchorage is excellent, and they ride in perfect fafety. Three veffels
of

of war, of about two hundred tons, and carrying from eight to twelve guns each, besides two or three merchant vessels, lay wind bound whilst we remained here. The little fort, with the surrounding houses built on the rocky shore, the vessels lying at anchor before it, the rich woods, the distant hills on the opposite side of the lake, and the vast lake itself, extending to the farthest part of the horizon, altogether formed an interesting and beautiful scene.

Whilst we were detained here by contrary winds, we regularly went on shore after breakfast to take a ramble in the woods; oftentimes also we amused ourselves with the diversion of hunting squirrels with dogs, amongst the shrubs and young trees on the borders of the lake, thousands of which animals we found in the neighbourhood of the fort. The squirrels, alarmed by the barking of the dogs, leap from tree to tree with wonderful swiftness; you follow them closely, shaking the trees, and striking against the branches with poles. Sometimes they will lead you a chace of a quarter of a mile and more; but sooner or later, terrified by your attentive pursuit, make a false leap, and come to the ground; the dogs, ever on the watch, then seize the opportunity to lay hold of them; frequently, however, the squirrels will elude their repeated snaps, and

mount

mount another tree before you can look round you. I have feldom known them to be hurt by their fall, notwithftanding that I have many times feen them tumble from branches of trees upwards of twenty feet from the ground.

In our rambles we ufed frequently to fall in with parties of the Seneka Indians, from the oppofite fide of the lake, that were amufing themfelves with hunting and fhooting thefe animals. They fhot them principally with bows and blow-guns, at the ufe of which laft the Senekas are wonderfully expert. The blow-gun is a narrow tube, commonly about fix feet in length, made of a cane reed, or of fome pithy wood, through which they drive fhort flender arrows by the force of the breath. The arrows are not much thicker than the lower ftring of a violin; they are headed generally with little triangular bits of tin, and round the oppofite ends, for the length of two inches, a quantity of the down of thiftles, or something very like it, is bound, fo as to leave the arrows at this part of fuch a thicknefs that they may but barely pafs into the tube. The arrows are put in at the end of the tube that is held next to the mouth, the down catches the breath, and with a fmart puff they will fly to the diftance of fifty yards. I have followed young Seneka Indians, whilft fhooting with blow-guns, for hours together, during which time

time I have never known them once to miſs their aim, at the diſtance of ten or fifteen yards, although they ſhot at the little red ſquirrels, which are not half the ſize of a rat; and with ſuch wonderful force uſed they to blow forth the arrows, that they frequently drove them up to the very thiſtle-down through the heads of the largeſt black ſquirrels. The effect of theſe guns appears at firſt like magic. The tube is put to the mouth, and in the twinkling of an eye you ſee the ſquirrel that is aimed at fall lifeleſs to the ground; no report, not the ſmalleſt noiſe even, is to be heard, nor is it poſſible to ſee the arrow, ſo quickly does it fly, until it appears faſtened in the body of the animal.

The Seneka is one of the ſix nations which formerly bore the general name of the Iroquois Indians. Their principal village is ſituated on Buffalo Creek, which falls into the eaſtern extremity of Lake Erie, on the New York ſhore. We took the ſhip's boat one morning, and went over to viſit it, but all the Indians, men, women, and children, amounting in all to upwards of ſix hundred perſons, had, at an early hour, gone down to Fort Niagara, to partake of a feaſt which was there prepared for them. We walked about in the neighbourhood of the village, dined on the graſs on ſome cold proviſions that we had taken with us, and in the evening, returned.

Oppoſite

Oppofite to the mouth of Buffalo Creek there is a very dangerous fand bar, which at times it is totally impoffible to pafs in any other veffels than bateaux; we found it no eafy matter to get over it in the fhip's long boat with four oars on going into the creek; and in returning the paffage was really tremendous. The wind, which was wefterly, and of courfe impelled the vaft body of water in the lake towards the mouth of the creek, had increafed confiderably whilft we had been on fhore, and the waves had begun to break with fuch fury over the bar, that it was not without a confiderable fhare of terror that we contemplated the profpect of paffing through them: the commodore of the King's fhips on the lake, who was at the helm, was determined, however, to crofs the bar that night, and accordingly, a ftrict filence having been enjoined, that the crew might hear his orders, we boldly entered into the midft of the breakers: the boat now rolled about in a moft alarming manner; fometimes it mounted into the air on the top of the mighty billows, at other times it came thumping down with prodigious force on the bar; at laft it ftuck quite faft in the fand; neither oars nor rudder were any longer of ufe, and for a moment we gave ourfelves over for loft; the waves that rolled towards us broke on all fides with a noife like that of thunder,

thunder, and we were expecting that the boat would be overwhelmed by fome one or other of them every inftant, when luckily a large wave, that rolled on a little farther than the reft without breaking into foam, fet us again afloat, and the oarfmen making at that moment the moft vigorous exertions, we once more got into deep water; it was not, however, until after many minutes that we were fafely out of the tremendous furf. A boat, with a pair of oars only, that attempted to follow us, was overwhelmed in an inftant by a wave which broke over her: it was in vain to think of attempting to give any affiftance to her crew, and we were obliged for a time to endure the painful thought that they might be ftruggling with death within a few yards of us; but before we loft fight of the fhore we had the fatisfaction of beholding them all ftanding in fafety on the beach, which they had reached by fwimming.

After having been detained about feven days at Fort Erie, the wind veered about in our favour, the fignal gun was fired, the paffengers repaired on board, and at half an hour before fun-fet we launched forth into the lake. It was much fuch another evening as that on which we left Kingfton; the vaft lake, bounded only by the horizon, glowed with the rich warm tints that were reflected in its unruffled
furface

surface from the western sky; and the top of the tall forest, adorning the shores, appeared fringed with gold, as the sun sunk down behind it. There was but little wind during the first part of the night; but afterwards a fresh breeze sprang up, and by ten o'clock the next morning we found ourselves forty miles distant from the fort: the prosperous gale, however, did not long continue, the sky became overcast, the waves began to roll with fury, and the captain judging it advisable to seek a place of shelter against the impending storm, the ship was put about, and with all possible expedition measured back the way which we had just made with so much pleasure. We did not return, however, the whole way to Fort Erie, but run into a small bay on the same side of the lake, about ten miles distant, sheltered by Point Abineau: by three o'clock in the afternoon the vessel was safely moored, and this business having been accomplished, we proceeded in the long boat to the shore, which was about two miles off.

Point Abineau is a long narrow neck of land, which projects into the lake nearly in a due south direction; on each side of it there is an extensive bay, which affords good anchorage; the extremity of the point is covered with rocks, lying horizontally in beds, and extending a considerable way into the lake, nearly even

even with the surface of the water, so that it is only in a few places that boats can approach the shore. The rocks are of a slate colour, but spotted and streaked in various directions with a dirty yellow; in many places they are perforated with small holes, as if they had been exposed to the action of fire. The shores of the bays, on the contrary, are covered with sand; on digging to the depth of a few feet, however, I should imagine that in most parts of the shore the same sort of rocks would be found as those seen on the extremity of the point; for where the sandy part of the shore commences, it is evident that the rocks have been covered by the sand which has been washed up by the waves of the lake: the northern shore of the lake abounds very generally with rocks of the same description.

On the western side of Point Abineau the strand differs in no wise, to appearance, from that of the ocean: it is strewed with a variety of shells of a large size; quantities of gulls are continually seen hovering over it; and during a gale of wind from the west, a surge breaks in upon it, as tremendous as is to be seen on any part of the coast of England. The mounds of sand accumulated on Point Abineau are truly astonishing; those next to the lake, that have been washed by the storms of late years, are totally devoid of verdure; but others, situated

situated behind them, towards the center of the point, seem coeval with the world itself, and are covered with oaks of the largest size from top to bottom. In general these mounds are of an irregular form; but in some places, of the greatest height, they are so even and straight that it appears as if they had been thrown up by the hand of art, and you may almost fancy them to be the old works of some vast fortification. These regular mounds extend in all directions, but chiefly from north to south, which demonstrates that westerly winds were as prevalent formerly in this part of the country as they are at the present day. I should suppose that some of these mounds are upwards of one hundred feet above the level of the lake.

The ground on the eastern side of the point is neither so much broken nor so sandy as that on the opposite one, and there we found two farm houses, adjoining to each of which were about thirty acres of cleared land. At one of these we procured a couple of sheep, some fowls, and a quantity of potatoes, to add to our store of provisions, as there was reason to apprehend that our voyage would not be speedily terminated: whilst the men were digging for the latter, the old woman of the house spread her little table, and prepared for us the best viands which her habitation afforded, namely, coarſe cake bread, roaſted potatoes, and bear's fleſh ſalted, which laſt we found by no means unpalatable. The haunch of a young cub is a diſh much eſteemed, and we frequently met with it at table in the upper country; it is extremely rich and oily, neverthelefs they ſay it never cloys the ſtomach.

Towards evening we returned to the veſſel, and the ſtorm being much abated, paſſed, not an, uncomfortable night.

At day break the next morning I took the boat, and went on ſhore to join a party that, as I had been informed the preceding evening, was going a bear-hunting. On landing, I found the men and dogs ready, and having loaded our guns we advanced into the woods. The people here, as in the back parts of the United States, devote a very great part of their time to hunting, and they are well ſkilled in the purſuit of game of every deſcription. They ſhoot almoſt univerſally with the rifle gun, and are as dextrous at the uſe of it as any men can be. The guns uſed by them are all imported from England. Thoſe in moſt eſtimation carry balls of the ſize of thirty to the pound; in the States the hunters very commonly ſhoot with balls of a much ſmaller ſize, ſixty of them not weighing more than one pound; but the people in Canada are of opinion that it is better to uſe the large balls,

balls, although more troublesome to carry through the woods, as they inflict much more destructive wounds than the others, and game seldom escapes after being wounded by them. Dogs of a large size are chosen for bear hunting: those most generally preferred seem to be of a breed between the blood hound and mastiff; they will follow the scent of the bear, as indeed most field dogs will, but their chief use is to keep the bear at bay when wounded, or to follow him if he attempt to make off whilst the hunter is reloading his gun. Bears will never attempt to attack a man or a dog while they can make their escape, but once wounded or closely hemmed in they will fight most furiously. The young ones, at sight of a dog, generally take to a tree; but the old ones, as if conscious of their ability to fight a dog, and at the same time that they cannot fail of becoming the prey of the hunter if they ascend a tree, never do so, unless indeed they see a hunter coming towards them on horseback, a sight which terrifies them greatly.

The Indians generally go in large parties to hunt bears, and on coming to the place where they suppose these animals are lurking, they form themselves into a large circle, and as they advance endeavour to rouse them. It is seldom that the white hunters muster together

gether in sufficient numbers to pursue their game in this manner; but whenever they have men enough to divide themselves so, they always do it. We proceeded in this manner at Point Abineau, where three or four men are amply sufficient to hem in a bear between the water and the main land. The point was a very favourable place for hunting this year, for the bears, intent, as I before mentioned, upon emigrating to the south, used, on coming down from the upper country, to advance to the extreme end of the point, as if desirous of getting as near as possible by land to the opposite side of the lake, and scarcely a morning came but what one or two of them were found upon it. An experienced hunter can at once discern the track of a bear, deer, or any other large animal, in the woods, and can tell with no small degree of precision how long a time before, it was, that the animal passed that way. On coming to a long valley, between two of the sand hills on the point, a place through which the bears generally passed in going towards the water, the hunters whom I accompanied at once told how many bears had come down from the upper country the preceding night, and also how many of them were cubs. To the eye of a common observer the track of these animals amongst the leaves is wholly imperceptible; indeed,

indeed, in many inſtances, even after the hunters had pointed them out to me, I could but barely perceive the prints of their feet on the cloſeſt inſpection; yet the hunters, on coming up to the place, ſaw theſe marks with a glance of the eye.

After killing a bear, the firſt care of the hunters is to ſtrip him of his ſkin. This buſineſs is performed by them in a very few minutes, as they always carry knives about them particularly ſuited for the purpoſe; afterwards the carcaſe is cut up, an operation in which the tomahawk, an inſtrument that they, moſtly, carry with them alſo, is particularly uſeful. The choiceſt parts of the animal are then ſelected and carried home, and the reſt left in the woods. The Indians hold the paws of the bear in great eſtimation; ſtewed with young puppies, they are ſerved up at all their principal feaſts. On killing the animal, the paws are gaſhed with a knife, and, afterwards, hung over a fire, amidſt the ſmoke, to dry. The ſkins of the bears are applied to numberleſs uſes, in the country, by the farmers, who ſet no ſmall value upon them. They are commonly cured by being ſpread upon a wall or between two trees, before the ſun, and in that poſition ſcraped with a knife, or piece of iron, daily, which brings out the greaſe or oil, a very conſiderable quantity of
which

which oozes from them. Racoon and deer skins, &c. are cured in a similar manner. The Indians have a method of dressing these different skins with the hair on, and of rendering them at the same time as pliable as a piece of cloth; this is principally effected by rubbing the skins, with the hand, in the smoke of a wood fire.

Towards the middle of the day, the hunt being over, the party returned to the habitation on the point. On arriving there I found my companions, who had just come on shore, and after having strolled about the woods for a time, we all went on board the ship to dine.

The sky had been very gloomy the whole of this day; it became more and more so as the evening approached, and the seamen foretold that before morning there would be a dreadful storm. At no time a friend to the watery element, I immediately formed the resolution of passing the night on shore; accordingly having got the boat manned after dinner, I took with me my servant, and landed at the head of the bay on the eastern side of the point. Here being left to ourselves, we pitched our tent by moonlight, under the shelter of one of the steep sand hills; and having kindled a large fire in the front of it, laid down, and were soon lulled to repose

pose by the hollow roar of the wind amidst the tall trees of the surrounding forest. Not so my companions, who visited me at an early hour the next morning, and lamented sorely that they had not accompanied me on shore. There had been a tremendous sea running in the lake all night; the wind had shifted somewhat to the southward, and Point Abineau, in consequence, affording but little protection to the vessel, she had rolled about in a most alarming manner: one of the stancheons at her bow started by her violent working; the water came pouring in as from a pump; a scene of confusion ensued, and the sailors were kept busily employed the greater part of the night in stopping the leak. The vessel being old, crazy, and on her last voyage, serious apprehensions were entertained lest some worse accident should befal her before morning, and neither the crew nor the passengers felt themselves at all easy until daylight appeared, when the gale abated. We amused ourselves this morning in rambling through the woods, and along the shores of the lake, with our fowling pieces. On the strand we found great numbers of gulls, and different birds of prey, such as hawks, kites, &c.; here also we met with large flocks of sand larks, as they are called by the people of the country, in colour somewhat resembling

the

the grey lapwing; their walk and manner alfo are fo very fimilar, that, when on the ground, they might be taken for the fame bird were they but of a larger fize; they are not much bigger than a fparrow. In the woods we fell in for the firft time with a large covey or flock of fpruce partridges or pheafants, as the people call them in this neighbourhood. In colour, they are not much unlike the Englifh partridge, but of a larger fize, and their flefh differs in flavour little from that of the Englifh pheafant. They are different in many refpects both from the partridge and pheafant found in Maryland and in the middle ftates, but in none more fo than in their wonderful tamenefs, or rather ftupidity. Before the flock took to flight I fhot three birds fingly from off one tree, and had I but been acquainted with the proper method of proceeding at the time, it is poffible I might have fhot them all in turn. It feems you muft always begin by fhooting the bird that fits loweft on the tree, and fo proceed upwards, in which cafe the furvivors are not at all alarmed. Ignorant, however, of this fecret, I fhot at one of the uppermoft birds, and the difturbance that he made in falling through the branches on which the others were perched put the flock to flight immediately.

On

On returning from our ramble in the woods to the margin of the lake, we were agreeably furprifed to find the wind quite favourable for profecuting our voyage, and in a few minutes afterwards heard the fignal gun, and faw the fhip's boat coming for the purpofe of taking us from fhore. We got on board in time for dinner, but did not proceed on our voyage until midnight; fo high a fea ftill continued running in the lake, that the captain thought it imprudent to venture out of the bay before that time. In the morning we found ourfelves under the rich bold lands on the fouthern fide of the lake; the water was fmooth, the fky ferene, and every one felt pleafed with the voyage. It was on this day that we beheld the cloud over the Falls of Niagara, as I before mentioned, at the great diftance of fifty-four miles.

Lake Erie is of an elliptical form; in length about three hundred miles, and in breadth, at the wideft part, about ninety. The depth of water in this lake is not more than twenty fathoms, and in calm weather veffels may fecurely ride at anchor in any part of it; but when ftormy, the anchorage in an open part of the lake is not fafe, the fands at bottom not being firm, and the anchors apt therefore to lofe their hold. Whenever there is a gale of wind the waters immediately become turbid,

owing

owing to the quantity of yellow sand that is washed up from the bottom of the lake; in calm weather the water is clear, and of a deep greenish colour. The northern shore of the lake is very rocky, as likewise are the shores of the islands, of which there are several clusters towards the western extremity of the lake; but along most parts of the southern shore is a fine gravelly beach. The height of the land bordering on the lake is very unequal; in some places long ranges of steep mountains rise from the very edge of the water; in others the shores are so flat and so low, that when the lake is raised a little above its usual level, in consequence of a strong gale of wind setting in towards the shore, the country is deluged for miles.

A young gentleman, who was sent in a bateau with dispatches across the lake, not long before we passed through the country, perished, with several of his party, owing to an inundation of this sort that took place on a low part of the shore. I must here observe, that when you navigate the lake in a bateau, it is customary to keep as close as possible to the land; and whenever there is any danger of a storm, you run the vessel on shore, which may be done with safety, as the bottom of it is perfectly flat. I before mentioned the peculiar advantage of a bateau over a keel boat in this respect. The young gentleman alluded

to

to was coasting along in this manner, when a violent storm suddenly arose. The bateau was instantaneously turned towards the shore; unfortunately, however, in running her upon the beach some mismanagement took place, and she overset. The waves had already begun to break in on the shore with prodigious impetuosity; each one of them rolled farther in than the preceding one; the party took alarm, and instead of making as strenuous exertions as it was supposed they might have made, to right the bateau, they took a few necessaries out of her, and attempted to save themselves by flight; but so rapidly did the water flow after them, in consequence of the increasing storm, that before they could proceed far enough up the country to gain a place of safety, they were all overwhelmed by it, two alone excepted, who had the presence of mind and ability to climb a lofty tree. To the very great irregularity of the height of the lands on both sides of it, is attributed the frequency of storms on Lake Erie. The shores of Lake Ontario are lower and more uniform than those of any of the other lakes; and that lake is the most tranquil of any, as has already been noticed.

There is a great deficiency of good harbours along the shores of this Lake. On its northern side there are but two places which afford shelter to vessels drawing more than
seven

seven feet water, namely, Long Point and Point Abineau; and thefe only afford a partial fhelter. If the wind fhould fhift to the fouthward whilft veffels happen to be lying under them, they are thereby expofed to all the dangers of a rocky lee fhore. On the fouthern fhore, the firft harbour you come to in going from Fort Erie, is that of Prefqu' Ifle. Veffels drawing eight feet water may there ride in perfect fafety; but it is a matter of no fmall difficulty to get into the harbour, owing to a long fand bar which extends acrofs the mouth of it. Prefqu' Ifle is fituated at the diftance of about fixty miles from Fort Erie. Beyond this, nearly midway between the eaftern and weftern extremities of the lake, there is another harbour, capable of containing fmall veffels, at the mouth of Cayahega River, and another at the mouth of Sandufky River, which falls into the lake within the north weftern territory of the States. It is very feldom that any of thefe harbours are made ufe of by the Britifh fhips; they, indeed, trade almoft folely between Fort Erie and Detroit River; and when in profecuting their voyages they chance to meet with contrary winds, againft which they cannot make head, they for the moft part return to Fort Erie, if bound to Detroit River; or to fome of the bays amidft the clufters of iflands fituated towards the weftern extremity of the lake

lake, if bound to Fort Erie. In going up the lake, it very often happens that veffels, even after they have got clofe under thefe iflands, the neareft of which is not lefs than two hundred and forty miles from Fort Erie, are driven back by ftorms the whole way to that fort. Juft as we were preparing to caft anchor under Middle Ifland, one of the neareft of them, a fquall fuddenly arofe, and it was not without very great difficulty that we could keep our ftation: the captain told us afterwards, that he really feared at one time, that we fhould have been driven back to our old quarters.

It was about two o'clock on the third day from that of our quitting Point Abineau, that we reached Middle Ifland. We lay at anchor until the next morning, when the wind fhifted a few points in our favour, and enabled us to proceed fome miles farther on, to a place of greater fafety, fheltered by iflands on all fides; but beyond this the wind did not permit us to advance for three days. It is very feldom that veffels bound from Fort Erie to any place on Detroit River accomplifh their voyage without ftopping amongft thefe iflands; for the fame wind favourable for carrying them from the eaftern to the weftern extremity of the lake will not waft them up the river. The river runs nearly in a fouth-weft direction; its current is very ftrong; and unlefs the wind blows frefh, fresh, and nearly in an opposite direction to it, you cannot proceed. The navigation of Lake Erie, in general, is very uncertain; and passengers that cross it in any of the King's, or principal merchant vessels, are not only called upon to pay double the sum for their passage, demanded for that across Lake Ontario, but anchorage money besides, that is, a certain sum per diem as long as the vessel remains wind bound at anchor in any harbour. The anchorage money is about three dollars per day for each cabin passenger.

The islands at the western end of the lake, which are of various sizes, lie very close to each other, and the scenery amongst them is very pleasing. The largest of them are not more than fourteen miles in circumference, and many would scarcely be found to admeasure as many yards round. They are all covered with wood of some kind or other, even to the very smallest. The larger islands produce a variety of fine timber, amongst which are found oaks, hiccory trees, and red cedars; the latter grow to a much larger size than in any part of the neighbouring country, and they are sent for even from the British settlements on Detroit River, forty miles distant. None of these islands are much elevated above the lake, nor are they diversified with any rising grounds; most of them, indeed, are as flat as if they had been

been overflowed with water, and in the interior parts of some of the largest of them there are extensive ponds and marshes. The fine timber, which these islands produce, indicates that the soil must be uncommonly fertile. Here are found in great numbers, amongst the woods, racoons, and squirrels; bears are also at times found upon some of the islands during the winter season, when the lake is frozen between the main land and the islands; but they do not remain continually, as the other animals do. All the islands are dreadfully infested with serpents, and on some of them rattlesnakes are so numerous, that in the height of summer it is really dangerous to land: it was now late in September; yet we had not been three minutes on shore on Bass Island, before several of these noxious reptiles were seen amongst the bushes, and a couple of them, of a large size, were killed by the seamen.

Two kinds of rattlesnakes are found in this part of the country; the one is of a deep brown colour, clouded with yellow, and is seldom met with more than thirty inches in length. It usually frequents marshes and low meadows, where it does great mischief amongst cattle, which it bites mostly in the lips as they are grazing. The other sort is of a greenish yellow colour, clouded with brown, and attains nearly twice the size of the other. It is most commonly found between three and four feet in length, and as thick as the wrist of a large man. The rattlesnake is much thicker in proportion to its length than any other snake, and it is thickest in the middle of the body, which approaches somewhat to a triangular form, the belly being flat, and the back bone rising higher than any other part of the animal. The rattle, with which this serpent is provided, is at the end of the tail; it is usually about half an inch in breadth, one quarter of an inch in thickness, and each joint about half an inch long. The joint consists of a number of little cases of a dry horny substance, inclosed one within another, and not only the outermost of these little cases articulates with the outermost case of the contiguous joint, but each case, even to the smallest one of all, at the inside, is connected by a sort of joint with the corresponding case in the next joint of the rattle. The little cases or shells lie very loosely within one another, and the noise proceeds from their dry and hard coats striking one against the other. It is said that the animal gains a fresh joint to its rattle every year; of this, however, I have great doubts, for the largest snakes are frequently found to have the fewest joints to their rattles. A medical gentleman in the neighbourhood of Newmarket, behind the Blue Mountains, in Virginia, had a rattle in his possession,

poſſeſſion, which contained no leſs than thirty-two joints; yet the ſnake from which it was taken ſcarcely admeaſured five feet; rattleſnakes, however, of the ſame kind, and in the ſame part of the country, have been found of a greater length with not more than ten rattles. One of the ſnakes, which we ſaw killed on Baſs Iſland, in Lake Erie, had no more than four joints in its rattle, and yet it was nearly four feet long.

The ſkin of the rattleſnake, when the animal is wounded, or otherwiſe enraged, exhibits a variety of beautiful tints, never ſeen at any other time. It is not with the teeth which the rattleſnake uſes for ordinary purpoſes that it ſtrikes its enemy, but with two long crooked fangs in the upper jaw, which point down the throat. When about to uſe theſe fangs, it rears itſelf up as much as poſſible, throws back its head, drops its under jaw, and ſpringing forward upon its tail, endeavours to hook itſelf as it were upon its enemy. In order to raiſe itſelf on its tail it coils itſelf up previouſly in a ſpiral line, with the head in the middle. It cannot ſpring farther forward than about half its own length.

The fleſh of the rattleſnake is as white as the moſt delicate fiſh, and is much eſteemed by thoſe who are not prevented from taſting it by prejudice. The ſoup made from it is ſaid to be delicious, and very nouriſhing.

In my rambles about the iflands under which we lay at anchor, I found many fpecimens of the exuviæ of thefe fnakes, which, in the opinion of the country people of Upper Canada, are very efficacious in the cure of the rheumatifm, when laid over the part afflicted, and faftened down with a bandage. The body of the rattlefnake dried to a cinder over the fire, and then finely pulverifed, and infufed in a certain portion of brandy, is alfo faid to be a never failing remedy againft that diforder. I converfed with many people who had made ufe of this medicine, and they were firmly perfuaded that they were indebted to it for a fpeedy cure. The liquor is taken inwardly, in the quantity of a wine glafs full at once, about three times a day. No effect, more than from taking plain brandy, is perceived from taking this medicine on the firft day; but at the end of the fecond day the body of the patient becomes fuffufed with a cold fweat, every one of his joints grow painful, and his limbs become feeble, and fcarcely able to fupport him; he grows worfe and worfe for a day or two; but perfevering in the ufe of the medicine for a few days, he gradually lofes his pains, and recovers his wonted ftrength of body.

Many different kinds of ferpents befides rattlefnakes are found on thefe iflands in Lake Erie. I killed feveral totally different from any

any that I had ever met with in any other part
of the country; amongst the number was one
which I was informed was venomous in the
highest degree: it was somewhat more than
three feet in length; its back was perfectly
black; its belly a vivid orange. I found it
amongst the rocks on Middle Island, and on
being wounded in the tail, it turned about
to defend itself with inconceivable fury. Mr.
Carver tells of a serpent that is peculiar to these
islands, called the hissing snake : " It is," says
he, " of the small speckled kind, and about
" eighteen inches long. When any thing ap-
" proaches it, it flattens itself in a moment,
" and its spots, which are of various dyes,
" become visibly brighter through rage; at the
" same time it blows from its mouth with
" great force a subtile wind that is reported to
" be of a nauseous smell, and if drawn in with
" the breath of the unwary traveller will in-
" fallibly bring on a decline, that in a few
" months must prove mortal, there being no
" remedy yet discovered which can counteract
" its baneful influence." Mr. Carver does not
inform us of his having himself seen this snake;
I am tempted, therefore, to imagine, that he
has been imposed upon, and that the whole
account he has given of it is fabulous. I made
very particular enquiries respecting the ex-
istence of such a snake, from those persons who
were

were in the habit of touching at these islands, and neither they nor any other person I met with in the country had ever seen or heard of such a snake, except in Mr. Carver's Travels. Were a traveller to believe all the stories respecting snakes that are current in the country, he must believe that there is such a snake as the whip snake, which, as it is said, pursues cattle through the woods and meadows, lashing them with its tail, till overcome with the fatigue of running they drop breathless to the ground, when it preys upon their flesh; he must also believe that there is such a snake as the hoop snake, which has the power of fixing its tail firmly in a certain cavity inside of its mouth, and then of rolling itself forward like a hoop or wheel with such wonderful velocity that neither man nor beast can possibly escape from its devouring jaws.

The ponds and marshes in the interior parts of these islands abound with ducks and other wild fowl, and the shores swarm with gulls. A few small birds are found in the woods; but I saw none amongst them that were remarkable either for their song or plumage.

At sun-set, on the last day of September, we left the islands, and the next morning entered Detroit River. The river, at its mouth, is about five miles wide, and continues nearly the same breadth for a considerable distance. The shores

shores are of a moderate height, and thickly wooded; but there was nothing particularly interesting in the prospect till we arrived within four or five miles of the new British post. Here the banks appeared diversified with Indian encampments and villages, and beyond them the British settlements were seen to great advantage. The river was crowded with Indian canoes and bateaux, and several pleasure boats belonging to the officers of the garrison, and to the traders, that had come out in expectation of meeting us, were seen cruizing about backwards and forwards. The two other vessels of war, which we had left behind us at Fort Erie, as well as the trading vessels, had overtaken us just as we entered the river, and we all sailed up together with every bit of canvass, that we could muster, full spread. The day was uncommonly clear, and the scene altogether was pleasing and interesting.

The other vessels proceeded up the river to the British post; but ours, which was laden with presents for the Indians, cast anchor opposite to the habitation of the gentleman in the Indian department, whom I before mentioned, which was situated in the district of Malden. He gave us a most cordial invitation to stay at his house whilst we should remain in this part of the country; we gladly accepted of it, and accordingly went with him on shore.

LETTER XXXIII.

Description of the District of Malden.—Establishment of a new British Post there.—Island of Bois Blanc.—Difference between the British and Americans respecting the Right of Possession.—Block Houses, how constructed.—Captain E—'s Farm.—Indians.—Description of Detroit River, and the Country bordering upon it.—Town of Detroit.—Head Quarters of the American Army.—Officers of the Western Army.—Unsuccessful Attempt of the Americans to impress upon the Minds of the Indians an Idea of their Consequence.—Of the Country round Detroit.—Doubts concerning our Route back to Philadelphia.—Determine to go by Presqu' Isle.—Departure from Detroit.

Malden, October.

MALDEN is a district of considerable extent, situated on the eastern side of Detroit River, about eighteen miles below the town of Detroit. At the lower end of the district there are but few houses, and these stand very widely asunder; but at the upper end, bordering upon the river, and adjoining to the new British post that has been established since the evacuation of Detroit, a little

town

town has been laid out, which already contains more than twenty houses; and is rapidly increasing. Hither several of the traders have removed who formerly resided at Detroit. This little town has as yet received no particular name, neither has the new post, but they merely go under the name of the new British post and town near the island of Bois-Blanc, an island in the river near two miles in length, and half a mile in breadth, that lies opposite to Malden.

When the evacuation of Detroit was first talked of, the island was looked to as an eligible situation for the new post, and orders were sent to purchase it from the Indians, and to take possession of it in the name of his Britannic Majesty. Accordingly a party of troops went down for that purpose from Detroit; they erected a small block house on the northern extremity of it, and left a serjeant's guard there for its defence. Preparations were afterwards making for building a fort on it; but in the mean time a warm remonstrance against such proceedings came from the government of the United States *, who insisted

---

* Notwithstanding that the government of the United States has thought it incumbent upon itself to remonstrate against our taking possession of this island, and thus to dispute every inch of ground respecting the right to which there could not be the smallest doubt, yet the generality of the people of the

States

insisted upon it that the island was not within the limits of the British dominions. The point,

States affect to talk of every such step as idle and unnecessary, inasmuch as they are fully persuaded, in their own minds, that all the British dominions in North America must, sooner or later, become a part of their empire. Thus Mr. Imlay, in his account of the north western territory: " It is certain, that as " the country has been more opened in America, and thereby " the rays of the sun have acted more powerfully upon the. " earth, these benefits have tended greatly to soften the winter " season; so that peopling Canada, for which we are much " obliged to you, is a double advantage to us. First, it is set- " tling and populating a country that must, sooner or later, " from the natural order of things, become a part of our em- " pire; and secondly, it is immediately meliorating the cli- " mate of the northern states," &c.

The greatest empires that have ever appeared on the face of the globe have dissolved in the course of time, and no one acquainted with history will, I take it for granted, presume to say that the extended empire of Britain, all powerful as it is at present, is so much more closely knit together than any other empire ever was before it, that it can never fall asunder; Canada, I therefore suppose, may, with revolving years, be disjointed from the mother country, as well as her other colonies; but whenever that period shall arrive, which I trust is far distant, I am humbly of opinion that it will not form an additional knot in that extensive union of states which at present subsist on the continent of North America; indeed, were the British dominions in North America to be dissevered from the other members of the empire the ensuing year, I am still tempted to imagine that they would not become linked with the present federal American states, and for the following reasons:

First, because the constitution of the federal states, which is the bond that holds them together, is not calculated for such a large territory as that which the present states, together with such an addition, would constitute.

The constitution of the states is that of the people, who, through their respective representatives assembled together at some

point, it was found, would admit of some dispute, and as it could not be determined immediately,

some one place, must decide upon every measure that is to be taken for the public weal. This place, it is evident, ought in justice to be as central as possible to every state; the necessity, indeed, of having the place so situated has been manifested in the building of the new federal city. Were it not for this step, many of the most enlightened characters in the states have given it as their opinion, that the union could not have remained many years entire, for the states so far removed from the seat of the legislature, before the new city was founded, had complained grievously of the distance which their delegates had to travel to meet congress, and had begun to talk of the necessity of a separation of the states : and now, on the other hand, that a central spot has been fixed upon, those states to the northward, conveniently situated to Philadelphia, the present seat of the federal government, say that the new city will be so far removed from them, that the sending of delegates thither will be highly inconvenient to them, and so much so, as to call for a separation of the union on their part. In a former letter I stated the various opinions that were entertained by the people of the United States on this subject, and I endeavoured to shew that the seat of congress would be removed to the new federal city without endangering a partition of the states; but I am fully persuaded, that were Canada to become an independent state, and a place were to be fixed on central to all the states, supposing her to be one, that neither she, nor the state at the remote opposite end, would long continue, if they ever did submit, to send their delegates to a place so far removed, that it would require more than a fourth part of the year for them (the delegates) to travel, even with the utmost possible expedition, backward and forward, between the district which they represented and the seat of congress.

Secondly, I think the two Canadas will never become connected with the present states, because the people of these provinces, and those of the adjoining states, are not formed for a close intimacy with each other.

The bulk of the people of Upper Canada are refugees, who
were

diately, the plan of building the fort was relinquished for the time. The block houfe on the

were driven from the ftates by the perfecution of the republican party; and though the thirteen years which have paffed over have nearly extinguifhed every fpark of refentment againft the Americans in the breafts of the people of England, yet this is by no means the cafe in Upper Canada; it is there common to hear, even from the children of the refugees, the moſt grofs invectives poured out againſt the people of the ſtates; and the people of the frontier ſtates, in their turn, are as violent againſt the refugees and their poſterity; and, indeed, whilſt Canada forms a part of the Britiſh empire, I am inclined, from what I have ſeen and heard in travelling through the country, to think that this ſpirit will not die away. In Lower Canada the fame acrimonious temper of mind is not obſervable amongſt the people, excepting indeed in thoſe few parts of the country where the inhabited parts of the ſtates approach cloſely to thoſe of the province; but here appears to be a general difinclination amongſt the inhabitants to have any political connection with the people of the ſtates, and the French Canadians affect to hold them in the greateſt contempt. Added to this, the prevalent language of the lower province, which has remained the fame for almoſt forty years, notwithſtanding the great pains that have been taken to change it, and which is therefore likely to remain fo ſtill, is another obſtacle in the way of any cloſe connection between the people of the lower province and thoſe of the ſtates. Even in conducting the affairs of the provincial legiſlative aſſembly, notwithſtanding that moſt of the Engliſh inhabitants are well acquainted with the French language, yet a confiderable degree of difficulty is experienced from the generality of the French delegates being totally ignorant of the Engliſh language, which, as I have already mentioned, they have an unconquerable averſion againſt learning.

Thirdly, I think the Britiſh dominions in North America will never be annexed to thoſe of the ſtates, becauſe they are by nature formed for conſtituting a ſeparate independent territory.

At

the ifland, however, ftill remains guarded, and poffeffion will be kept of it until the matter in difpute

At prefent the boundary line between the Britifh dominions and the States runs along the river St. Croix, thence along the high lands bordering upon New England till it meets the forty-fifth parallel of north latitude, and afterwards along the faid parallel until it ftrikes the River St. Lawrence, or Cataragui, or Iroquois. Now the dominions fouth of the St. Lawrence are evidently not feparated from the United States by any bold determinate boundary line; I therefore fuppofe that they may, in fome manner, be connected with them; but the country to the northward, bounded on the north by Hudfon's Bay, on the eaft by the ocean, on the fouth and weft by the St. Lawrence, and that vaft chain of lakes which extends to the weftward, is feparated from the United States by one of the moft remarkable boundary lines that is to be found on the face of the globe between any two countries on the fame continent; and from being bounded in fuch a remarkable manner, and thus detached as it were by nature from the other parts of the continent, it appears to me that it is calculated for forming a diftinct feparate ftate, or diftinct union of ftates, from the prefent American federal ftates; that is, fuppofing, with the revolutions of time, that this arm of the Britifh empire fhould be fome time or other lopped off. I confefs it appears ftrange to me, that any perfon fhould fuppofe, after looking attentively over a map of North America, that the Britifh dominions, fo extenfive and fo unconnected with them, could ever become joined in a political union with the prefent federal ftates on the continent. There is more reafon to imagine that the Floridas, and the Spanifh poffeffions to the eaft of the Miffiffippi, will be united therewith; for as the rivers which flow through the Spanifh dominions are the only channels whereby the people of fome of the weftern ftates can convey the produce of their own country to the ocean with convenience, it is natural to fuppofe that the people of thefe ftates will be anxious to gain poffeffion of thefe rivers, for which purpofe they muft poffefs themfelves of the country through which they pafs. But there are certain bounds, beyond

dispute be adjudged by the commissioners appointed, pursuant to the late treaty, for the purpose of determining the exact boundaries of the British dominions in this part of the continent, which were by no means clearly ascertained by the definitive treaty of peace between the States and Great Britain.

In this particular instance the dispute arises respecting the true meaning of certain words of the treaty. " The boundary line," it says, " is to run through the middle of Lake Erie " until it arrive at the water communication " between that lake and Lake Huron; thence " along the middle of the said water commu-" nication." The people of the States construe the middle of the water communication to be the middle of the most approved and most frequented channel of the river; we, on the contrary, construe it to be the middle of the river, provided there is a tolerable channel on each side. Now the island of Bois Blanc clearly lies between the middle of the river and the British main; but then the deepest and most approved channel for ships of burthen is between the island and the British shore. In

yond which a representative government cannot extend, and the ocean on the east and south, the St. Lawrence and the lakes on the north, and the Mississippi on the west, certainly appear to set bounds to the jurisdiction of the government of the United States, if indeed it can extend even so far.

BLOCK HOUSE. 177

our acceptation of the word, therefore, the ifland unqueftionably belongs to us; in that of the people of the States, to them. It appears to me, that our claim in this inftance is certainly the moft juft; for although the beft and moft commodious channel be on our fide, yet the channel on the oppofite fide of the ifland is fufficiently deep to admit through it, with perfect fafety, the largeft of the veffels at prefent on the lakes, and indeed as large veffels as are deemed fuitable for this navigation.

Plans for a fort on the main land, and for one on the ifland of Bois Blanc, have been drawn; but as only the one fort will be erected, the building of it is poftponed until it is determined to whom the ifland belongs: if within the Britifh dominions, the fort will be erected on the ifland, as there is a ftill more advantageous pofition for one there than on the main land; in the mean time a large block houfe, capable of accommodating, in every refpect comfortably, one hundred men and officers, has been erected on the main land, around which about four acres or more of ground have been referved for his Majefty's ufe, in cafe the fort fhould not be built on the ifland.

A block houfe, which I have fo frequently mentioned, is a building, whofe walls are

Vol. II.   N   formed

formed of thick square pieces of timber. It is usually built two stories high, in which case the upper story is made to project about two or three feet beyond the walls of the lower one, and loop holes are left in the floor round the edge of it, so that if an attempt were made to storm the house, the garrison could fire directly down upon the heads of the assailants. Loop holes are left also in various parts of the walls, some of which are formed, as is the case at this new block house at Malden, of a size sufficient to admit a small cannon to be fired through them. The loop holes are furnished with large wooden stoppers or wedges, which in the winter season, when there is no danger of an attack, are put in, and the interstices closely caulked, to guard against the cold; and indeed, to render the house warm, they are obliged to take no small pains in caulking the seams between the timber in every part. A block house, built on the most approved plan, is so constructed, that if one half of it were shot away, the other half would stand firm. Each piece of timber in the roof and walls is jointed in such a manner as to be rendered independent of the next piece to it; one wall is independent of the next wall, and the roof is in a great measure independent of all of them, so that if a piece of artillery were played upon the house,

that

that bit of timber alone againſt which the ball ſtruck would be diſplaced, and every other one would remain uninjured. A block houſe is proof againſt the heavieſt fire of muſquetry. As theſe houſes may be erected in a very ſhort time, and as there is ſuch an abundance of timber in every part of the country, wherewith to build them, they are met with in North America at almoſt every military out-poſt, and indeed in almoſt every fortreſs throughout the country. There are ſeveral in the upper town of Quebec.

Amongſt the ſcattered houſes at the lower end of the diſtrict of Malden, there are ſeveral of a reſpectable appearance, and the farms adjoining to them are very conſiderable. The farm belonging to our friend, Captain E———, under whoſe roof we tarry, contains no leſs than two thouſand acres. A very large part of it is cleared, and it is cultivated in a ſtyle which would not be thought meanly of even in England. His houſe, which is the beſt in the whole diſtrict, is agreeably ſituated, at the diſtance of about two hundred yards from the river; there is a full view of the river, and of the iſland of Bois Blanc, from the parlour windows, and the ſcene is continually enlivened by the number of Indian canoes that paſs and repaſs before it. In front of the houſe there is a neat little lawn, paled in, and ornamented with clumps of trees, at the bottom of which, not far from the water, ſtands a large Indian wigwam, called the council houſe, in which the Indians are aſſembled whenever there are any affairs of importance to be tranſacted between them and the officers in the Indian department. Great numbers of theſe people come from the iſland of Bois Blanc, where no leſs than five hundred families of them are encamped, to viſit us daily; and we in our turn go frequently to the iſland, to have an opportunity of obſerving their native manners and cuſtoms.

Our friend has told them, that we have croſſed the big lake, the Atlantic, on purpoſe to come and ſee them. This circumſtance has given them a very favourable opinion of us; they approve highly of the undertaking, and ſay that we have employed our time to a good purpoſe. No people on earth have a higher opinion of their own conſequence; indeed, they eſteem themſelves ſuperior to every other race of men.

We remained for a ſhort time in Malden, and then ſet off for Detroit in a neat little pleaſure boat, which one of the traders obligingly lent to us. The river between the two places varies in breadth from two miles to half a mile. The banks are moſtly very low, and in ſome places large marſhes extend along the ſhores,

shores, and far up into the country. The shores are adorned with rich timber of various kinds, and bordering upon the marshes, where the trees have full scope to extend their branches, the woodland scenery is very fine. Amidst the marshes, the river takes some very confiderable bends, and it is diverfified at the fame time with feveral large iflands, which occafion a great diverfity of profpect.

Beyond Malden no houfes are to be feen on either fide of the river, except indeed the few miferable little huts in the Indian villages, until you come within four miles or thereabouts of Detroit. Here the fettlements are very numerous on both fides, but particularly on that belonging to the Britifh. The country abounds with peach, apple, and cherry orchards, the richeft I ever beheld; in many of them the trees, loaded with large apples of various dyes, appeared bent down into the very water. They have many different forts of excellent apples in this part of the country, but there is one far fuperior to all the reft, and which is held in great eftimation, called the pomme caille. I do not recollect to have feen it in any other part of the world, though doubtlefs it is not peculiar to this neighbourhood. It is of an extraordinary large fize, and deep red colour; not confined merely to the fkin, but extending to the very core of the apple: if the

skin

skin be taken off delicately, the fruit appears nearly as red as when entire. We could not resist the temptation of stopping at the first of these orchards we came to, and for a few pence we were allowed to lade our boat with as much fruit as we could well carry away. The peaches were nearly out of season now, but from the few I tasted, I should suppose that they were of a good kind, far superior in flavour, size, and juicinefs to those commonly met with in the orchards of the middle states.

The houses in this part of the country are all built in a similar style to those in Lower Canada; the lands are laid out and cultivated also similarly to those in the lower province; the manners and persons of the inhabitants are the same; French is the predominant language, and the traveller may fancy for a moment, if he pleases, that he has been wafted by enchantment back again into the neighbourhood of Montreal or Three Rivers. All the principal posts throughout the western country, along the lakes, the Ohio, the Illinois, &c. were established by the French; but, except at Detroit and in the neighbourhood, and in the Illinois country, the French settlers have become so blended with the greater number who spoke English, that their language has every where died away.

Detroit

Detroit contains about three hundred houses, and is the largest town in the western country. It stands contiguous to the river, on the top of the banks, which are here about twenty feet high. At the bottom of them there are very extensive wharfs for the accommodation of the shipping, built of wood, similar to those in the Atlantic sea-ports. The town consists of several streets that run parallel to the river, which are interfected by others at right angles. They are all very narrow, and not being paved, dirty in the extreme whenever it happens to rain: for the accommodation of passengers, however, there are footways in most of them, formed of square logs, laid transversely close to each other. The town is surrounded by a strong stockade, through which there are four gates; two of them open to the wharfs, and the two others to the north and south side of the town respectively. The gates are defended by strong block houses, and on the west side of the town is a small fort in form of a square, with bastions at the angles. At each of the corners of this fort is planted a small field-piece; and these constitute the whole of the ordnance at present in the place. The British kept a considerable train of artillery here, but the place was never capable of holding out for any length of time against a regular force: the fortifications, indeed, were constructed

ſtructed chiefly as a defence againſt the Indians.

Detroit is at preſent the head-quarters of the weſtern army of the States; the garriſon conſiſts of three hundred men, who are quartered in barracks. Very little attention is paid by the officers to the minutiæ of diſcipline, ſo that however well the men may have acquitted themſelves in the field, they make but a poor appearance on parade. The belles of the town are quite au deſeſpoir at the late departure of the Britiſh troops; though the American officers tell them they have no reaſon to be ſo, as they will find them much more ſenſible agreeable men than the Britiſh officers when they know them; a ſtyle of converſation, which, ſtrange as it may appear to us, is yet not at all uncommon amongſt them. Three months, however, have not altered the firſt opinion of the ladies. I cannot better give you an idea of the unpoliſhed, coarſe, diſcordant manners of the generality of the officers of the weſtern army of the States, than by telling you, that they cannot agree ſufficiently amongſt themſelves to form a regimental meſs; repeated attempts have been made ſince their arrival at Detroit to eſtabliſh one, but their frequent quarrels would never ſuffer it to remain permanent. A duelliſt and an officer of the weſtern army were nearly ſynonimous terms

terms, at one period, in the United States, owing to the very great number of duels that took place amongſt them when cantoned at Grenville.

About two thirds of the inhabitants of Detroit are of French extraction, and the greater part of the inhabitants of the ſettlements on the river, both above and below the town, are of the ſame deſcription. The former are moſtly engaged in trade, and they all appear to be much on an equality. Detroit is a place of very conſiderable trade; there are no leſs than twelve trading veſſels belonging to it, brigs, ſloops, and ſchooners, of from fifty to one hundred tons burthen each. The inland navigation in this quarter is indeed very extenſive, Lake Erie, three hundred miles in length, being open to veſſels belonging to the port, on the one ſide; and lakes Michigan and Huron, the firſt upwards of two hundred miles in length, and ſixty in breadth, and the ſecond, no leſs than one thouſand miles in circumference, on the oppoſite ſide; not to ſpeak of Lake St. Clair and Detroit River, which connect theſe former lakes together, or of the many large rivers which fall into them. The ſtores and ſhops in the town are well furniſhed, and you may buy fine cloth, linen, &c. and every article of wearing apparel, as good in their kind, and nearly on as reaſonable terms, as you can purchafe them at New York or Philadelphia.

The inhabitants are well fupplied with provifions of every defcription; the fifh in particular, caught in the river and neighbouring lakes, are of a very fuperior quality. The fifh held in moft eftimation is a fort of large trout, called the Michillimakinac white fifh, from its being caught moftly in the ftraits of that name. The inhabitants of Detroit and the neighbouring country, however, though they have provifions in plenty, are frequently much diftreffed for one very neceffary concomitant, namely, falt. Until within a fhort time paft they had no falt but what was brought from Europe; but falt fprings have been difcovered in various parts of the country, from which they are now beginning to manufacture that article for themfelves. The beft and moft profitable of the fprings are retained in the hands of government, and the profits arifing from the fale of the falt are to be paid into the treafury of the province. Throughout the weftern country they procure their falt from fprings, fome of which throw up fufficient water to yield feveral hundred bufhels in the courfe of one week.

There is a large Roman catholic church in the town of Detroit, and another on the oppofite fide, called the Huron church, from its

having

having been devoted to the ufe of the Huron Indians. The ftreets of Detroit are generally crowded with Indians of one tribe or other, and amongft them you fee numberlefs old fquaws leading about their daughters, ever ready to difpofe of them, pro tempore, to the higheft bidder. At night all the Indians, except fuch as get admittance into private houfes, and remain there quietly, are turned out of the town, and the gates fhut upon them.

The American officers here have endeavoured to their utmoft to imprefs upon the minds of the Indians an idea of their own fuperiority over the Britifh; but as they are very tardy in giving thefe people any prefents, they do not pay much attention to their words. General Wayne, from continually promifing them prefents, but at the fame time always poftponing the delivery when they come to afk for them, has fignificantly been nicknamed by them, General Wabang, that is General Tomorrow.

The country around Detroit is very much cleared, and fo likewife is that on the Britifh fide of the river for a confiderable way above the town. The fettlements extend nearly as far as Lake Huron; but beyond the River La Trenche, which falls into Lake St. Clair, they are fcattered very thinly along the fhores. The banks of the River La Trenche, or Thames, as it is now called, are increaſing very faſt in population, as I before mentioned, owing to the great emigration thither of people from the neighbourhood of Niagara, and of Detroit alſo ſince it has been evacuated by the Britiſh. We made an excurſion, one morning, in our little boat as far as Lake St. Clair, but met with nothing, either amongſt the inhabitants, or in the face of the country, particularly deſerving of mention. The country round Detroit is uncommonly flat, and in none of the rivers is there a fall ſufficient to turn even a griſt mill. The current of Detroit River itſelf is ſtronger than that of any others, and a floating mill was once invented by a Frenchman, which was chained in the middle of that river, where it was thought the ſtream would be ſufficiently ſwift to turn the water wheel: the building of it was attended with conſiderable expence to the inhabitants, but after it was finiſhed it by no means anſwered their expectations. They grind their corn at preſent by wind mills, which I do not remember to have ſeen in any other part of North America.

The ſoil of the country bordering upon Detroit River is rich though light, and it produces good crops both of Indian corn and wheat. The climate is much more healthy than that of the country in the neighbourhood

of

of Niagara River; intermittent fevers however are by no means uncommon diforders. The fummers are intenfely hot, Fahrenheit's thermometer often rifing above 100; yet a winter feldom paffes over but what fnow remains on the ground for two or three months.

Whilft we remained at Detroit, we had to determine upon a point of fome moment to us travellers, namely, upon the route by which to return back towards the Atlantic. None of us felt much inclined to crofs the lake again to Fort Erie, we at once therefore laid afide all thoughts of returning that way. Two other routes then prefented themfelves for our confideration; the one was to proceed by land from Detroit, through the north weftern territory of the United States, as far as the head waters of fome one of the rivers which fall into the Ohio, having reached which, we might afterwards have proceeded upwards or downwards, as we found moft expedient: the other was to crofs by water to Prefqu' Ifle, on the fouth fide of Lake Erie, and thence go down French Creek and the Alleghany River, as far as Pittfburgh on the Ohio, where being arrived we fhould likewife have had the choice of defcending the Ohio and Miffiffippi, or of going on to Philadelphia, through Pennfylvania, according as we fhould find circumftances moft convenient. The firft of thefe

routes

routes was moſt ſuited to our inclination, but we ſoon found that we muſt give over all thoughts of proceeding by it. The way to have proceeded would have been to ſet out on horſeback, taking with us ſufficient proviſions to laſt for a journey through a foreſt of upwards of two hundred miles in length, and truſting our horſes to the food which they could pick up for themſelves amongſt the buſhes. There was no poſſibility of procuring horſes, however, for hire at Detroit or in the neighbourhood, and had we purchaſed them, which could not have been done but at a moſt exorbitant price, we ſhould have found it a difficult matter perhaps to have got rid of them when we had ended our land journey, unleſs indeed we choſe to turn them adrift in the woods, which would not have been perfectly ſuitable to our finances. But independent of this conſideration there was another obſtacle in our way, and that was the difficulty of procuring guides. The Indians were all preparing to ſet out on their hunting excurſions, and had we even been able to have procured a party of them for an eſcort, there would have been ſome riſk, we were told, of their deſerting us before we reached our journey's end. If they fell in on their journey with a hunting party that had been very ſuccefsful; if they came to a place where there was great abund-

ance

ance of game; or, in fhort, if we did not proceed juſt according to their fancy, impatient of every reſtraint, and without caring in the leaſt for the hire we had promiſed them, they would, perhaps, leave us in the whim of moment to fhift for ourſelves in the woods, a ſituation we had no defire to fee ourfelves reduced to: we determined therefore to proceed by Preſqu' Ifle. But now another difficulty aroſe, namely, how we were to get there: a fmall veſſel, a very unufual circumſtance indeed, was juſt about to fail, but it was fo crowded with paſſengers, that there was not a fingle birth vacant, and moreover, if there had been, we did not wifh to depart fo abruptly from this part of the country. One of the principal traders, however, at Detroit, to whom we had carried letters, foon accommodated matters to our fatisfaction, by promifing to give orders to the mafter of one of the lake veſſels, of which he was in part owner, to land us at that place. The veſſel was to fail in a fortnight; we immediately therefore fecured a paſſage in her, and having fettled with the mafter that he fhould call for us at Malden, we fet off once more for that place in our little boat, and in a few hours, from the time we quitted Detroit, arrived there.

LETTER XXXIV.

Presents delivered to the Indians on the Part of the British Government.—Mode of distributing them.—Reasons why given.—What is the best Method of conciliating the good Will of the Indians.—Little pains taken by the Americans to keep up a good Understanding with the Indians.—Consequences thereof.—War between the Americans and Indians.—A brief Account of it.—Peace concluded by General Wayne.—Not likely to remain permanent.—Why.—Indian Manner of making Peace described.

Malden, October.

ADJOINING to our friend's house at Malden stands an extensive range of storehouses, for the reception of the presents yearly made by government to the Indians in this part of the country, in which several clerks are kept constantly employed. Before we had been long at Malden we had an opportunity of seeing some of the presents delivered out. A number of chiefs of different tribes had previously come to our friend, who is at the head of the department in this quarter, and had given to him, each, a bundle of little bits of cedar wood, about the thickness of a small pocket book pencil, to remind him of the exact number

number of individuals in each tribe that expected to fhare the bounty of their great father. The fticks in thefe bundles were of different lengths, the longeft denoted the number of warriors in the tribe, the next in fize the number of women, and the fmalleft the number of children. Our friend on receiving them handed them over to his clerks, who made a memorandum in their books of the contents of each bundle, and of the perfons that gave them, in order to prepare the prefents accordingly. The day fixed upon for the delivery of the prefents was bright and fair, and being in every refpect favourable for the purpofe, the clerks began to make the neceffary arrangements accordingly.

A number of large ftakes were firft fixed down in different parts of the lawn, to each of which was attached a label, with the name of the tribe, and the number of perfons in it, who were to be provided for; then were brought out from the ftores feveral bales of thick blankets, of blue, fcarlet, and brown cloth, and of coarfe figured cottons, together with large rolls of tobacco, guns, flints, powder, balls, fhot, cafe-knives, ivory and horn combs, looking-glaffes, pipe-tomahawks, hatchets, fciffars, needles, vermilion in bags, copper and iron pots and kettles, the whole valued at about £. 500 fterling. The bales of goods being

being opened, the blankets, cloths, and cottons were cut up into small pieces, each sufficient to make for one person a wrapper, a shirt, a pair of leggings, or whatever else it was intended for; and the portions of the different articles intended for each tribe were thrown together in a heap, at the bottom of the stake which bore its name. This business took up several hours, as there were no less than four hundred and twenty Indians to be served. No liquor, nor any silver ornaments, except to favourite chiefs in private, are ever given on the part of government to the Indians, notwithstanding they are so fond of both; and a trader who attempts to give these articles to them in exchange for the presents they have received from government, or, indeed, who takes from them on any conditions, their presents, is liable to a very heavy penalty for every such act, by the laws of the province.

The presents having been all prepared, the chiefs were ordered to assemble their warriors, who were loitering about the grounds at the outside of the lawn. In a few minutes they all came, and having been drawn up in a large circle, our friend delivered a speech on the occasion, without which ceremony no business, according to Indian custom, is ever transacted. In this they were told, " That their great and good Father, who lived on the oppsite side of the

the big lake (meaning thereby the king) was ever attentive to the happinefs of all his faithful people; and that, with his accuftomed bounty, he had fent the prefents which now lay before them to his good children the Indians; that he had fent the guns, the hatchets, and the ammunition for the young men, and the clothing for the aged, women, and children; that he hoped the young men would have no occafion to employ their weapons in fighting againft enemies, but merely in hunting; and that he recommended it to them to be attentive to the old, and to fhare bountifully with them what they gained by the chace; that he trufted the great fpirit would give them bright funs and clear fkies, and a favourable feafon for hunting; and that when another year fhould pafs over, if he ftill continued to find them good children, he would not fail to renew his bounties, by fending them more prefents from acrofs the big lake.

This fpeech was delivered in Englifh, but interpreters attended, who repeated it to the different tribes in their refpective languages, paragraph by paragraph, at the end of every one of which the Indians fignified their fatisfaction by a loud coarfe exclamation of " Hoah! Hoah!" The fpeech ended, the chiefs were called forward, and their feveral heaps were fhewn to them, and committed to their care. They received them with thanks; and beckoning to their warriors, a number of young men quickly started from the crowd, and in less than three minutes the presents were conveyed from the lawn, and laden on board the canoes, in waiting to convey them to the island and adjacent villages. The utmost regularity and propriety was manifested on this occasion in the behaviour of every Indian; there was not the smallest wrangling amongst them about their presents; nor was the least spark of jealousy observable in any one tribe about what the other had received; each one took up the heap allotted to it, and departed without speaking a word.

Besides the presents, such as I have described, others of a different nature again, namely, provisions, were dealt out this year amongst certain tribes of the Indians that were encamped on the island of Bois Blanc. These were some of the tribes that had been at war with the people of the United States, whose villages, fields of corn, and stores of provisions had been totally destroyed during the contest by General Wayne, and who having been thereby bereft of every means of support, had come, as soon as peace was concluded, to beg for subsistence from their good friends the British. " Our enemies," said they, have de-
" stroyed our villages and stores of provisions;
" our women and children are left without
" food;

"food; do you then, who call yourselves our "friends, shew us now that you really are so, "and give them food to eat till the sun ripens "our corn, and the great spirit gives another "prosperous season for hunting." Their request was at once complied with; a large storehouse was erected on the island, and filled with provisions at the expence of government for their use, and regularly twice a week the clerks in the Indian department went over to distribute them. About three barrels of salted pork or beef, as many of flour, beans or peas, Indian corn, and about two carcases of fresh beef, were generally given out each time. These articles of provision the Indians received, not in the thankful manner in which they did the other presents, but seemingly as if they were due to them of right. One nation they think ought never to hesitate about giving relief to another in distress, provided it was not at enmity with it; and indeed, were their white brethren, the British, to be reduced by any calamity to a similar state of distress, the Indians would with the utmost cheerfulness share with them their provisions to the very last.

The presents delivered to the Indians, together with the salaries of the officers in the Indian department, are computed to cost the crown, as I before mentioned, about £.100,000 sterling,

sterling, on an average, per annum. When we first gained possession of Canada, the expence of the presents was much greater, as the Indians were then more numerous, and as it was also found necessary to bestow upon them, individually, much larger presents than are now given, in order to overcome the violent prejudices against us which had been instilled into their minds by the French. These prejudices having happily been removed, and the utmost harmony having been established between them and the people on our frontiers, presents of a less value even than what are now distributed amongst them would perhaps be found sufficient to keep up that good understanding which now subsists between us; it could not, however, be deemed a very advisable measure to curtail them, as long as a possibility remained that the loss of their friendship might be incurred thereby: and, indeed, when we consider what a happy and numerous people the Indians were before Europeans intruded themselves into the territories allotted to them by nature; when we consider how many thousands have perished in battle, embroiled in our contests for power and dominion, and how many thousands more have perished by the use of the poisonous beverages which we have introduced amongst them; when we consider how many artificial wants have been
raised

raised in the minds of the few nations of them that yet remain, and how sadly the morals of these nations have been corrupted by their intercourse with the whites; when we consider, finally, that in the course of fifty years more no vestige even of these once virtuous and amiable people will probably be found in the whole of that extensive territory which lies between the Mississippi and the Atlantic, and was formerly inhabited solely by them; instead of wishing to lessen the value or the number of the few trifles that we find are acceptable to them in their present state, we ought rather to be desirous of contributing still more largely to their comfort and happiness.

Acceptable presents are generally found very efficacious in conciliating the affections of any uncivilized nation: they have very great influence over the minds of the Indians; but to conciliate their affections to the utmost, presents alone are not sufficient; you must appear to have their interest at heart in every respect; you must associate with them; you must treat them as men that are your equals, and, in some measure, even adopt their native manners. It was by such steps as these that the French, when they had possession of Canada, gained their favour in such a very eminent manner, and acquired so wonderful an ascendency over them. The old Indians still say, that

that they never were so happy as when the French had possession of the country; and, indeed, it is a very remarkable fact, which I before mentioned, that the Indians, if they are sick, if they are hungry, if they want shelter from a storm, or the like, will always go to the houses of the old French settlers in preference to those of the British inhabitants. The necessity of treating the Indians with respect and attention is strongly inculcated on the minds of the English settlers, and they endeavour to act accordingly; but still they cannot banish wholly from their minds, as the French do, the idea that the Indians are an inferior race of people to them, to which circumstance is to be attributed the predilection of the Indians for the French rather than them; they all live together, however, on very amicable terms, and many of the English on the frontiers have indeed told me, that if they were but half as honest, and half as well conducted towards one another, as the Indians are towards them, the state of society in the country would be truly enviable.

On the frontiers of the United States little pains have hitherto been taken by the government, and no pains by the people, to gain the good will of the Indians; and the latter, indeed, instead of respecting the Indians as an independent neighbouring nation, have in too many

many inftances violated their rights as men in the moft flagrant manner. The confequence has been, that the people on the frontiers have been involved in all the calamities that they could have fuffered from an avengeful and cruel enemy. Nightly murders, robberies, maffacres, and conflagrations have been common. They have hardly ventured to ftir, at times, beyond the walls of their little habitations; and for whole nights together have they been kept on the watch, in arms, to refift the onfet of the Indians. They have never dared to vifit their neighbours unarmed, nor to proceed alone, in open day, on a journey of a few miles. The gazettes of the United States have daily teemed with the fhocking accounts of the barbarities committed by the Indians, and volumes would fcarcely fuffice to tell the whole of the dreadful tales.

It has been faid by perfons of the States, that the Indians were countenanced in committing thefe enormities by people on the Britifh frontiers, and liberal abufe has been beftowed on the government for having aided, by diftributing amongft them guns, tomahawks, and other hoftile weapons. That the Indians were incited by prefents, and other means, to act againft the people of the colonies, during the American war, muft be admitted; but that, after peace was concluded, the

the same line of conduct was pursued towards them, is an aspersion equally false and malicious. To the conduct of the people of the States themselves alone, and to no other cause, is unquestionably to be attributed the continuance of the warfare between them and the Indians, after the definitive treaty of peace was signed. Instead of then taking the opportunity to reconcile the Indians, as they might easily have done by presents, and by treating them with kindness, they still continued hostile towards them; they looked upon them, as indeed they still do, merely as wild beasts, that ought to be banished from the face of the earth; and actuated by that insatiable spirit of avarice, and that restless and dissatisfied turn of mind, which I have so frequently noticed, instead of keeping within their territories, where millions of acres remained unoccupied, but no part, however, of which could be had without being paid for, they crossed their boundary lines, and fixed themselves in the territory of the Indians, without ever previously gaining the consent of these people. The Indians, nice about their boundary line beyond any other nations, perhaps, in the world, that have such extensive dominions in proportion to their numbers, made no scruple to attack, to plunder, and even to murder these intruders, when a fit opportunity

opportunity offered. The whites endeavoured to repel their attacks, and shot them with as much unconcern as they would either a wolf or a bear. In their expeditions againſt the white ſettlers, the Indians frequently were driven back with loſs; but their ill ſucceſs only urged them to return with redoubled fury, and their well-known revengeful diſpoſition leading them on all occaſions to ſeek blood for blood, they were not merely ſatisfied with murdering the whole families of the ſettlers who had wounded or killed their chiefs or warriors, but oftentimes, in order to appeaſe the manes of their comrades, they croſſed their boundary line in turn, and committed moſt dreadful depredations amongſt the peaceable white inhabitants in the States, who were in no manner implicated in the ill conduct of the men who had encroached upon the Indian territories. Here alſo, if they happened to be repulſed, or to loſe a friend, they returned to ſeek freſh revenge; and as it ſeldom happened that they did eſcape without loſs, their exceſſes and barbarities, inſtead of diminiſhing, were becoming greater every year. The attention of the government was at laſt directed towards the melancholy ſituation of the ſettlers on the frontiers, and the reſult was, that congreſs determined that an army ſhould be raiſed, at the expence of the States, to repel the foe.

An

An army was accordingly raised some time about the year 1790, which was put under the command of General St. Clair. It consisted of about fifteen hundred men; but these were not men that had been accustomed to contend against Indians, nor was the General, although an experienced officer, and well able to conduct an army against a regular force, at all qualified, as many persons had foreseen, and the event proved, to command on an expedition of such a nature as he was now about to be engaged in.

St. Clair advanced with his army into the Indian territory; occasional skirmishes took place, but the Indians still kept retreating before him, as if incapable of making any resistance against such a powerful force. Forgetful of the stratagems of the artful enemy he had to contend with, he boldly followed, till at last, having been drawn far into their territory, and to a spot suitable to their purpose, the Indians attacked him on all sides; his men were thrown into confusion; in vain he attempted to rally them. The Indians, emboldened by the disorder they saw in his ranks, came rushing down with their tomahawks and scalping knives. A dreadful havoc ensued. The greater part of the army was left dead on the fatal field; and of those that escaped the knife, the most were taken prisoners.

foners. All the cannon, ammunition, baggage, and horfes of St. Clair's army fell into the hands of the Indians on this occafion.

A great many young Canadians, and in particular many that were born of Indian women, fought on the fide of the Indians in this action, a circumftance which confirmed the people of the States in the opinion they had previoufly formed, that the Indians were encouraged and abetted in their attacks upon them by the Britifh. I can fafely affirm, however, from having converfed with many of thefe young men who fought againft St. Clair, that it was with the utmoft fecrecy they left their homes to join the Indians, fearful left the government fhould cenfure their conduct; and that in efpoufing the quarrel of the Indians, they were actuated by a defire to affift a people whom they conceived to be injured, more than by an unextinguifhed fpirit of refentment againft men, whom they had formerly viewed in the light of rebels.

As the revenge of the Indians was completely glutted by this victory over St. Clair, it is not improbable, but that if pains had been taken immediately to negociate a peace with them, it might have been obtained on eafy terms; and had the boundary line then determinately agreed upon been faithfully obferved afterwards by the people of the States, there is

great

great reafon to imagine that the peace would have been a permanent one. As this, however, was a queftionable meafure, and the general opinion was, that a peace could be made on better terms if preceded by a victory on the part of the States, it was determined to raife another army. Liberal fupplies for that purpofe were granted by congrefs, and three thoufand men were foon collected together.

Great pains were taken to enlift for this new army men from Kentucky, and other parts of the frontiers, who had been accuftomed to the Indian mode of fighting; and a fufficient number of rifle-men from the frontier were collected, to form a very large regiment. The command of the new army was given to the late General Wayne. Upon being appointed to it, his firft care was to introduce ftrict difcipline amongft his troops; he afterwards kept the army in motion on the frontier, but he did not attempt to penetrate far into the Indian country, nor to take any offenfive meafures againft the enemy for fome time. This delay the General conceived would be attended with two great advantages; firft, it would ferve to banifh from the minds of his men all recollection of the defeat of the late army; and fecondly, it would afford him an opportunity of training perfectly to the Indian mode of fighting fuch of his men as were ignorant

norant of it; for he saw no hopes of succefs but in fighting the Indians in their own way.

When the men were sufficiently trained he advanced, but it was with the utmost caution. He seldom proceeded farther than twelve miles in one day; the march was always ended by noon, and the afternoon was regularly employed in throwing up strong intrenchments round the camp, in order to secure the army from any sudden attack ; and the spot that had been thus fortified on one day was never totally abandoned until a new encampment had been made on the ensuing one. Moreover, strong posts were established at the distance of forty miles, or thereabouts, from each other, in which guards were left, in order to ensure a safe retreat to the army in case it should not be successful. As he advanced, General Wayne sent detachments of his army to destroy all the Indian villages that were near him, and on these occasions the deepest stratagems were made use of. In some instances his men threw off their clothes, and by painting their bodies, disguised themselves so as to resemble Indians in every respect, then approaching as friends, they committed dreadful havoc. Skirmishes also frequently took place, on the march, with the Indians who hovered round the army. These terminated with various succefs, but mostly in favour of the Americans; as in their

conduct,

conduct, the knowledge and difcipline of regular troops were combined with all the cunning and ftratagem of their antagonifts.

All this time the Indians kept retreating, as they had done formerly before St. Clair; and without being able to bring on a decifive engagement, General Wayne proceeded even to the Miami of the Lakes, fo called in contradiftinction to another River Miami, which empties itfelf into the Ohio. Here it was that that curious correfpondence in refpect to Fort Miami took place, the fubftance of which was related in moft of the Englifh and American prints, and by which General Wayne expofed himfelf to the cenfure of many of his countrymen, and General, then Colonel Campbell, who commanded in the fort, gained the public thanks of the traders in London.

The Miami Fort, fituated on the river of the fame name, was built by the Englifh in the year 1793, at which time there was fome reafon to imagine that the difputes exifting between Great Britain and the United States would not have been quite fo amicably fettled, perhaps, as they have been; at leaft that doubtlefs muft have been the opinion of government, otherwife they would not have given orders for the conftruction of a fort within the boundary line of the United States, a circumftance which could not fail to excite the indignation

nation of the people thereof. General Wayne, it would appear, had received no pofitive orders from his government to make himfelf mafter of it: could he have gained poffeffion of it, however, by a coup-de-main, without incurring any lofs, he thought that it could not but have been deemed an acceptable piece of fervice by the public, from whom he fhould have received unbounded applaufe. Vanity was his ruling paffion, and actuated by it on this occafion, he refolved to try what he could do to obtain poffeffion of the fort. Colonel Campbell, however, by his fpirited and manly anfwer to the fummons that was fent him, to furrender the fort on account of its being fituated within the boundary line of the States, foon convinced the American general that he was not to be fhaken by his remonftrances or intimidated by his menaces, and that his two hundred men, who compofed the garrifon, had fufficient refolution to refift the attacks of his army of three thoufand, whenever he thought proper to march againft the fort. The main divifion of the American army, at this time, lay at the diftance of about four miles from the fort; a fmall detachment from it, however, was concealed in the woods at a very little diftance from the fort, to be ready at the call of General Wayne, who, ftrange to tell, when he found he was not likely to get poffeffion of it it in consequence of the summons he sent, was so imprudent, and departed so much from the dignity of the general and the character of the soldier, as to ride up to the fort, and to use the most gross and illiberal language to the British soldiers on duty in it. His object in doing so was, I should suppose, to provoke the garrison to fire upon him, in which case he would have had a pretext for storming the fort.

Owing to the great prudence, however, of Colonel Campbell, who had issued the strictest orders to his men and officers to remain silent, notwithstanding any insults that were offered to them, and not to attempt to fire, unless indeed an actual attack were made on the place, Wayne's plan was frustrated, much bloodshed certainly saved, and a second war between Great Britain and America perhaps averted.

General Wayne gained no great personal honour by his conduct on this occasion; but the circumstance of his having appeared before the British fort in the manner he did operated strongly in his favour in respect to his proceedings against the Indians. These people had been taught to believe by the young Canadians that were amongst them, that if any part of the American army appeared before the fort, it would certainly be fired upon; for they had no idea that the Americans would have

have come in sight of it without taking offensive measures, in which case resistance would certainly have been made. When, therefore, it was heard that General Wayne had not been fired upon, the Indians complained grievously of their having been deceived, and were greatly disheartened on finding that they were to receive no assistance from the British. Their native courage, however, did not altogether forsake them; they resolved speedily to make a stand, and accordingly having chosen their ground, awaited the arrival of General Wayne, who followed them closely.

Preparatory to the day on which they expected a general engagement, the Indians, contrary to the usages of most nations, observe a strict fast; nor does this abstinence from all sorts of food diminish their exertions in the field, as from their early infancy they accustom themselves to fasting for long periods together. The day before General Wayne was expected, this ceremony was strictly attended to, and afterwards, having placed themselves in ambush in the woods, they waited for his arrival. He did not, however, come to the ground on the day that they had imagined, from the reports given them by their scouts of his motions, he would have done; but having reason to think he would come on the subsequent day, they did not move from their ambush. The second

second day passed over without his drawing nearer to them; but fully persuaded that he would come up with them on the next, they still lay concealed in the same place. The third day proved to be extremely rainy and tempestuous; and the scouts having brought word, that from the movements General Wayne had made there was no likelihood of his marching towards them that day, the Indians, now hungry after having fasted for three entire days, determined to rise from their ambush in order to take some refreshment. They accordingly did so, and having no suspicion of an attack, began to eat their food in security.

Before they began to eat, the Indians had divided themselves, I must observe, into three divisions, in order to march to another quarter, where they hoped to surprise the army of the States. In this situation, however, they were themselves surprised by General Wayne. He had received intelligence from his scouts, now equally cunning with those of the Indians, of their proceedings, and having made some motions as if he intended to move to another part of the country, in order to put them off their guard, he suddenly turned, and sent his light horse pouring down on them when they least expected it. The Indians were thrown into confusion, a circumstance which with them never fails to occasion a defeat; they made but

a faint

a faint refiftance, and then fled with precipitancy.

On his arrival at Philadelphia, in the beginning of the year 1796, I was introduced to General Wayne, and I had then an opportunity of feeing the plan of all his Indian campaigns. A moft pompous account was given of this victory, and the plan of it excited, as indeed it well might, the wonder and admiration of all the old officers who faw it. The Indians were reprefented as drawn up in three lines, one behind the other, and after receiving with firmnefs the charge of the American army, as endeavouring with great fkill and adroitnefs to turn its flanks, when, by the fudden appearance of the Kentucky riflemen and the light cavalry, they were put to flight. From the regularity with which the Indians fought on this occafion, it was argued that they muft doubtlefs have been conducted by Britifh officers of fkill and experience. How abfurd this whole plan was, however, was plainly to be deduced from the following circumftance, allowed both by the general and his aides de camp, namely, that during the whole action the American army did not fee fifty Indians; and indeed every perfon who has read an account of the Indians muft know that they never come into the field in fuch regular array, but always fight under covert,

behind

behind trees or bushes, in the most irregular manner. Notwithstanding the great pains that were taken formerly, both by the French and English, they never could be brought to fight in any other manner. It was in this manner, and no other, as I heard from several men who were in the action with them, that they fought against General Wayne; each one, as soon as the American troops were descried, instantly sheltered himself, and in retreating they still kept under covert. It was by fighting them also in their own way, and by sending parties of his light troops and cavalry to rout them from their lurking places, that General Wayne defeated them; had he attempted to have drawn up his army in the regular order described in the plan, he could not but have met with the same fate as St. Clair, and general Braddock did on a former occasion.

Between thirty and forty Indians, who had been shot or bayoneted as they attempted to run from one tree to another, were found dead on the field by the American army. It is supposed that many more were killed, but the fact of the matter could never be ascertained by them: a profound silence was observed on the subject by the Indians, so that I never could learn accurately how many of them had fallen; that however is an immaterial circumstance; suffice it to say that the engagement soon

soon induced the Indians to sue for a peace. Commissioners were deputed by the government of the United States to meet their chiefs; the preliminaries were soon arranged, and a treaty was concluded, by which the Indians relinquished a very considerable part of their territory, bordering upon that of the United States.

The last and principal ceremony observed by the Indians in concluding a peace, is that of burying the hatchet. When this ceremony came to be performed, one of the chiefs arose, and lamenting that the last peace concluded between them and the people of the States had remained unbroken for so short a time, and expressing his desire that this one should be more lasting, he proposed the tearing up of a large oak that grew before them, and the burying of the hatchet under it, where it would for ever remain at rest. Another chief said, that trees were liable to be levelled by the storms; that at any rate they would decay; and that as they were desirous that a perpetual peace should be established between them and their late enemies, he conceived it would be better to bury the hatchet under the tall mountain which arose behind the wood. A third chief in turn addressed the assembly: " As " for me," said he, " I am but a man, and I " have not the strength of the great spirit to
" tear

"tear up the trees of the foreſt by the roots, or to remove mountains, under which to bury the hatchet; but I propoſe that the hatchet may be thrown into the deep lake, where no mortal can ever find it, and where it will remain buried for ever." This propoſal was joyfully accepted by the aſſembly, and the hatchet was in conſequence caſt with great ſolemnity into the water. The Indians now tell you, in their figurative language, that there muſt be peace for ever. "On former times," ſay they, "when the hatchet was buried, it was only ſlightly covered with a little earth and a few leaves, and being always a very troubleſome reſtleſs creature, it ſoon contrived to find its way aboveground, where it never failed to occaſion great confuſion between us and our white brethren, and to knock a great many good people on the head; but now that it has been thrown into the deep lake, it can never do any more miſchief amongſt us; for it cannot riſe of itſelf to the ſurface of the lake, and no one can go to the bottom to look for it." And that there would be a permanent peace between them I have no doubt, provided that the people of the States would obſerve the articles of the treaty as punctually as the Indians; but it requires little ſagacity to predict that this will not be the caſe, and that ere long the hatchet

hatchet will be again refumed. Indeed, a little time before we reached Malden, meffengers from the fouthern Indians had arrived to found the difpofition of thofe who lived near the lake, and try if they were ready and willing to enter into a frefh war. Nor is this eagernefs for war to be wondered at, when from the report of the commiffioners, who were fent down by the federal government to the new ftate of Tenaffee, in order to put the treaty into effect, and to mark out the boundaries of that ftate in particular, it appeared that upwards of five thoufand people, contrary to the ftipulation of the treaty lately entered into with the Indians, had encroached upon, and fettled themfelves down in Indian territory, which people, the commiffioners faid, could not be perfuaded to return, and in their opinion could not be forced back again into the States without very great difficulty *.

A large portion of the back fettlers, living upon the Indian frontiers, are, according to the beft of my information, far greater favages than the Indians themfelves. It is nothing uncommon, I am told, to fee hung up in their chimney corners, or nailed againft the door of

* The fubftance of this report appeared in an extract of a letter from Lexington, in Kentucky, which I myfelf faw, and which was publifhed in many of the newfpapers in the United States.

their habitations, fimilarly to the ears or brufh of a fox, the fcalps which they have themfelves torn from the heads of the Indians whom they have fhot; and in numberlefs publications in the United States I have read accounts of their having flayed the Indians, and employed their fkins as they would have done thofe of a wild beaft, for whatever purpofe they could be applied to. An Indian is confidered by them as nothing better than a deftructive ravenous wild beaft, without reafon, without a foul, that ought to be hunted down like a wolf wherever it makes its appearance; and indeed, even amongft the bettermoft fort of the inhabitants of the weftern country, the moft illiberal notions are entertained refpecting thefe unfortunate people, and arguments for their banifhment, or rather extirpation, are adopted, equally contrary to juftice and to humanity. " The Indian," fay they, " who has " no idea, or at leaft is unwilling to apply him-
" felf to agriculture, requires a thoufand acres
" of land for the fupport of his family; an hun-
" dred acres will be enough for one of us and
" our children; why then fhould thefe hea-
" thens, who have no notion of arts and ma-
" nufactures, who never have made any im-
" provement in fcience, and have never been
" the inventors of any thing new or ufeful to
" the human fpecies, be fuffered to encumber
" the

" the foil?" " The settlements making in the
" upper parts of Georgia, upon the fine lands
" of the Oconec and Okemulgee rivers, will,"
says Mr. Imlay, speaking of the probable destination of the Indians of the south western
territory, " bid defiance to them in that quar-
" ter. The settlements of French Broad, aided
" by Holston, have nothing to fear from them;
" and the Cumberland is too puissant to appre-
" hend any danger. The Spaniards are in
" possession of the Floridas (how long they
" will remain so must depend upon their mo-
" deration and good manners) and of the set-
" tlements at the Natchez and above, which
" will soon extend to the southern bounda-
" ries of Cumberland, so that they (the In-
" dians) will be completely enveloped in a few
" years. Our people (alluding to those of the
" United States) will continue to *encroach* upon
" them on three sides, and *compel* them to live
" more domestic lives, and assimilate them to
" our mode of living, or cross to the western
" side of the Mississippi."

O Americans! shall we praise your justice
and your love of liberty, when thus you talk
of encroachments and compulsion? Shall we
commend your moderation, when we see ye
eager to gain fresh possessions, whilst ye have
yet millions of acres within your own territories unoccupied? Shall we reverence your regard

gard for the rights of human nature, when we fee ye bent upon banifhing the poor Indian from the land where reft the bones of his anceftors, to him more precious than your cold hearts can imagine, and when we fee ye tyrannizing over the haplefs African, becaufe nature has ftamped upon him a complexion different from your own?

The conduct of the people of the States towards the Indians appears the more unreafonable and the more iniquitous, when it is confidered that they are dwindling faft away of themfelves; and that in the natural order of things there will not probably be a fingle tribe of them found in exiftence in the weftern territory by the time that the numbers of the white inhabitants of the country become fo numerous as to render land one half as valuable there as it is at prefent within ten miles of Philadelphia or New York. Even in Canada, where the Indians are treated with fo much kindnefs, they are difappearing fafter, perhaps, than any people were ever known to do before them, and are making room every year for the whites; and it is by no means improbable, but that at the end of fifty years there will not be a fingle Indian to be met with between Quebec and Detroit, except the few perhaps that may be induced to lead quiet domeftic lives, as a fmall number now does in

the

the village of Lorette near Quebec, and at some other places in the lower province.

It is well known, that before Europeans got any footing in North America, the increase of population amongst the Indian nations was very slow, as it is at this day amongst those who remain still unconnected with the whites. Various reasons have been assigned for this. It has been asserted, in the first place, that the Indian is of a much cooler temperament than the white man, has less ardour in pursuit of the female, and is furnished with less noble organs of generation. This assertion is perhaps true in part: they are chaste to a proverb when they come to Philadelphia, or any other of the large towns, though they have a predilection in general for white women, and might there readily indulge their inclination; and there has never been an instance that I can recollect, of their offering violence to a female prisoner, though oftentimes they have carried off from the settlements very beautiful women; that, however, they should not have been gifted by the Creator with ample powers to propagate their species would be contrary to every thing we see either in the animal or the vegetable world; it seems to be with more justice that their slow increase is ascribed to the conduct of the women. The dreadful practice amongst them, of prostituting themselves at a

very

very early age, cannot fail, I should imagine, to vitiate the humours, and must have a tendency to occasion sterility. Added to this, they suckle the few children they have for several years, during which time, at least amongst many of the tribes, they avoid all connection with their husbands; moreover, finding great inconveniency attendant upon a state of pregnancy, when they are following their husbands, in the hunting season, from one camp to another, they have been accused of making use of certain herbs, the specific virtues of which they are well acquainted with, in order to procure abortion.

If one or more of these causes operated against the rapid increase of their numbers before the arrival of Europeans on the continent, the subsequent introduction of spirituous liquors amongst them, of which both men and women drink to the greatest excess whenever an opportunity offers, was sufficient in itself not only to retard this slow increase, but even to occasion a diminution of their numbers. Intermittent fevers and various other disorders, whether arising from an alteration in the climate, owing to the clearing of the woods, or from the use of the poisonous beverages introduced amongst them by the whites, it is hard to say, have likewise contributed much of late years to diminish their numbers. The Shawnese,

Shawnefe, one of the moft warlike tribes, has been leffened nearly one half by ficknefs. Many other reafons could be adduced for their decreafe, but it is needlefs to enumerate them. That their numbers have gradually leffened, as thofe of the whites' have increafed, for two centuries paft, is incontrovertible; and they are too much attached to old habits to leave any room to imagine that they will vary their line of conduct, in any material degree, during years to come, fo that they muft of confequence ftill continue to decreafe.

In my next letter I intend to communicate to you a few obfervations that I have made upon the character, manners, cuftoms, and perfonal and mental qualifications, &c. of the Indians. So much has already been written on thefe fubjects, that I fear I fhall have little to offer to your perufal but what you may have read before. I am induced to think, however, that it will not be wholly unpleafing to you to hear the obfervations of others confirmed by me, and if you fhould meet with any thing new in what I have to fay, it will have the charm of novelty at leaft to recommend it to your notice. I am not going to give you a regular detail of Indian manners, &c.; it would be abfurd in me, who have only been with them for a few weeks, to attempt to do fo. If you wifh to have an account of

Indian

Indian affairs at large, you must read Le P. Charlevoix, Le P. Hennipin, Le Hontan, Carver, &c. &c. who have each written volumes on the subject.

LETTER XXXV.

A brief Account of the Persons, Manners, Character, Qualifications, mental and corporeal, of the Indians; interspersed with Anecdotes.

Malden.

WHAT I shall first take notice of in the persons of the Indians, is the colour of their skins, which, in fact, constitutes the most striking distinction between their persons and ours. In general their skin is of a copper cast; but a most wonderful difference of colour is observable amongst them; some, in whose veins there is no reason to think that any other than Indian blood flows, not having darker complexions than natives of the south of France or of Spain, whilst others, on the contrary, are nearly as black as negroes. Many persons, and particularly some of the most respectable of the French missionaries, whose long residence amongst the Indians ought to have

have made them competent judges of the matter, have been of opinion, that their natural colour does not vary from ours; and that the darkness of their complexion arises wholly from their anointing themselves so frequently with unctuous substances, and from their exposing themselves so much to the smoke of wood fires, and to the burning rays of the sun. But although it is certain that they think a dark complexion very becoming; that they take great pains from their earliest age to acquire such an one; and that many of them do, in process of time, contrive to vary their original colour very considerably; although it is certain likewise, that when first born their colour differs but little from ours; yet it appears evident to me, that the greater part of them are indebted for their different hues to nature alone. I have been induced to form this opinion from the following consideration, namely; that those children which are born of parents of a dark colour are almost universally of the same dark cast as those from whom they sprang. Nekig, that is, The Little Otter, an Ottoway chief of great notoriety, whose village is on Detroit River, and with whom we have become intimately acquainted, has a complexion that differs but little from that of an African; and his little boys, who are the very image of the father, are just as black as himself. With regard to Indian children being white on their first coming into the world, it ought by no means to be concluded from thence, that they would remain so if their mothers did not bedaub them with grease, herbs, &c. as it is well known that negro children are not perfectly black when born, nor indeed for many months afterwards, but that they acquire their jetty hue gradually, on being exposed to the air and sun, just as in the vegetable world the tender blade, on first peeping above ground, turns from white to a pale greenish colour, and afterwards to a deeper green.

Though I remarked to you in a former letter, that the Missisaguis, who live about Lake Ontario, were of a much darker cast than any other tribe of Indians I met with, yet I do not think that the different shades of complexion observable amongst the Indians are so much confined to particular tribes as to particular families; for even amongst the Missisaguis I saw several men that were comparatively of a very light colour. Judging of the Creeks, Cherokees, and other southern Indians, from what I have seen of them at Philadelphia, and at other towns in the States, whither they often come in large parties, led either by business or curiosity, it appears to me that their skin has a redder tinge, and more warmth of colouring in it, if I may ufe the expreffion, than that of the Indians in the neighbourhood of the lakes; it appears to me alfo, that there is lefs difference of colour amongft them than amongft thofe laft mentioned.

Amongft the female Indians alfo, in general, there is a much greater famenefs of colour than amongft the men. I do not recollect to have feen any of a deeper complexion than what might be termed a dirty copper colour.

The Indians univerfally have long, ftraight, black, coarfe hair, and black eyes, rather fmall than full fized; they have, in general, alfo, high prominent cheek bones, and fharp fmall nofes, rather inclining to an aquiline fhape; they have good teeth, and their breath, in general, is as fweet as that of a human being can be. The men are for the moft part very well made; it is a moft rare circumftance to meet with a deformed perfon amongft them: they are remarkably ftraight; have full open chefts; their walk is firm and erect, and many amongft them have really a dignified deportment. Very few of them are under the middle ftature, and none of them ever become very fat or corpulent. You may occafionally fee amongft them ftout robuft men, clofely put together, but in general they are but flightly made. Their legs, arms, and hands, are for the moft part extremely well fhaped; and very many

many amongſt them would be deemed handſome men in any country in the world.

The women, on the contrary, are moſtly under the middle ſize; and have higher cheek bones, and rounder faces than the men. They have very ungraceful carriages; walk with their toes turned conſiderably inwards, and with a ſhuffling gait; and as they advance in years they grow remarkably fat and coarſe. I never ſaw an Indian woman of the age of thirty, but what her eyes were ſunk, her forehead wrinkled, her ſkin looſe and ſhrivelled, and her whole perſon, in ſhort, forbidding; yet, when young, their faces and perſons are really pleaſing, not to ſay ſometimes very captivating. One could hardly imagine, without witneſſing it, that a few years could poſſibly make ſuch an alteration as it does in their perſons This ſudden change is chiefly owing to the drudgery impoſed on them by the men after a certain age; to their expoſing themſelves ſo much to the burning rays of the ſun; ſitting ſo continually in the ſmoke of wood fires; and, above all, to the general cuſtom of proſtituting themſelves at a very early age.

Though the Indians are profuſely furniſhed with hair on their heads, yet on none of the other parts of the body, uſually covered with it amongſt us, is the ſmalleſt ſign of hair viſible, except, indeed, on the chins of old men, where a few a few slender straggling hairs are sometimes seen, not different from what may be occasionally seen on women of a certain age in Europe. Many persons have supposed that the Indians have been created without hair on those parts of the body where it appears wanting; others, on the contrary, are of opinion, that nature has not been less bountiful to them than to us; and that this apparent deficiency of hair is wholly owing to their plucking it out themselves by the roots, as soon as it appears above the skin. It is well known, indeed, that the Indians have a great dislike to hair, and that such of the men as are ambitious of appearing gayer than the rest, pluck it not only from their eye-brows and eye-lashes, but also from every part of the head, except one spot on the back part of the crown, where they leave a long lock. For my own part, from every thing I have seen and heard, I am fully persuaded, that if an Indian were to lay aside this custom of plucking out the hair, he would not only have a beard, but likewise hair on the same parts of the body as white people have; I think, however, at the same time, that this hair would be much finer, and not grow as thickly as upon our bodies, notwithstanding that the hair of their heads is so much thicker than ours. The few hairs that are seen on the faces of old men are to be attributed to the carelessness of old people about their external appearance.

To pluck out their hair, all such as have any connection with the traders make use of a pliable worm, formed of flattened brass wire. This instrument is closely applied, in its open state, to the surface of the body where the hair grows; it is then compressed by the finger and thumb; a great number of hairs are caught at once between the spiral evolutions of the wire, and by a sudden twitch they are all drawn out by the roots. An old squaw, with one of these instruments, would deprive you of your beard in a very few minutes, and a slight application of the worm two or three times in the year would be sufficient to keep your chin smooth ever afterwards. A very great number of the white people, in the neighbourhood of Malden and Detroit, from having submitted to this operation, appear at first sight as little indebted to nature for beards as the Indians. The operation is very painful, but it is soon over, and when one considers how much time and trouble is saved and ease gained by it in the end, it is only surprising that more people do not summon up resolution, and patiently submit to it.

The long lock of hair on the top of the head, with the skin on which it grows, constitutes the true scalp; and in scalping a person that has a full head of hair, an experienced warrior never thinks of taking off more of the skin than

than a bit of about the fize of a crown piece, from the part of the head where this lock is ufually left. They ornament this folitary lock of hair with beads, filver trinkets, &c. and on grand occafions with feathers. The women do not pluck any of the hair from off their heads, and pride themfelves upon having it as long as poffible. They commonly wear it neatly platted up behind, and divided in front on the middle of the forehead. When they wifh to appear finer than ufual, they paint the fmall part of the fkin, which appears on the feparation of the hair, with a ftreak of vermilion; when neatly done, it looks extremely well, and forms a pleafing contraft to the jetty black of their hair.

The Indians, who have any dealings with the Englifh or American traders, and all of them have that live in the neighbourhood, and to the eaft of the Miffiffippi, and in the neighbourhood of the great lakes to the north-weft, have now totally laid afide the ufe of furs and fkins in their drefs, except for their fhoes or moccafins, and fometimes for their leggings, as they find they can exchange them to advantage for blankets and woollen cloths, &c. which they confider likewife as much more agreeable and commodious materials for wearing apparel. The moccafin is made of the fkin of the deer, elk, or buffalo, which is commonly

drefied

dreffed without the hair, and rendered of a deep brown colour by being expofed to the fmoke of a wood fire. It is formed of a fingle piece of leather, with a feam from the toe to the inftep, and another behind, fimilar to that in a common fhoe; by means of a thong, it is faftened round the inftep, juft under the anklebone, and is thus made to fit very clofe to the foot. Round that part where the foot is put in, a flap of the depth of an inch or two is left, which hangs loofely down over the ftring by which the moccafin is faftened; and this flap, as alfo the feam, are taftefully ornamented with porcupine quills and beads: the flap is edged with tin or copper tags filled with fcarlet hair, if the moccafin be intended for a man, and with ribands if for a woman. An ornamented moccafin of this fort is only worn in drefs, as the ornaments are expenfive, and the leather foon wears out; one of plain leather anfwers for ordinary ufe. Many of the white people on the Indian frontiers wear this kind of fhoe; but a perfon not accuftomed to walk in it, or to walk barefoot, cannot wear it abroad, on a rough road, without great inconvenience, as every unevennefs of furface is felt through the leather, which is foft and pliable: in a houfe it is the moft agreeable fort of fhoe that can be imagined: the Indians wear it univerfally.

Above

Above the moccafin all the Indians wear what are called leggings, which reach from the inftep to the middle of the thigh. They are commonly made of blue or fcarlet cloth, and are formed fo as to fit clofe to the limbs, like the modern pantaloons; but the edges of the cloth annexed to the feam, inftead of being turned in, are left on the outfide, and are ornamented with beads, ribands, &c. when the leggings are intended for drefs. Many of the young warriors are fo defirous that their leggings fhould fit them neatly, that they make the fquaws, who are the tailors, and really very good ones, fow them tight on their limbs, fo that they cannot be taken off, and they continue to wear them conftantly till they are reduced to rags. The leggings are kept up by means of two ftrings, one on the outfide of each thigh, which are faftened to a third, that is tied round the waift.

They alfo wear round the waift another ftring, from which are fufpended two little aprons, fomewhat more than a foot fquare, one hanging down before and the other behind, and under thefe a piece of cloth, drawn clofe up to the body between the legs, forming a fort of trufs. The aprons and this piece of cloth, which are all faftened together, are called the breech cloth. The utmoft ingenuity of the fquaws is exerted in adorning the little aprons with beads, ribands, &c.

The

The moccafins, leggings, and breech cloth conftitute the whole of the drefs which they wear when they enter upon a campaign, except indeed it be a girdle, from which hangs their tobacco pouch and fcalping knife, &c.; nor do they wear any thing more when the weather is very warm; but when it is cool, or when they drefs themfelves to vifit their friends, they put on a fhort fhirt, loofe at the neck and wrifts, generally made of coarfe figured cotton or callico of fome gaudy pattern, not unlike what would be ufed for window or bed curtains at a common inn in England. Over the fhirt they wear either a blanket, large piece of broad cloth, or elfe a loofe coat made fomewhat fimilarly to a common riding frock; a blanket is more commonly worn than any thing elfe. They tie one end of it round their waift with a girdle, and then drawing it over their fhoulders, either faften it acrofs their breafts with a fkewer, or hold the corners of it together in the left hand. One would imagine that this laft mode of wearing it could not but be highly inconvenient to them, as it muft deprive them in a great meafure of the ufe of one hand; yet it is the mode in which it is commonly worn, even when they are fhooting in the woods; they generally, however, keep the right arm difengaged when they carry a gun, and draw the blanket over the left fhoulder.

The dress of the women differs but very little from that of the men. They wear moccasins, leggings, and loose short shirts, and like them they throw over their shoulders, occasionally, a blanket or piece of broad cloth, but most generally the latter; they do not tie it round their waist, however, but suffer it to hang down so as to hide their legs; instead also of the breech cloth, they wear a piece of cloth folded closely round their middle, which reaches from the waist to the knees. Dark blue or green cloths in general are preferred to those of any other colour; a few of the men are fond of wearing scarlet.

The women in warm weather appear in the villages without any other covering above their waists than these shirts, or shifts if you please so to call them, though they differ in no respect from the shirts of the men; they usually, however, fasten them with a broach round the neck. In full dress they also appear in these shirts, but then they are covered entirely over with silver broaches, about the size of a sixpenny piece. In full dress they likewise fasten pieces of ribands of various colours to their hair behind, which are suffered to hang down to their very heels. I have seen a young squaw, that has been a favourite with the men, come forth at a dance with upwards of five guineas worth of ribands streaming from her hair.

On

On their wrifts the women wear filver bracelets when they can procure them; they alfo wear filver ear-rings; the latter are in general of a very fmall fize; but it is not merely one pair which they wear, but feveral. To admit them, they bore a number of holes in their ears, fometimes entirely round the edges. The men wear ear-rings likewife, but of a fort totally different from thofe worn by the women; they moftly confift of round flat thin pieces of filver, about the fize of a dollar, perforated with holes in different patterns; others, however, equally large, are made in a triangular form. Some of the tribes are very felect in the choice of the pattern, and will not wear any but the one fort of pendants. Inftead of boring their ears, the men flit them along the outward edge from top to bottom, and as foon as the gafh is healed hang heavy weights to them in order to ftretch the rim thus feparated as low down as poflible. Some of them are fo fuccefsful in this operation, that they contrive to draw the rims of the ear in form of a bow, down to their very fhoulders, and their large ear-rings hang dangling on their breafts. To prevent the rim thus extended from breaking, they bind it with brafs wire; however, I obferved that there was not one in fix that had his ears perfect; the leaft touch, indeed, is

fufficient

sufficient to break the skin, and it would be most wonderful if they were able to preserve it entire, engaged so often as they are in drunken quarrels, and so often liable to be entangled in thickets whilst pursuing their game.

Some of the men wear pendants in their noses, but these are not so common as earrings. The chiefs and principal warriors wear breast plates, consisting of large pieces of silver, sea shells, or the like. Silver gorgets, such as are usually worn by officers, please them extremely, and to favourite chiefs they are given out, amongst other presents, on the part of government. Another sort of ornament is likewise worn by the men, consisting of a large silver clasp or bracelet, to which is attached a bunch of hair dyed of a scarlet colour, usually taken from the knee of the buffalo. This is worn on the narrow part of the arm above the elbow, and it is deemed very ornamental, and also a badge of honour, for no person wears it that has not distinguished himself in the field. Silver ornaments are universally preferred to those of any other metal.

The Indians not only paint themselves when they go to war, but likewise when they wish to appear full dressed. Red and black are their favourite colours, and they daub themselves in the most fantastic manner. I have seen

seen some with their faces entirely covered with black, except a round spot in the center, which included the upper lip and end of the nose, which was painted red; others again I have seen with their heads entirely black, except a large red round spot on each ear; others with one eye black and the other red, &c.; but the most common style of painting I observed, was to black their faces entirely over with charcoal, and then wetting their nails, to draw parallel undulating lines on their cheeks. They generally carry a little looking glass about them to enable them to dispose of their colours judiciously. When they go to war they rub in the paint with grease, and are much more particular about their appearance, which they study to render as horrible as possible; they then cover their whole body with red, white, and black paint, and seem more like devils than human beings. Different tribes have different methods of painting themselves.

Though the Indians spend so much of their time in adorning their persons, yet they take no pains to ornament their habitations, which for the most part are wretched indeed. Some of them are formed of logs, in a style somewhat similar to the common houses in the United States; but the greater part of them are of a moveable nature, and formed of bark. The bark

bark of the birch tree is deemed preferable to every other fort, and where it is to be had is always made ufe of; but in this part of the country not being often met with, the bark of the elm tree is ufed in its ftead. The Indians are very expert in ftripping it from a tree; and frequently take the entire bark from off the trunk in one piece. The fkeletons of their huts confift of flender poles, and on them the bark is faftened with ftrips of the tough rind of fome young tree: this, if found, proves a very effectual defence againft the weather. The huts are built in various forms: fome of them have walls on every fide, doors, and alfo a chimney in the middle of the roof; Others are open on one fide, and are nothing better than fheds. When built in this laft ftyle, four of them are commonly placed together, fo as to form a quadrangle, with the open parts towards the infide, and a fire common to them all is kindled in the middle. In fine weather thefe huts are agreeable dwellings; but in the depth of winter they muft be dreadfully uncomfortable. Others of their huts are built in a conical fhape. The Nandoweffies, Mr. Carver tells us, live entirely in tents formed of fkins. A great many of the families that were encamped on the ifland of Bois Blanc, I obferved, lived in the canvas tents which they had taken from St. Clair's army. Many of the

the Indian nations have no permanent place of refidence, but move about from one fpot to another, and in the hunting feafon they all have moveable encampments, which laft are in general very rude, and infufficient to give them even tolerable fhelter from a fall of rain or fnow. The hunting feafon commences on the fall of the leaf, and continues till the fnow diffolves.

In the depth of winter, when the fnow is frozen on the ground, they form their hunting fheds of the fnow itfelf; a few twigs platted together being fimply placed overhead to prevent the fnow which forms the roof from falling down. Thefe fnowy habitations are much more comfortable, and warmer in winter time than any others that can be erected, as they effectually fcreen you from the keen piercing blafts of the wind, and a bed of fnow is far from being uncomfortable. To accuftom the troops to encamp in this ftyle, in cafe of a winter campaign, a party of them, headed by fome of the young officers, ufed regularly to be fent from Quebec by the late governor, into the woods, there to fhift for themfelves during the month of February. Care was always taken, however, to fend with them two or three experienced perfons, to fhew them how to build the huts, otherwife death might have been the confequence to many.

In

In thefe encampments they always fleep with their feet to the fire; and indeed in the Indian encampments in general, during cold weather, they fleep on the ground with their feet to the fire; during mild weather, many of them fleep on benches of bark in their huts, which are raifed from two to four feet from the ground.

The utenfils in an Indian hut are very few; one or two brafs or iron kettles procured from the traders, or, if they live removed from them, pots formed of ftone, together with a few wooden fpoons and difhes made by themfelves conftitute in general the whole of them. A ftone of a very foft texture, called the *foap ftone*, is very commonly found in the back parts of North America, particularly fuited for Indian workmanfhip. It receives its name from appearing to the touch as foft and fmooth as a bit of foap; and indeed it may be cut with a knife almoft equally eafily. In Virginia they ufe it powdered for the boxes of their wheels inftead of greafe. Soft, however, as is this ftone; it will refift fire equally with iron. The foap ftone is of a dove colour; others nearly of the fame quality, are found in the country, of a black and red colour, which are ftill commonly ufed by the Indians for the bowls of their pipes.

The bark canoes, which the Indians use in this part of the country, are by no means so neatly formed as those made in the country upon, and to the north of, the River St. Lawrence: they are commonly formed of one entire piece of elm bark, taken from the trunk of the tree, which is bound on ribs formed of slender rods of tough wood. There are no ribs, however, at the ends of these canoes, but merely at the middle part, where alone it is that passengers ever sit. It is only the center, indeed, which rests upon the water; the ends are generally raised some feet above the surface, the canoes being of a curved form. They bring them into this shape by cutting, nearly midway between the stem and stern, two deep slits, one on each side, in the back, and by lapping the disjointed edges one over the other. No pains are taken to make the ends of the canoes water tight, since they never touch the water.

On first inspection you would imagine, from its miserable appearance, that an elm bark canoe, thus constructed, were not calculated to carry even a single person safely across a smooth piece of water; it is nevertheless a remarkably safe sort of boat, and the Indians will resolutely embark in one of them during very rough weather. They are so light that they ride securely over every wave, and the only precaution

caution neceffary in navigating them is to fit
fteady. I have feen a dozen people go fecurely
in one, which might be eafily carried by a
fingle able-bodied man. When an Indian
takes his family to any diftance in a canoe, the
women, the girls, and boys, are furnifhed each
with a paddle, and are kept bufily at work;
the father of the family gives himfelf no
trouble but in' fteering the veffel.

The Indians that are connected with the
traders have now, very generally, laid afide
bows and arrows, and feldom take them into
their hands, except it be to amufe themfelves
for a few hours, when they have expended
their powder and fhot : their boys, however,
ftill ufe them univerfally, and fome of them
fhoot with wonderful dexterity. I faw a young
Shawnefe chief, apparently not more than ten
years old, fix three arrows running in the body
of a fmall black fquirrel, on the top of a very
tall tree, and during an hour or two that I followed him through the woods, he fcarcely
miffed his mark half a dozen times. It is
aftonifhing to fee with what accuracy, and at
the fame time with what readinefs, they mark
the fpot where their arrows fall. They will
fhoot away a dozen arrows or more, feemingly
quite carelefs about what becomes of them, and
as inattentive to the fpot where they fall as if
they never expected to find them again, yet

afterwards

afterwards they will run and pick them every one up without hesitation. The southern Indians are much more expert at the use of the bow than those near the lakes, as they make much greater use of it.

With the gun, it seems to be generally allowed, that the Indians are by no means so good marksmen as the white people. I have often taken them out shooting with me, and I always found them very slow in taking aim; and though they generally hit an object that was still, yet they scarcely ever touched a bird on the wing, or a squirrel that was leaping about from tree to tree.

The expertness of the Indians in throwing the tomahawk is well known. At the distance of ten yards they will fix the sharp edge of it in an object nearly to a certainty. I have been told, however, that they are not fond of letting it out of their hands in action, and that they never attempt to throw it but when they are on the point of overtaking a flying foe, or are certain of recovering it. Some of them will fasten a string of the length of a few feet to the handle of the tomahawk, and will launch it forth, and draw it back again into their hand with great dexterity; they will also parry the thrust or cuts of a sword with the tomahawk very dexterously.

The common tomahawk is nothing more than

TOMAHAWKS.

than a light hatchet, but the moft approved fort has on the back part of the hatchet, and connected with it in one piece, the bowl of a pipe, fo that when the handle is perforated, the tomahawk anfwers every purpofe of a pipe: the Indians, indeed, are fonder of fmoking out of a tomahawk than out of any other fort of pipe. That formerly given to the Indians by the French traders, inftead of a pipe, had a large fpike on the back part of the hatchet; very few of thefe inftruments are now to be found amongft them; I never faw but one. The tomahawk is commonly worn by the left fide, ftuck in a belt.

For the favourite chiefs, very elegant pipe tomahawks, inlaid with filver, are manufactured by the armourers in the Indian department. Captain E—— has given me one of this kind, which he had made for himfelf; it is fo much admired by the Indians, that when they have feen it with me, they have frequently afked me to lend it to them for an hour or fo to fmoke out of, juft as children would afk for a pretty plaything; they have never failed to return it very punctually.

The armourers here alluded to are perfons kept at the expence of government to repair the arms of the Indians when they happen to break, which is very commonly the cafe.

An Indian child, foon after it is born, is
fwathed

swathed with cloths or skins, and being then laid on its back, is bound down on a piece of thick board, spread over with soft mofs. The board is left somewhat longer and broader than the child, and bent pieces of wood, like pieces of hoops, are placed over its face to protect it, so that if the machine were suffered to fall the child would not probably be injured. The women, when they go abroad, carry their children thus tied down on their backs, the board being suspended by a broad band, which they wear round their foreheads. When they have any business to transact at home, they hang the board on a tree, if there be one at hand, and set them a swinging from side to side, like a pendulum, in order to exercise the children; sometimes also, I observed, they unloosened the children from the boards, and putting them each into a sort of little hammock, fastened them between two trees, and there suffered them to swing about. As soon as they are strong enough to crawl about on their hands and feet they are liberated from all confinement, and suffered, like young puppies, to run about, stark naked, into water, into mud, into snow, and, in short, to go wheresoever their choice leads them; hence they derive that vigour of constitution which enables them to support the greatest fatigue, and that indifference to the changes of the weather which

they

they poſſeſs in common with the brute creation. The girls are covered with a looſe garment as ſoon as they have attained four or five years of age, but the boys go naked till they are conſiderably older.

The Indians, as I have already remarked, are for the moſt part very ſlightly made, and from a ſurvey of their perſons one would imagine that they were much better qualified for any purſuits that required great agility than great bodily ſtrength. This has been the general opinion of moſt of thoſe who have written on this ſubject. I am induced, however, from what I have myſelf been witneſs to, and from what I have collected from others, to think that the Indians are much more remarkable for their muſcular ſtrength than for their agility. At different military poſts on the frontiers, where this ſubject has been agitated, races, for the ſake of experiment, have frequently been made between ſoldiers and Indians, and provided the diſtance was not great, the Indians have almoſt always been beaten; but in a long race, where ſtrength of muſcle was required, they have without exception been victorious; in leaping alſo the Indians have been infallibly beaten by ſuch of the ſoldiers as poſſeſſed common activity: but the ſtrength of the Indians is moſt conſpicuous in the carrying of burthens on their backs;

they esteem it nothing to walk thirty miles a day for several days together under a load of eight stone, and they will walk an entire day under a load without taking any refreshment. In carrying burdens they make use of a sort of frame, somewhat similar to what is commonly used by a glazier to carry glass; this is fastened by cords, or strips of tough bark or leather, round their shoulders, and when the load is fixed upon the broad ledge at the bottom of the frame, two bands are thrown round the whole, one of which is brought across the forehead, and the other across the breast, and thus the load is supported. The length of way an Indian will travel in the course of the day, when unencumbered with a load, is astonishing. A young Wyandot, who, when peace was about to be made between the Indians and General Wayne, was employed to carry a message from his nation to the American officer, travelled but little short of eighty miles on foot in one day; and I was informed by one of the general's aids-de-camp, who saw him when he arrived at the camp, that he did not appear in the least degree fatigued.

Le P. Charlevoix observes, that the Indians seem to him to possess many personal advantages over us; their senses, in particular, he thinks much finer than ours; their sight is, indeed, quick and penetrating, and it does not fail

fail them till they are far advanced in years, notwithstanding that their eyes are exposed so many months each winter to the dazzling whiteness of the snow, and to the sharp irritating smoke of wood fires. Disorders in the eyes are almost wholly unknown to them; nor is the slightest blemish ever seen in their eyes, excepting it be a result from some accident. Their hearing is very acute, and their sense of smelling so nice, that they can tell when they are approaching a fire long before it is in sight.

The Indians have most retentive memories; they will preserve to their deaths a recollection of any place they have once passed through; they never forget a face that they have attentively observed but for a few seconds; at the end of many years they will repeat every sentence of the speeches that have been delivered by different individuals in a public assembly; and has any speech been made in the council house of the nation, particularly deserving of remembrance, it will be handed down with the utmost accuracy from one generation to another, though perfectly ignorant of the use of hieroglyphicks and letters; the only memorials of which they avail themselves are small pieces of wood, such as I told you were brought by them to Captain E——, preparatory to the delivery of the presents, and belts of wampum;
the

the former are only used on trifling occasions, the latter never but on very grand and solemn ones. Whenever a conference, or a talk as they term it, is about to be held with any neighbouring tribe, or whenever any treaty or national compact is about to be made, one of these belts, differing in some respect from every other that has been made before, is immediately constructed; each person in the assembly holds this belt in his hand whilst he delivers his speech, and when he has ended, he presents it to the next person that rises, by which ceremony each individual is reminded, that it behoves him to be cautious in his discourse, as all he says will be faithfully recorded by the belt. The talk being over, the belt is deposited in the hands of the principal chief.

On the ratification of a treaty, very broad splendid belts are reciprocally given by the contracting parties, which are deposited amongst the other belts belonging to the nation. At stated intervals they are all produced to the nation, and the occasions upon which they were made are mentioned; if they relate to a talk, one of the chiefs repeats the substance of what was said over them; if to a treaty, the terms of it are recapitulated. Certain of the squaws, also, are entrusted with the belts, whose business it is to relate the history of each one of them to the younger branches of the

the tribe; this they do with great accuracy, and thus it is that the remembrance of every important tranfaction is kept up.

The wampum is formed of the infide of the clam fhell, a large fea fhell bearing fome fimilitude to that of a fcallop, which is found on the coafts of New England and Virginia. The fhell is fent in its original rough ftate to England, and there cut into fmall pieces, exactly fimilar in fhape and fize to the modern glafs bugles worn by ladies, which little bits of fhell conftitute wampum. There are two forts of wampum, the white and the purple; the latter is moft efteemed by the Indians, who think a pound weight of it equally valuable with a pound of filver. The wampum is ftrung upon bits of leather, and the belt is compofed of ten, twelve, or more ftrings, according to the importance of the occafion on which it is made; fometimes alfo the wampum is fowed in different patterns on broad belts of leather.

The ufe of wampum appears to be very general amongft the Indian nations, but how it became fo, is a queftion that would require difcuffion, for it is well known that they are a people obftinately attached to old cuftoms, and that would not therefore be apt to adopt, on the moft grand and folemn occafion, the ufe of an article that they had never feen until brought to them by ftrangers; at the fame time

time it seems wholly impossible that they should ever have been able to have made wampum from the clam shell for themselves; they fashion the bowls of tobacco pipes, indeed, from stone, in a very curious manner, and with astonishing accuracy, considering that they use no other instrument than a common knife, but then the stone which they commonly carve thus is of a very soft kind; the clam shell, however, is exceedingly hard, and to bore and cut it into such small pieces as are necessary to form wampum, very fine tools would be wanting. Probably they made some use of the clam shell, and endeavoured to reduce it to as small bits as they could with their rude instruments before we came amongst them, but on finding that we could cut it so much more neatly than they could, laid aside the wampum before in use for that of our manufacture. Mr. Carver tells us, that he found sea shells very generally worn by the Indians who resided in the most interior parts of the continent, who never could have visited a sea shore themselves, and could only have procured them at the expence of much trouble from other nations.

The Indians are exceedingly sagacious and observant, and by dint of minute attention, acquire many qualifications to which we are wholly strangers. They will traverse a trackless forest, hundreds of miles in extent, without deviating from the ſtraight courſe, and will reach to a certainty the ſpot whither they intended to go on ſetting out: with equal ſkill they will croſs one of the large lakes, and though out of ſight of the ſhores for days, will to a certainty make the land at once, at the very place they deſired. Some of the French miſſionaries have ſuppoſed that the Indians are guided by inſtinct, and have pretended that Indian children can find their way through a foreſt as eaſily as a perſon of maturer years; but this is a moſt abſurd notion. It is unqueſtionably by a cloſe attention to the growth of the trees, and poſition of the ſun, that they find their way. On the northern ſide of a tree, there is generally the moſt moſs, and the bark on that ſide in general differs from that on the oppoſite one. The branches towards the ſouth are for the moſt part more luxuriant than thoſe on the other ſides of trees, and ſeveral other diſtinctions alſo ſubſiſt between the northern and ſouthern ſides, conſpicuous to Indians, who are taught from their infancy to attend to them, which a common obſerver would perhaps never notice. Being accuſtomed from their childhood, likewiſe, to pay great attention to the poſition of the ſun, they learn to make the moſt accurate allowance for its apparent motion from one part of the heavens to another, and in any part of the day they will

point

point to the part of the heavens where it is, although the sky be obscured by clouds or mists.

An instance of their dexterity in finding their way through an unknown country came under my observation when I was at Staunton, situated behind the Blue Mountains, Virginia. A number of the Creek nation had arrived at that town in their way to Philadelphia, whither they were going upon some affairs of importance, and had stopped there for the night. In the morning some circumstance or another, what could not be learned, induced one half of the Indians to set off without their companions, who did not follow until some hours afterwards. When these last were ready to pursue their journey, several of the towns-people mounted their horses to escort them part of the way. They proceeded along the high road for some miles, but all at once, hastily turning aside into the woods, though there was no path, the Indians advanced confidently forward; the people who accompanied them, surprised at this movement, informed them that they were quitting the road to Philadelphia, and expressed their fears lest they should miss their companions, who had gone on before. They answered, that they knew better; that the way through the woods was the shortest to Philadelphia ; and that they knew very well that their companions had entered the

the woods at the very place they did. Curiofity led fome of the horfemen to go on, and to their aftonifhment, for there was apparently no track, they overtook the other Indians in the thickeft part of the wood; but what appeared moft fingular was, that the route which they took was found, on examining a map, to be as direct for Philadelphia as if they had taken the bearings by a mariner's compafs. From others of their nation, who had been at Philadelphia at a former period, they had probably learned the exact direction of that city from their village, and had never loft fight of it, although they had already travelled three hundred miles through woods, and had upwards of four hundred miles more to go before they could reach the place of their deftination.

Of the exactnefs with which they can find out a ftrange place that they have been once directed to by their own people, a ftriking example is furnifhed us, I think, by Mr. Jefferfon, in his account of the Indian graves in Virginia. Thefe graves are nothing more than large mounds of earth in the woods, which, on being opened, are found to contain fkeletons in an erect pofture: the Indian mode of fepulture has been too often defcribed to remain unknown to you. But to come to my ftory. A party of Indians that were paffing on to fome of the fea ports on the Atlantic, juft just as the Creeks above mentioned were going to Philadelphia, were observed, all on a sudden, to quit the straight road by which they were proceeding, and without asking any questions, to strike through the woods in a direct line to one of these graves, which lay at the distance of some miles from the road. Now very near a century must have passed over since the part of Virginia, in which this grave was situated, had been inhabited by Indians; and these Indian travellers, who went to visit it by themselves, had, unquestionably, never been in that part of the country before; they must have found their way to it simply from the description of its situation that had been handed down to them by tradition.

The Indians, for the most part, are admirably well acquainted with the geography of their own country. Ask them any questions relative to the situation of a particular place in it, and if there be a convenient spot at hand, they will, with the utmost facility, trace upon the ground with a stick a map, by no means inaccurate, of the place in question, and the surrounding country; they will point out the course of the rivers, and by directing your attention to the sun, make you acquainted with the different bearings. I happened once to be sitting in a house at the western extremity of Lake Erie, whilst we were detained there by contrary

contrary winds, and was employed in looking over a pocket map of the state of New York, when a young Seneka warrior entered. His attention was attracted by the sight of the map, and he seemed at once to comprehend the meaning of it; but never having before seen a general map of the state of New York, and being wholly ignorant of the use of letters, he could not discover to what part of the country it had a reference; simply, however, by laying my finger upon the spot where we then were, and by shewing to him the line that denoted Buffalo Creek, on which his village was situated, I gave him the clue to the whole, and having done so, he quickly ran over the map, and with the utmost accuracy pointed out by name, every lake and river for upwards of two hundred miles distant from his village. All the lakes and rivers in this part of the country still retain the Indian names, so that had he named them wrong, I could have at once detected him. His pleasure was so great on beholding such a perfect map of the country, that he could not refrain from calling some of his companions, who were loitering at the door, to come and look at it. They made signs to me to lend it to them; I did so, and having laid it on a table, they sat over it for more than half an hour, during which time I observed they frequently testified their pleasure to one another on finding particular places accurately laid down, which they had been acquainted with. The older men also seemed to have many stories to tell the others, probably respecting the adventures they had met with at distant parts of the country, and which they were now glad of having an opportunity of elucidating by the map before them.

Whenever a track of ground is about to be purchased by government from the Indians, for no private individuals can purchase lands from them by the laws of the province, a map of the country is drawn, and the part about to be contracted for, is particularly marked out. If there be any mistakes in these maps, the Indians will at once point them out; and after the bargain is made, they will, from the maps, mark out the boundaries of the lands they have ceded with the greatest accuracy, notching the trees, if there be any, along the boundary line, and if not, placing stakes or stones in the ground to denote where it runs. On these occasions regular deeds of sale are drawn, with accurate maps of the lands which have been purchased attached to them, and these deeds are signed in form by the contracting parties. I saw several of them in possession of our friend Captain E———, which were extremely curious on account of the Indian signatures. The Indians, for the most part, take upon them
the

the name of some animal, as, The Blue Snake; The Little Turkey; The Big Bear; The Mad Dog, &c. and their fignatures confift of the outline, drawn with a pen, of the different animals whofe names they bear. Some of the fignatures at the bottom of thefe deeds were really well executed, and were lively reprefentations of the animals they were intended for.

The Indians in general poffefs no fmall fhare of ingenuity. Their domeftic wooden utenfils, bows and arrows, and other weapons, &c. are made with the utmoft neatnefs; and indeed the workmanfhip of them is frequently fuch as to excite aftonifhment, when it is confidered that a knife and a hatchet are the only inftruments they make ufe of. On the handles of their tomahawks, on their powder horns, on the bowls of their pipes, &c. you oftentimes meet with figures extremely well defigned, and with fpecimens of carving far from contemptible. The embroidery upon their moccafins and other garments fhews that the females are not lefs ingenious in their way than the men. Their porcupine quill work would command admiration in any country in Europe. The foft young quills of the porcupine are thofe which they ufe, and they dye them of the moft beautiful and brilliant colours imaginable. Some of their dyes have been difcovered, but many of them yet remain unknown, as do alſo many of the medicines with which they perform ſometimes moſt miraculous cures. Their dyes and medicines are all procured from the vegetable world.

But though the Indians prove by their performances, that they have ſome reliſh for the works of art, yet they are by no means ready to beſtow commendations on every thing curious for its workmanſhip that is ſhewn to them. Trinkets or ornaments for dreſs, though ever ſo gaudy, or ever ſo neatly manufactured, they deſpiſe, unleſs ſomewhat ſimilar in their kind to what they themſelves are accuſtomed to wear, and faſhioned exactly to their own taſte, which has remained nearly the ſame ſince Europeans firſt came amongſt them; nor will they praiſe any curious or wonderful piece of mechaniſm, unleſs they can ſee that it is intended to anſwer ſome uſeful purpoſe. Nothing that I could ſhew them attracted their attention, I obſerved, ſo much as a light double-barrelled gun, which I commonly carried in my hand when walking about their encampments. This was ſomething in their own way; they at once perceived the benefit that muſt accrue to the ſportſman from having two barrels on the one ſtock, and the contrivance pleaſed them; well acquainted alſo with the qualities of good locks, and the advantages attending them, they expreſſed great ſatisfaction

tion at finding thofe upon my piece fo fuperior to what they perhaps had before feen.

It is not every new fcene either, which to them, one would imagine, could not fail to appear wonderful, that will excite their admiration.

A French writer, I forget who, tells us of fome Iroquois Indians that walked through feveral of the fineft ftreets of Paris, but without expreffing the leaft pleafure at any thing they faw, until they at laft came to a cook's fhop; this called forth their warmeft praife; a fhop where a man was always fure of getting fomething to fatisfy his hunger, without the trouble and fatigue of hunting and fifhing, was in their opinion one of the moft admirable inftitutions poffible: had they been told, however, that they muft have paid for what they eat, they would have expreffed equal indignation perhaps at what they faw. In their own villages they have no idea of refufing food to any perfon that enters their habitation in quality of a friend.

The Indians, whom curiofity or bufinefs leads to Philadelphia, or to any other of the large towns in the States, find, in general, as little deferving of notice in the ftreets and houfes there as thefe Iroquois at Paris; and there is not one of them but what would prefer his own wigwam to the moft fplendid habita-

tions they fee in any of thefe places. The
fhipping, however, at Philadelphia and the
other fea-ports, feldom fails to excite their admiration,
becaufe they at once fee the utility
and advantage of large veffels over canoes,
which are the only veffels they have. The
young Wyandot, whom I before mentioned, as
having made fuch a wonderful day's journey
on foot, happened to be at Philadelphia when
I was there, and he appeared highly delighted
with the river, and the great number of fhips
of all fizes upon it; but the tide attracted his
attention more than any thing elfe whatfoever.
On coming to the river the firft day, he looked
up at the fun, and made certain obfervations
upon the courfe of the ftream, and general
fituation of the place, as the Indians never
fail to do on coming to any new or remarkable
fpot. The fecond time, however, he went
down to the water, he found to his furprife
that the river was running with equal rapidity
in a contrary direction to what he had feen
it run the day before. For a moment he imagined
that by fome miftake he muft have got
to the oppofite fide of it; but foon recollecting
himfelf, and being perfuaded that he ftood on
the very fame fpot from whence he had viewed
it the day before, his aftonifhment became great
indeed. To obtain information upon fuch an
interefting point, he immediately fought out

an

an aid-de-camp of General Wayne, who had brought him to town. This gentleman, however, only rendered the appearance still more myfterious to him, by telling him, that the great fpirit, for the convenience of the white men, who were his particular favourites, had made the rivers in their country to run two ways; but the poor Wyandot was fatisfied with the anfwer, and replied, " Ah, my friend, " if the great fpirit would make the Ohio to " run two ways for us, we fhould very often " pay you a vifit at Pittfburgh *." During his ftay at Philadelphia he never failed to vifit the river every day.

Amongft the public exhibitions at Philadelphia, the performances of the horfe riders and tumblers at the amphitheatre appear to afford them the greateft pleafure; they entertain the higheft opinion of thefe people who are fo diftinguifhed for their feats of activity, and rank them amongft the ableft men in the nation. Nothing, indeed, gives more delight to the Indians than to fee a man that excels in any bodily exercife; and tell them even of a perfon that is diftinguifhed for his great ftrength, for his fwiftnefs in running, for his dexterous management of the bow or the gun, for his cunning in hunting, for his intrepid

* A town fituated at the very head of the Ohio.

and firm conduct in war, or the like, they will liften to you with the greateft pleafure, and readily join in praifes of the hero.

The Indians appear, on the firft view, to be of a very cold and phlegmatic difpofition, and you muft know them for fome time before you can be perfuaded to the contrary. If you fhew them any artificial production which pleafes them, they fimply tell you, with feeming indifference, " that it is pretty;" " that they like " to look at it;" " that it is a clever inven- " tion:" nor do they teftify their fatisfaction and pleafure by emotions feemingly much warmer in their nature, on beholding any new or furprifing fpectacle, or on hearing any happy piece of intelligence. The performances at the amphitheatre at Philadelphia, though unqueftionably highly interefting to them, never drew forth from them, I obferved, more than a fmile or a gentle laugh, followed by a remark in a low voice to their friend fitting next to them. With equal indifference do they behold any thing terrible, or liften to the accounts of any dreadful cataftrophe that has befallen their families or their nation. This apathy, however, is only affumed, and certainly does not proceed from a real want of feeling: no people on earth are more alive to the calls of friendfhip; no people have a greater affection for their offspring in their tender years; no

people

people are more fenfible of an injury: a word in the flighteft degree infulting will kindle a flame in their breafts, that can only be extinguifhed by the blood of the offending party; and they will traverfe forefts for hundreds of miles, expofed to the inclemency of the fevereft weather, and to the pangs of hunger, to gratify their revenge; they will not ceafe for years daily to vifit, and filently to mourn over the grave of a departed child; and they will rifk their lives, and facrifice every thing they poffefs, to affift a friend in diftrefs; but at the fame time, in their opinion, no man can be efteemed a good warrior or a dignified character that openly betrays any extravagant emotions of furprife, of joy, of forrow, or of fear, on any occafion whatfoever. The excellence of appearing thus indifferent to what would excite the ftrongeft emotions in the minds of any other people, is forcibly inculcated on them from their earlieft youth; and fuch an aftonifhing command do they acquire over themfelves, that even at the ftake, when fuffering the fevereft tortures that can be inflicted on the human body by the flames and the knife, they appear unmoved, and laugh, as it is well-known, at their tormentors.

This affected apathy on the part of the Indians makes them appear uncommonly grave and referved in the prefence of ftrangers; in their

their own private circles, however, they frequently keep up gay and sprightly conversations; and they are possessed, it is said, of a lively and ready turn of wit. When at such a place as Philadelphia, notwithstanding their appearing so indifferent to every thing before them whilst strangers are present, yet, after having retired by themselves to an apartment for the night, they will frequently sit up for hours together, laughing and talking of what they have seen in the course of the day. I have been told by persons acquainted with their language, that have overheard their discourse on such occasions, that their remarks are most pertinent, and that they sometimes turn what has passed before them into such ludicrous points of view, that it is scarcely possible to refrain from laughter.

But though the Indians, in general, appear so reserved in the presence of strangers, yet the firmness of their dispositions forbids them from ever appearing embarrassed, and they would sit down to table in a palace, before the first crowned head on the face of the earth, with as much unconcern as they would sit down to a frugal meal in one of their own cabins. They deem it highly becoming in a warrior, to accommodate his manners to those of the people with whom he may happen to be, and as they are wonderfully observant,

you

you will feldom perceive any thing of awkwardnefs or vulgarity in their behaviour in the company of ftrangers. I have feen an Indian, that had lived in the woods from his infancy, enter a drawing room in Philadelphia, full of ladies, with as much eafe and as much gentility as if he had always lived in the city, and merely from having been told, preparatory to his entering, the form ufually obferved on fuch occafions. But the following anecdote will put this matter in a ftronger point of view.

Our friend Nekig, the Little Otter, had been invited to dine with us at the houfe of a gentleman at Detroit, and he came accordingly, accompanied by his fon, a little boy of about nine or ten years of age. After dinner a variety of fruits were ferved up, and amongft the reft fome peaches, a difh of which was handed to the young Indian. He helped himfelf to one with becoming propriety; but immediately afterwards he put the fruit to his mouth, and bit a piece out of it. The father eyed him with indignation, and fpoke fome words to him in a low voice, which I could not underftand, but which, on being interpreted by one of the company, proved to be a warm reprimand for his having been fo deficient in obfervation as not to peel his peach, as he faw the gentleman oppofite to

him

him had done. The little fellow was extremely afhamed of himfelf; but he quickly retrieved his error, by drawing a plate towards him, and pealing the fruit with the greateft neatnefs.

Some port wine, which he was afterwards helped to, not being by any means agreeable to his palate, the little fellow made a wry face, as a child might naturally do, after drinking it. This called forth another reprimand from the father, who told him, that he defpaired of ever feeing him a great man or a good warrior if he appeared then to diflike what his hoft had kindly helped him to. The boy drank the reft of his wine with feeming pleafure.

The Indians fcarcely ever lift their hands againft their children; but if they are unmindful of what is faid to them, they fometimes throw a little water in their faces, a fpecies of reprimand of which the children have the greateft dread, and which produces an inftantaneous good effect. One of the French miflionaries tells us of his having feen a girl of an advanced age fo vexed at having fome water thrown in her face by her mother, as if fhe was ftill a child, that fhe inftantly retired, and put an end to her exiftence. As long as they remain children, the young Indians are attentive in the extreme to the advice of their parents;

parents; but arrived at the age of puberty, and able to provide for themselves, they no longer have any respect for them, and they will follow their own will and pleasure in spite of all their remonstrances, unless, indeed, their parents be of an advanced age. Old age never fails to command their most profound veneration.

No people are possessed of a greater share of natural politeness than the Indians: they will never interrupt you whilst you are speaking; nor, if you have told them any thing which they think to be false, will they bluntly contradict you; " We dare say brother," they will answer, " that you yourself believe what " you tell us to be true; but it appears to us " so improbable that we cannot give our assent " to it."

In their conduct towards one another nought but gentleness and harmony is observable. You are never witness, amongst them, to such noisy broils and clamorous contentions as are common amongst the lower classes of people in Europe; nor do you perceive amongst them any traces of the coarse vulgar manners of these latter people; they behave on all occasions like gentlemen, and could not so many glaring proofs be adduced to the contrary, you never could imagine that they were that ferocious savage people in war which they are
said

said to be. It must be understood, however, that I only speak now of the Indians in their sober state; when intoxicated with spirits, which is but too often the case, a very different picture is presented to our view, and they appear more like devils incarnate than human beings; they roar, they fight, they cut each other, and commit every sort of outrage; indeed so sensible are they of their own infirmities in this state, that when a number of them are about to get drunk, they give up their knives and tomahawks, &c. to one of the party, who is on honour to remain sober, and to prevent mischief, and who generally does behave according to this promise. If they happen to get drunk without having taken this precaution, their squaws take the earliest opportunity to deprive them of their weapons.

The Indians prefer whiskey and rum to all other spirituous liquors; but they do not seem eager to obtain these liquors so much for the pleasure of gratifying their palates as for the sake of intoxication. There is not one in a hundred that can refrain from drinking to excess if he have it in his power; and the generality of them having once got a taste of any intoxicating liquor, will use every means to gain more; and to do so they at once become mean, servile, deceitful, and depraved, in every sense of the word. Nothing can make
amends

amends to thefe unfortunate people for the introduction of fpirituous liquors amongft them. Before their acquaintance with them, they were diftinguifhed beyond all other nations for their temperance in eating and drinking; for their temperance in eating, indeed, they are ftill remarkable; they efteem it indecorous in the higheft degree even to appear hungry; and on arriving at their villages, after having fafted, perhaps, for feveral days preceding, they will fit down quietly, and not afk for any food for a confiderable time; and having got wherewith to fatisfy their appetite, they will eat with moderation, as though the calls of hunger were not more prefling than if they had feafted the hour before. They never eat on any occafion in a hurry.

The Indians are by nature of a very hofpitable generous difpofition, where no particular circumftances operate to the contrary; and, indeed, even when revenge would fain perfuade them to behave differently, yet having once profeffed a friendfhip for a ftranger, and pledged themfelves for his fafety, nothing can induce them to deviate from their word. Of their generofity I had numberlefs proofs in the prefents which they gave me; and though it muft be allowed, that when they make prefents they generally expect others in return, yet I am convinced, from the manner in which
they

they prefented different trifles to me, that it was not with an expectation of gaining more valuable prefents in return that they gave them to me, but merely through friendfhip. It is notorious, that towards one another they are liberal in the extreme, and for ever ready to fupply the deficiencies of their neighbours with any fuperfluities of their own. They have no idea of amaffing wealth for themfelves individually; and they wonder that perfons can be found in any fociety, fo deftitute of every generous fentiment, as to enrich themfelves at the expence of others, and to live in eafe and affluence, regardlefs of the mifery and wretchednefs of members of the fame community to which they themfelves belong. Their dreffes, domeftic utenfils, and weapons, are the only articles of property to which they lay an exclufive claim; every thing elfe is the common property of the tribe, in promoting the general welfare in which every individual feels himfelf deeply interefted. The chiefs are actuated by the fame laudable fpirit, and inftead of being the richeft, are, in many inftances, the pooreft perfons in the community; for whilft others have leifure to hunt, &c. it frequently happens that the whole of their time is occupied in fettling the public affairs of the nation.

The generality of the Indian nations appear to have two forts of chiefs; council chiefs, and

war

war chiefs. The former are hereditary, and are employed principally in the management of their civil affairs; but they may be war chiefs at the fame time: the latter are chofen from amongft thofe who have diftinguifhed themfelves the moft in battle, and are folely employed in leading the warriors in the field. The chiefs have no power of enforcing obedience to their commands, nor do they ever attempt to give their orders in an imperious manner; they fimply advife. Each private individual conceives that he is born in a ftate of perfect liberty, and he difdains all controul, but that which his own reafon fubjects him to. As they all have one intereft, however, at heart, which is the general welfare of the nation, and as it is well known that the chiefs are actuated by no other motives, whatever meafures they recommend are generally attended to, and at once adopted. Savages as they are, yet in no civilized community, I fear, on earth, fhall we find the fame public fpirit, the fame difintereftednefs, and the fame regard to order, where order is not enforced by the feverity of laws, as amongft the Indians.

The Indians have the moft fovereign contempt for any fet of people that have tamely relinquifhed their liberty; and they confider fuch as have loft it, even after a hard ftruggle,

as unworthy any rank in fociety above that of
old women: to this caufe, and not to the difference that fubfifts between their perfons, is
to be attributed, I conceive, the rooted aver-
fion which the Indians univerfally have for
negroes. You could not poffibly affront an
Indian more readily, than by telling him that
you think he bears fome refemblance to a negro; or that he has negro blood in his veins:
they look upon them as animals inferior to the
human fpecies, and will kill them with as
much unconcern as a dog or a cat.

An American officer, who, during the war
with Great Britain, had been fent to one of
the Indian nations refident on the weftern
frontier of the States, to perfuade them to remain neuter in the conteft, informed me, that
whilft he remained amongft them fome agents
arrived in their village to negociate, if poffible,
for the releafe of fome negro flaves whom they
had carried off from the American fettlements.
One of thefe negroes, a remarkably tall hand-
fome fellow, had been given to an Indian woman of fome confequence in the nation, in
the manner in which prifoners are ufually difpofed of amongft them. Application was
made to her for his ranfom. She liftened
quietly to what was faid; refolved at the fame
time, however, that the fellow fhould not have
his liberty, fhe ftepped afide into her cabin,
and

and having brought out a large knife, walked up to her flave, and without more ado plunged it into his bowels: " Now," fays fhe, addreffing herfelf coolly to the agents; " now " I give you leave to take away your negro." The poor creature that had been ftabbed fell to the ground, and lay writhing about in the greateft agonies, until one of the warriors took compaffion on him, and put an end to his mifery by a blow of a tomahawk.

At Detroit, Niagara, and fome other places in Upper Canada, a few negroes are ftill held in bondage. Two of thefe haplefs people contrived, whilft we remained at Malden, to make their efcape from Detroit, by ftealing a boat, and proceeding in the night down the river. As the wind would not permit them to crofs the lake, it was conjectured that they would be induced to coaft along the fhore until they reached a place of fafety; in hopes, therefore, of being able to recover them, the proprietor came down to Malden, and there procured two trufty Indians to go in queft of them. The Indians, having received a defcription of their perfons, fet out; but had fcarcely proceeded an hundred yards, when one of them, who could fpeak a few words of Englifh, returned, to afk the proprietor if he would give him permiffion to fcalp the negroes if they were at all refractory, or refufed coming.

His requeſt was peremptorily refuſed, for it was well known that, had it been granted, he would have at once killed them to avoid the trouble of bringing them back. " Well," ſays he, " if you will not let me ſcalp both, " you won't be angry with me, I hope, if I " ſcalp one." He was told in anſwer, that he muſt bring them both back alive. This circumſtance appeared to mortify him extremely, and he was beginning to heſitate about going, when, ſorry am I to ſay, the proprietor, fearful leſt the fellows ſhould eſcape from him, gave his aſſent to the Indian's requeſt, but at the ſame time he begged that he would not deſtroy them if he could poſſibly avoid it. What the reſult was I never learned; but from the apparent ſatisfaction with which the Indian ſet out after he had obtained his dreadful permiſſion, there was every reaſon to imagine that one of the negroes at leaſt would be ſacrificed.

This indifference in the mind of the Indians about taking away the life of a fellow creature, makes them appear, it muſt be confeſſed, in a very unamiable point of view. I fear alſo, that in the opinion of many people, all the good qualities which they poſſeſs, would but ill atone for their revengeful diſpoſition, and for the cruelties which, it is well known, they ſometimes inflict upon the priſoners who have fallen into their power in battle. Great pains have

have been taken, both by the French and English miffionaries, to reprefent to them the infamy of torturing their prifoners; nor have thefe pains been beftowed in vain; for though in fome recent inftances it has appeared that they ftill retain a fondnefs for this horrid practice, yet I will venture, from what I have heard, to affert, that of late years not one prifoner has been put to the torture, where twenty would have been a hundred years ago. Of the prifoners that fell into their hands on St. Clair's defeat, I could not learn, although I made ftrict enquiries on the fubject, that a fingle man had been faftened to the ftake. As foon as the defeat was known, rewards were held out by the Britifh officers, and others that had influence over them, to bring in their prifoners alive, and the greater part of them were delivered up unhurt; but to irradicate wholly from their breafts the fpirit of revenge has been found impoffible. You will be enabled to form a tolerable idea of the little good effect which education has over their minds in this refpect, from the following anecdotes of Captain Jofeph Brandt, a war chief of the Mohawk nation.

This Brandt, at a very early age, was fent to a college in New England, where, being poffeffed of a good capacity, he foon made very confiderable progrefs in the Greek and Latin

Latin languages. Uncommon pains were taken to inftil into his mind the truths of the gofpel. He profeffed himfelf to be a warm admirer of the principles of chriftianity, and in hopes of being able to convert his nation on returning to them, he abfolutely tranflated the gofpel of St. Matthew into the Mohawk language; he alfo tranflated the eftablifhed form of prayer of the church of England. Before Brandt, however, had finifhed his courfe of ftudies, the American war broke out, and fired with that fpirit of glory which feems to have been implanted by nature in the breaft of the Indian, he immediately quitted the college, repaired to his native village, and fhortly afterwards, with a confiderable body of his nation, joined fome Britifh troops under the command of Sir John Johnfton. Here he diftinguifhed himfelf by his valour in many different engagements, and was foon raifed, not only to the rank of a war chief, but alfo to that of a captain in his Majefty's fervice.

It was not long, however, before Brandt fullied his reputation in the Britifh army. A fkirmifh took place with a body of American troops; the action was warm, and Brandt was fhot by a mufquet-ball in the heel; but the Americans in the end were defeated, and an officer with about fixty men taken prifoners. The officer, after having delivered up his fword, sword, had entered into converfation with Colonel Johnston, who commanded the British troops, and they were talking together in the moſt friendly manner, when Brandt, having ſtolen ſlily behind them, laid the American officer lifeleſs on the ground with a blow of his tomahawk. The indignation of Sir John Johnſton, as may readily be ſuppoſed, was rouſed by ſuch an act of treachery, and he reſented it in the warmeſt language. Brandt liſtened to him unconcernedly, and when he had finiſhed, told him, that he was ſorry what he had done had cauſed his diſpleaſure, but that indeed his heel was extremely painful at the moment, and he could not help revenging himſelf on the only chief of the party that he ſaw taken. Since he had killed the officer, his heel, he added, was much leſs painful to him than it had been before.

When the war broke out, the Mohawks reſided on the Mohawk River, in the ſtate of New York, but on peace being made, they emigrated into Upper Canada, and their principal village is now ſituated on the Grand River, which falls into Lake Erie on the north ſide, about ſixty miles from the town of Newark or Niagara; there Brandt at preſent reſides. He has built a comfortable habitation for himſelf, and any ſtranger that viſits him may reſt aſſured of being well received, and of finding

a plentiful table well served every day. He
has no less than thirty or forty negroes, who
attend to his horses, cultivate his grounds, &c.
These poor creatures are kept in the greatest
subjection, and they dare not attempt to make
their escape, for he has assured them, that if
they did so he would follow them himself,
though it were to the confines of Georgia, and
would tomahawk them wherever he met them.
They know his disposition too well not to
think that he would adhere strictly to his
word.

Brandt receives from government half pay
as a captain, besides annual presents, &c. which
in all amount, it is said, to £.500 per annum.
We had no small curiosity, as you may well
imagine, to see this Brandt, and we procured
letters of introduction to him from the governor's secretary, and from different officers
and gentlemen of his acquaintance, with an intention of proceeding from Newark to his village. Most unluckily, however, on the day
before that of our reaching the town of Newark or Niagara, he had embarked on board a
vessel for Kingston, at the opposite end of the
lake. You may judge of Brandt's consequence,
when I tell you, that a lawyer of Niagara, who
crossed Lake Ontario in the same vessel with
us, from Kingston, where he had been detained
for some time by contrary winds, informed us,

the

the day after our arrival at Niàgara, that by his not having reached that place in time to tranfact some law bufinefs for Brandt, and which had confequently been given to another perfon, he fhould be a lofer of one hundred pounds at leaft.

Brandt's fagacity led him, early in life, to difcover that the Indians had been made the dupe of every foreign power that had got footing in America; and, indeed, could he have had any doubts on the fubject, they would have been removed when he faw the Britifh, after having demanded and received the affiftance of the Indians in the American war, fo ungeneroufly and unjuftly yield up the whole of the Indian territories, eaft of the Miffiffippi and fouth of the lakes, to the people of the United States; to the very enemies, in fhort, they had made to themfelves at the requeft of the Britifh. He perceived with regret that the Indians, by efpoufing the quarrels of the whites, and by efpoufing different interefts, were weakening themfelves; whereas, if they remained aloof, and were guided by the one policy, they would foon become formidable, and be treated with more refpect; he formed the bold fcheme, therefore, of uniting the Indians together in one grand confederacy, and for this purpofe fent meffengers to different chiefs, propofing that a general meeting fhould be
held

held of the heads of every tribe, to take the
subject into consideration; but certain of the
tribes, suspicious of Brandt's designs, and fearful that he was bent upon acquiring power for
himself by this measure, opposed it with all
their might. Brandt has in consequence become extremely obnoxious to many of the most
warlike, and with such a jealous eye do they
now regard him, that it would not be perfectly safe for him to venture to the upper
country.

He has managed the affairs of his own people with great ability, and leased out their superfluous lands for them, for long terms of
years, by which measure a certain annual revenue is ensured to the nation, probably as
long as it will remain a nation. He wisely
judged, that it was much better to do so than
to suffer the Mohawks, as many other tribes
had done, to sell their possessions by piecemeal,
the sums of money they received for which,
however great, would soon be dissipated if paid
to them at once.

Whenever the affairs of his nation shall permit him to do so, Brandt declares it to be his
intention to sit down to the further study of
the Greek language, of which he professes himself to be a great admirer, and to translate from
the original, into the Mohawk language, more
of the New Testament; yet this same man,
shortly

shortly before we arrived at Niagara, killed his only son with his own hand. The son, it seems, was a drunken good for nothing fellow, who had often avowed his intention of destroying his father. One evening he absolutely entered the apartment of his father, and had begun to grapple with him, perhaps with a view to put his unnatural threats into execution, when Brandt drew a short sword, and felled him to the ground. Brandt speaks of this affair with regret, but at the same time without any of that emotion which another person than an Indian might be supposed to feel. He consoles himself for the act, by thinking that he has benefitted the nation, by ridding them of a rascal.

Brandt wears his hair in the Indian style, and also the Indian dress; instead of the wrapper, or blanket, he wears a short coat, such as I have described, similar to a hunting frock.

Though infinite pains have been taken by the French Roman Catholics, and other missionaries, to propagate the gospel amongst the Indians, and though many different tribes have been induced thereby to submit to baptism, yet it does not appear, except in very few instances, that any material advantages have resulted from the introduction of the Christian religion amongst them. They have learned to repeat certain forms of prayer; they have
learned

learned to attend to certain outward ceremonies; but they still continue to be swayed by the same violent passions as before, and have imbibed nothing of the genuine spirit of christianity.

The Moravian missionaries have wrought a greater change in the minds of the Indians than any others, and have succeeded so far as to induce some of them to abandon their savage mode of life, to renounce war, and to cultivate the earth. It is with the Munsies, a small tribe resident on the east side of Lake St. Clair, that they have had the most success; but the number that have been so converted is small indeed. The Roman Catholics have the most adherents, as the outward forms and parade of their religion are particularly calculated to strike the attention of the Indians, and as but little restraint is laid on them by the missionaries of that persuasion, in consequence of their profession of the new faith. The Quakers, of all people, have had the least success amongst them; the doctrine of non-resistance, which they set out with preaching, but ill accords with the opinion of the Indian; and amongst some tribes, where they have attempted to inculcate it, particularly amongst the Shawnese, one of the most warlike tribes to the north of the Ohio, they have

have been expofed to very imminent danger*.

The Indians, who yet remain ignorant of divine revelation, feem almoft univerfally to believe in the exiftence of one fupreme, beneficent, all wife, and all powerful fpirit, and likewife in the exiftence of fubordinate fpirits, both good and bad. The former, having the good of mankind at heart, they think it needlefs to pay homage to them, and it is only to the evil ones, of whom they have an innate dread, that they pay their devotions, in order to avert their ill intentions. Some diftant tribes, it is faid, have priefts amongft them, but it does not appear that they have any regular

---

* The great difficulty of converting the Indians to chriftianity does not arife from their attachment to their own religion, where they have any, fo much as from certain habits which they feem to have imbibed with the very milk of their mothers.

A French miffionary relates, that he was once endeavouring to convert an Indian, by defcribing to him the rewards that would attend the good, and the dreadful punifhment which muft inevitably await the wicked, in a future world, when the Indian, who had fome time before loft his deareft friend, fuddenly interrupted him, by afking him, whether he thought his departed friend was gone to heaven or to hell. I fincerely truft, anfwered the miffionary, that he is in heaven. Then I will do as you bid me, added the Indian, and lead a fober life, for I fhould like to go to the place where my friend is. Had he, on the contrary, been told that his friend was in hell, all that the reverend father could have faid to him of fire and brimftone would have been of little avail in perfuading him to have led any other than the moft diffolute life, in hopes of meeting with his friend to fympathife with him under his fufferings.

forms

forms of worship. Each individual repeats a prayer, or makes an offering to the evil spirit, when his fear and apprehensions suggest the necessity of his so doing.

The belief of a future state, in which they are to enjoy the same pleasures as they do in this world, but to be exempted from pain, and from the trouble of procuring food, seems to be very general amongst them. Some of the tribes have much less devotion than others; the Shawnese, a warlike daring nation, have but very little fear of evil spirits, and consequently have scarcely any religion amongst them. None of this nation, that I could learn, have ever been converted to Christianity.

It is a very singular and remarkable circumstance, that notwithstanding the striking similarity which we find in the persons, manners, customs, dispositions, and religion of the different tribes of Indians from one end of the continent of North America to the other, a similarity so great as hardly to leave a doubt on the mind but that they must all have had the same origin, the languages of the different tribes should yet be so materially different. No two tribes speak exactly the same language; and the languages of many of those, who live at no great distance asunder, vary so much, that they cannot make themselves at all understood to each other. I was informed

that

that the Chippeway language was by far the moſt general, and that a perſon intimately acquainted with it would ſoon be able to acquire a tolerable knowledge of any other language ſpoken between the Ohio and Lake Superior. Some perſons, who have made the Indian languages their ſtudy, aſſert, that all the different languages ſpoken by thoſe tribes, with which we have any connection, are but dialects of three primitive tongues, viz. the Huron, the Algonquin, and the Sioux; the two former of which, being well underſtood, will enable a perſon to converſe, at leaſt ſlightly, with the Indians of any tribe in Canada or the United States. All the nations that ſpeak a language derived from the Sioux, have, it is ſaid, a hiſſing pronunciation; thoſe who ſpeak one derived from the Huron, have a guttural pronunciation; and ſuch as ſpeak any one derived from the Algonquin, pronounce their words with greater ſoftneſs and eaſe than any of the others. Whether this be a juſt diſtinction or not I cannot pretend to determine; I ſhall only obſerve, that all the Indian men I ever met with, as well thoſe whoſe language is ſaid to be derived from the Huron, as thoſe whoſe language is derived from the Algonquin, appear to me to have very few labial ſounds in their language, and to pronounce the words from the throat, but not ſo much from the

upper

upper as the lower part of the throat towards the breast. A flight degree of hesitation is observable in their speech, and they articulate seemingly with difficulty, and in a manner somewhat similar to what a person, I should suppose, would be apt to do if he had a great weight laid on his chest, or had received a blow on his breast or back so violent as to affect his breath. The women, on the contrary, speak with the utmost ease, and the language, as pronounced by them, appears as soft as the Italian. They have, without exception, the most delicate harmonious voices I ever heard, and the most pleasing gentle laugh that it is possible to conceive. I have oftentimes sat amongst a group of them for an hour or two together, merely for the pleasure of listening to their conversation, on account of its wonderful softness and delicacy.

The Indians, both men and women, speak with great deliberation, and never appear to be at a loss for words to express their sentiments.

The native music of the Indians is very rude and indifferent, and equally devoid of melody and variety. Their famous war song is nothing better than an insipid recitative. Singing and dancing with them go hand in hand; and when a large number of them, collected together, join in the one song, the few wild

wild notes of which it confifts, mingled with the found of their pipes and drums, fometimes produce, when heard at a diftance, a pleafing effect on the ear; but it is then and then only that their mufic is tolerable.

The firft night of our arrival at Malden, juft as we were retiring to reft, near midnight, we were moft agreeably entertained in this manner with the found of their mufic on the ifland of Bois Blanc. Eager to hear more of it, and to be witnefs to their dancing, we procured a boat, and immediately croffed the river to the fpot where they were affembled. Three elderly men, feated under a tree, were the principal muficians. One of thefe beat a fmall drum, formed of a piece of a hollow tree covered with a fkin, and the two others marked time equally with the drum, with rattles formed of dried fquafhes or gourds filled with peafe. At the fame time thefe men fung, indeed they were the leaders of the fong, which the dancers joined in. The dancers confifted folely of a party of fquaws, to the number of twenty or thereabouts, who, ftanding in a circle, with their faces inwards and their hands folded round each other's necks, moved, thus linked together, fideways, with clofe fhort fteps, round a fmall fire. The men and women never dance together, unlefs indeed a pretty fquaw be introduced by fome young fellow

fellow into one of the men's dances, which is confidered as a very great mark of favour. This is of a piece with the general conduct of the Indians, who look upon the women in a totally different light from what we do in Europe, and condemn them as flaves to do all the drudgery. I have feen a young chief with no lefs than three women attendant on him to run after his arrows, when he was amufing himfelf with fhooting fquirrels; I have alfo feen Indians, when moving for a few miles from one place to another, mount their horfes and canter away at their eafe, whilft their women were left not only to walk, but to carry very heavy loads on their backs after them.

After the women had danced for a time, a larger fire was kindled, and the men affembled from different parts of the ifland, to the number of fifty or fixty, to amufe themfelves in their turn. There was little more variety in their dancing than in that of the women. They firft walked round the fire in a large circle, clofely, one after another, marking time with fhort fteps to the mufic; the beft dancer was put at their head, and gave the ftep; he was alfo the principal finger in the circle. After having made one round, the ftep was altered to a wider one, and they began to ftamp with great vehemence upon the ground; and every third or fourth round,

making

making little leaps off the ground with both feet, they turned their faces to the fire and bowed their heads, at the fame time going on fideways. At laft, having made a dozen or two rounds, towards the end of which each one of them had begun to ftamp on the ground with inconceivable fury, but more particularly the principal dancer, they all gave a loud fhout at once, and the dance ended.

In two or three minutes another dance was begun, which ended as foon, and nearly in the fame way as the other. There was but little difference in the figures of any of them, and the only material difference in the fongs was, that in fome of them the dancers, inftead of finging the whole of the air, came in fimply with refponfes to the airs fung by the old men. They beckoned to us to join them in their dance, which we immediately did, as it was likely to pleafe them, and we remained on the ifland with them till two or three o'clock in the morning. There is fomething inconceivably terrible in the fight of a number of Indians dancing thus round a fire in the depths of thick woods, and the loud fhrieks at the end of every dance adds greatly to the horror which their firft appearance infpires.

Scarcely a night paffed over but what there were dances, fimilar to thofe I have defcribed, on the ifland. They never think of dancing till the night is confiderably advanced, and they keep it up till daybreak. In the day time they lie fleeping in the fun, or fit fmoking tobacco, that is, when they have nothing particular to engage them. Though the moft diligent perfevering people in the world when roufed into action, yet when at peace with their neighbours, and having got wherewith to fatisfy the calls of hunger, they are the moft flothful and indolent poffible.

The dances mentioned are fuch as the Indians amufe themfelves with in common. On grand occafions they have a variety of others much more interefting to a fpectator. The dances which you fee in common amongft the Shawnefe, and certain other tribes, are alfo, it is faid, much more entertaining than thofe I have defcribed. There were feveral families of the Shawnefe encamped on the ifland of Bois Blanc when we were there; but as there was not a fufficient number to form a dance by themfelves, we were never gratified with a fight of their performances.

Of their grand dances the war dance muft undoubtedly, from every account I have received of it, for I never had any opportunity of feeing it myfelf, be the one moft worthy the attention of a ftranger. It is performed both on fetting out and returning from their war parties, and likewife at other times, but never except

except on some very particular and solemn occasion. The chiefs and warriors who are about to join in this dance dress and paint themselves as if actually out on a warlike expedition, and they carry in their hands their warlike weapons. Being assembled, they seat themselves down on their hams, in a circle, round a great fire, near to which is placed a large post; after remaining a short time in this position, one of the principal chiefs rises, and placing himself in the center, begins to rehearse, in a sort of recitative, all the gallant actions which he has ever performed; he dwells particularly on the number of enemies he has killed, and describes the manner in which he scalped them, making gestures all the time, and brandishing his weapons, as if actually engaged in performing the horrid operation. At the end of every remarkable story he strikes his war club on the post with great fury. Every chief and warrior tells of his deeds in turn. The song of one warrior often occupies several hours, and the dance itself sometimes lasts for three or four entire days and nights. During this period no one is allowed to sleep, a person who stands at the outside of the circle being appointed (whose business it is) to rouse any warrior that appears in the least drowsy. A deer, a bear, or some other large animal is put to roast at the fire as soon as the dance begins, and while it lafts each warrior rifes at will to help himfelf to a piece of it. After each perfon in the circle has in turn told of his exploits, they all rife, and join in a dance truly terrifying; they throw themfelves into a variety of poftures, and leaping about in the moft frantic manner, brandifh their knives and other weapons; at the fame time they fet up the war hoop, and utter the moft dreadful yells imaginable. In this manner the dance terminates.

The Indian flute or pipe is formed of a thick cane, fimilar to what is found on the banks of the Miffiffippi, and in the fouthern parts of the United States. It is about two feet or more in length, and has eight or nine holes in it, in one row. It is held in the fame manner as the oboe or clarinet, and the found is produced by means of a mouth piece not unlike that of a common whiftle. The tones of the inftrument are by no means unharmonious, and they would admit of a pleafing modulation, but I never met with an Indian that was able to play a regular air upon it, not even any one of the airs which they commonly fing, although I faw feveral that were extremely fond of amufing themfelves with the inftrument, and that would fit for hours together over the embers of their cabin fires, playing over a few wild melancholy notes. Every Indian that can bring a found

out

out of the inftrument, and ftop the holes, which any one may do, thinks himfelf mafter of it; and the notes which they commonly produce are as unconnected and unmeaning as thofe which a child would bring forth from a halfpenny whiftle.

In addition to what I have faid on the fubject of the Indians, I fhall only obferve, that notwithftanding they are fuch a very friendly hofpitable people, yet few perfons, who had ever tafted of the pleafures and comforts of civilized life, would feel any inclination to refide amongft them, on becoming acquainted with their manner of living. The filthinefs and wretchednefs of their fmoky habitations, the naufeoufnefs of their common food to a perfon not even of a delicate palate, and their general uncleanlinefs, would be fufficient, I think, to deter any one from going to live amongft them from choice, fuppofing even that no other reafons operated againft his doing fo. For my own part, I had fully determined in my own mind, when I firft came to America, not to leave the continent without fpending a confiderable time amongft them, in the interior parts of the country, in order to have an opportunity of obferving their native manners and cuftoms in their utmoft purity; but the famples I have feen of them during my ftay in this part of the country, although it has given me a moft favourable

vourable opinion of the Indians themselves, has induced me to relinquish my purpose. Content therefore with what I have seen myself, and with what I have heard from others, if chance should not bring me again into their way in prosecuting my journey into the settled parts of the States, I shall take no further pains to cultivate a more intimate acquaintance with them.

LETTER XXXVI.

Departure from Malden.—Storm on Lake Erie.—Driven back amongst the Islands.—Shipwreck narrowly avoided.—Voyage across the Lake.—Land at Fort Erie.—Proceed to Buffalo Creek.—Engage Indians to go through the Woods.—Set out on Foot.—Journey through the Woods.—Description of the Country beyond Buffalo Creek.—Vast Plains.—Grand Appearance of the Trees here.—Indian Dogs.—Arrival at the Settlements on Genesee River.—First Settlers.—Their general Character.—Description of the Country bordering on Genesee River.—Fevers common in Autumn.—Proceed on Foot to Bath.

Bath, November.

TOWARDS the latter end of the month of October, the schooner in which we had engaged a passage to Presqu' Isle made her

DEPARTURE FROM MALDEN.

her appearance before Malden, where she was obliged to lay at anchor for three days, the wind not being favourable for going farther down the river; at the end of that time, however, it veered about, and we repaired on board, after having taken a long farewel of our friend Captain E——, whose kindness to us had been unbounded, and was doubly grateful, inasmuch as it was totally unexpected by us young strangers, who had not the slightest acquaintance with him previous to our coming into the country, and had not been introduced to him even by letter.

The wind, though favourable, was very light on the morning of our embarkation, but the current being strong we were soon carried down to the lake. In the afternoon we passed the islands, which had the most beautiful appearance imaginable. The rich woods with which the shores were adorned, now tinged with the hues of autumn, afforded in their decline a still more pleasing variety to the eye than when they were clothed in their fullest verdure; and their gaudy colours, intermingled with the shadows of the rocks, were seen fancifully reflected in the unruffled surface of the surrounding lake. At day-break the next morning we found ourselves entirely clear of the land; but instead of the azure sky and gentle breezes which had favoured us the preceding

ceding day, we had thick hazy weather, and every appearance in the heavens indicated that before many hours were over we should have to contend with some of those dangerous storms that are so frequent on Lake Erie. It was not long indeed ere the winds began to blow, and the waves to rise in a tremendous manner, and we soon became spectators of a number of those confused and disgusting scenes which a gale of wind never fails to occasion in a small vessel crowded with passengers. A number of old French ladies, who were going to see their grandchildren in Lower Canada, and who now for the first time in their lives found themselves on the water, occupied the cabin. The hold of the vessel, boarded from end to end, and divided simply by a sail suspended from one of the beams, was filled on one side with steerage passengers, amongst which were several women and children; and on the opposite one with passengers who had paid cabin price, but were unable to get any better accommodation, amongst which number was our party. Not including either the old ladies in the cabin, or the steerage passengers, we sat down to dinner each day twenty-six in number, which circumstance, when I inform you that the vessel was only seventy tons burthen, will best enable you to conceive how much we must have been crowded. The

greater

greater part of the paffengers, drooping under fea-ficknefs, begged for heaven's fake that the captain would put back; but bent upon performing his voyage with expedition, which was a matter of the utmoft confequence indeed, now that the feafon was fo far advanced, and there was a poffibility that he might be blocked up by the ice on his return, he was deaf to their entreaties. What the earneft entreaties, however, of the paffengers could not effect, the ftorm foon compelled him to. It was found abfolutely neceffary to feek for a place of fhelter to avoid its fury; and accordingly the helm having been ordered up, we made the beft of our way back again to the iflands, in a bay between two of which we caft anchor. This bay, fituated between the Bafs Iflands, which are among the largeft in the clufter, is called, from its being fo frequently reforted to by veffels that meet with contrary winds in going down the lake, Put-in-Bay, vulgarly termed by the failors Pudding Bay.

Here we lay fecurely fheltered by the land until four o'clock the next morning, when the watch upon deck gave the alarm that the veffel was driving from her anchor, and going faft towards the fhore. The captain ftarted up, and perceiving that the wind had fhifted, and the land no longer afforded any protection to the veffel, he immediately gave orders to flip the cable, and hoift the jib, in order to wear the veffel round, and thus get free, if poffible, of the fhore. In the hurry and confufion of the moment, however, the mainfail was hoifted at the fame time with the jib, the veffel was put aback, and nothing could have faved her from going at once on fhore but the letting fall of another anchor inftantaneoufly. I can only account for this unfortunate miftake by fuppofing that the men were not fufficiently roufed from their flumbers, on coming upon deck, to hear diftinctly the word of command. Only one man had been left to keep the watch, as it was thought that the veffel was riding in perfect fafety, and from the time that the alarm was firft given until the anchor was dropped fcarcely four minutes elapfed.

The dawn of day only enabled us to fee all the danger of our fituation. We were within one hundred yards of a rocky lee fhore, and depending upon one anchor, which, if the gale increafed, the captain feared very much would not hold. The day was wet and fqually, and the appearance of the fky gave us every reafon to imagine that the weather, inftead of growing moderate, would become ftill more tempeftuous than it either was or had been; neverthelefs, buoyed up by hope, and by a good

good share of animal spirits, we eat our breakfasts regardless of the impending danger, and afterwards sat down to a game of cards; but scarcely had we played for one hour when the dismal cry was heard of, "All hands aloft," as the vessel was again drifting towards the shore. The day being very cold, I had thrown a blanket over my shoulders, and had fastened it round my waist with a girdle, in the Indian fashion; but being incapable of managing it like an Indian, I stopped to disencumber myself of it before I went on deck, so that, as it happened, I was the last man below. The readiest way of going up was through the hatchway, and I had just got my foot upon the ladder, in order to ascend, when the vessel struck with great force upon the rocks. The women shrieking now flocked round me, begging for God's sake that I would stay by them; at the same time my companions urged me from above to come up with all possible speed. To my latest hour I shall never forget the emotions which I felt at that moment; to have staid below would have been useless; I endeavoured, therefore, to comfort the poor creatures that clung to me, and then disengaging myself from them, forced my way upon deck, where I was no sooner arrived than the hatches were instantly shut down upon the wretched females, whose shrieks resounded ed through the veffel, notwithftanding all the buftle of the feamen, and the tremendous roaring of the breakers amongft the adjacent rocks.

Before two minutes had paffed over, the veffel ftruck a fecond time, but with a ftill greater fhock; and at the end of a quarter of an hour, during which period fhe had gradually approached nearer towards the fhore, fhe began to ftrike with the fall of every wave.

The general opinion now feemed to be in favour of cutting away the mafts, in order to lighten the veffel; and the axes were actually upraifed for that purpofe, when one of my companions, who poffeffed a confiderable fhare of nautical knowledge from having been in the navy, oppofed the meafure. It appeared to him, that as the pumps were ftill free, and as the veffel had not yet made more water than could be eafily got under, the cutting away of the mafts would only be to deprive ourfelves of the means of getting off the rock if the wind fhould veer about; but he advifed the captain to have the yards and topmafts cut away. The mafts were fpared, and his advice was in every other refpect attended to. The wind unfortunately, however, ftill continued to blow from the fame point, and the only alteration obfervable in it was its blowing with ftill greater force than ever.

As

As the storm increased, the waves began to roll with greater turbulence than before; and with such impetuosity did they break over the bows of the vessel, that it was with the very utmost difficulty that I, and half a dozen more who had taken our station on the forecastle, could hold by our hands fast enough to save ourselves from being carried overboard. For upwards of four hours did we remain in this situation, expecting every instant that the vessel would go to pieces, and exposed every three or four minutes to the shock of one of the tremendous breakers which came rolling towards us. Many of the billows appeared to be half as high as the foretop, and sometimes, when they burst over us, our breath was nearly taken away by the violence of the shock. At last, finding ourselves so benumbed with cold that it would be impossible for us to make any exertions in the water to save ourselves if the vessel was wrecked, we determined to go below, there to remain until we should be again forced up by the waves.

Some of the passengers now began to write their wills on scraps of paper, and to inclose them in what they imagined would be most likely to preserve them from the water; others had begun to take from their trunks what they deemed most valuable; and one unfortunate thoughtless man, who was moving with his family

family from the upper country, we difcovered in the very act of loading himfelf with dollars from head to foot, fo that had he fallen into the water in the ftate we found him, he muft inevitably have been carried to the bottom.

Words can convey no idea of the wildnefs that reigned in the countenance of almoft every perfon as the night approached; and many, terrified with the apprehenfions of a nightly fhipwreck, began to lament that the cable had not been at once cut, fo as to have let the veffel go on fhore whilft day-light remained: this indeed had been propofed a few hours after the veffel began to ftrike; but it was over-ruled by the captain, who very properly refufed to adopt a meafure tending to the immediate and certain deftruction of his veffel, whilft a poffibility remained that fhe might efcape.

Till nine o'clock at night the veffel kept ftriking every minute, during which time we were kept in a ftate of the moft dreadful fufpence about our fate; but then happily the wind fhifted one or two points in our favour, which occafioned the veffel to roll inftead of ftriking. At midnight the gale grew fomewhat more moderate; and at three in the morning it was fo far abated, that the men were enabled to haul on the anchor, and in a fhort time to bring the veffel once more into
deep

DAMAGE DONE THE SHIP.

deep water, and out of all danger. Great was the joy, as may well be imagined, which this circumstance diffused amongst the passengers; and well pleased was each one, after the fatigue and anxiety of the preceding day, to think he might securely lay himself down to rest.

The next morning the sun arose in all his majesty from behind one of the distant islands. The azure sky was unobscured by a single cloud, the air felt serenely mild, and the birds, as if equally delighted with man that the storm was over, sweetly warbled forth their songs in the adjacent woods; in short, had it not been for the disordered condition in which we saw our vessel, and every thing belonging to us, the perils we had gone through would have appeared like a dream.

The first object of examination was the rudder. The tiller was broken to atoms; and the sailors who went over the stern reported, that of the four gudgeons or hooks on which the rudder was suspended, only one was left entire, and that one was much bent. On being unshipped, the bottom of it was found to be so much shivered that it actually resembled the end of a broom. The keel, there was every reason to suppose, was in the same shattered condition; nevertheless the vessel, to the great astonishment of every person on board, did not make much water. Had she been half as crazy as the King's vessel in which we went up the lake, nothing could have saved her from destruction.

A consultation was now held upon what was best to be done. To proceed on the voyage appeared totally out of the question; and it only remained to determine which way was the easiest and readiest to get back to Malden. All was at a stand, when an officer in the American service proposed the beating out of an iron crow bar, and the manufacturing of new gudgeons. This was thought to be impracticable; but necessity, the mother of invention, having set all our heads to work, an anvil was formed of a number of axes laid upon a block of wood; a large fire was kindled, and a party of us acting as smiths in turns, by the end of three hours contrived to hammer out one very respectable gudgeon.

In the mean time others of the passengers were employed in making a new tiller, and others undertook to fish for the cable and anchor that had been slipped, whilst the sailors were kept busily employed at the rigging. By nightfall the vessel was so far refitted that no apprehensions were any longer entertained about our being able to reach Malden in safety, and some began to think there would be no danger in prosecuting the voyage down the lake.

lake. The captain faid that his conduct muft be regulated entirely by the appearance of the weather on the following day.

Early the next morning, whilft we yet remained ftretched in our births, our party was much furprifed at hearing the found of ftrange voices upon deck; but our furprife was ftill greater, when on a nearer approach we recognized them to be the voices of two young friends of ours, who, like ourfelves, had croffed the Atlantic to make a tour of the continent of North America, and whom, but a few days before we had quitted Philadelphia, we had accompanied fome miles from that city on their way towards the fouth. They had travelled, it feemed, from Philadelphia to Virginia, afterwards to Kentucky, and had found their way from the Ohio to Detroit on horfeback, after encountering numberlefs inconveniences. There they had engaged a paffage in a little floop bound to Fort Erie, the laft veffel which was to quit that port during the prefent feafon. They had embarked the preceding day, and in the night had run in to Put-in-Bay, as the wind was not favourable for going down the lake. The commander of the floop offered to ftay by our veffel, and to give her every affiftance in his power, if our captain chofe to proceed down the lake with him. The offer was gladly accepted, and it was agreed that the two veſſels ſhould ſail together as ſoon as the wind was favourable.

After having breakfaſted, we proceeded with our young friends, in the ſhip's boat, to that part of the iſland off which we had been expoſed to ſo much danger. Here we found the ſhore ſtrewed with the oars, ſpars, &c. which had been waſhed overboard, and from the dreadful manner in which they were ſhattered, no doubt remained on our minds, but that if the veſſel had been wrecked, two thirds of the paſſengers at leaſt muſt have periſhed amidſt the rocks and breakers. We ſpent the day rambling about the woods, and recounting to each other our adventures ſince the laſt ſeparation, and in the evening returned to our reſpective ſhips. About midnight the wind became fair, and whilſt we lay wrapt in ſleep the veſſels put to ſea.

All hopes of being able to get on ſhore at Preſqu' Iſle were now over, for the captain, as our veſſel was in ſuch a tickliſh condition, was fearful of venturing in there, leſt he might loſe ſight of the ſloop; we made up our minds, therefore, for being carried once more to our old quarters, Fort Erie; and after a moſt diſagreeable paſſage of four days, during which we encountered ſeveral ſqualls not a little alarming, landed there in ſafety.

Our friends immediately ſet out for Newark, from

from whence, if the feafon would admit of it, and a favourable opportunity offered, they propofed to fail to Kingfton, and proceed afterwards to Lower Canada; we, on the contrary, defirous of returning by a different route from that by which we had come up the country, croffed over to Buffalo Creek, in hopes of being able to procure horfes at the Indian village there, to carry us through the Genefee country. To our difappointment we found, that all the Indians of the village who had horfes had already fet out with them on their hunting expedition; but the interpreters told us, that if we would confent to walk through the woods, as far as the fettlements of the white people, the neareft of which was ninety miles from Buffalo Creek, he did not doubt but that he could find Indians in the village who would undertake to carry our baggage for us; and that once arrived at the back fettlements, we fhould find it no difficult matter to hire horfes. We readily agreed to his propofals, and he in confequence foon picked out from the Indians five men, amongft which was a war chief, on whom he told us we might place every reliance, as he was a man of an excellent character. The Indians, it was fettled, were to have five dollars apiece for their fervices, and we were to furnifh them with provifions and liquor. The interpreter, who was a white man, put us on our guard againſt giving them too much of the latter; but he adviſed us always to give them ſome whenever we took any ourſelves, and adviſed us alſo to eat with them, and to behave towards them in every reſpect as if they were our equals. We had already ſeen enough of the Indians, to know that this advice was good, and indeed to have adopted of ourſelves the line of conduct which he recommended, even if he had ſaid nothing on the ſubject.

Having arranged every thing to our ſatisfaction, we returned to Fort Erie; there we diſpoſed of all our ſuperfluous baggage, and having made ſome addition to the ſtores of dried proviſions and biſcuits which our kind friend Captain E—— had furniſhed us with on leaving his hoſpitable roof, we embarked, with all belonging to us, in the ſhip's boat, for the village on Buffalo Creek, where we had ſettled to paſs the night, in order to be ready to ſtart early the next morning.

The Indians were with us according to appointment at day break; they divided the baggage, faſtened their loads each on their carrying frames, and appeared perfectly ready to depart, when their chief requeſted, through the interpreter, " that we would give them before " they ſet out a little of that precious water " we poſſeſſed, to waſh their eyes with, which " would diſpel the miſts of ſleep that ſtill hung
" over

"over them, and thus enable them to find out
"with certainty the intricate path through
"the thick foreſt we were about to traverſe;"
in other words, that we would give them ſome
brandy. It is always in figurative language of
this kind that the Indians aſk for ſpirits. We
diſpenſed a glaſs full of the precious liquor,
according to their deſire, to each of them, as
well as to their ſquaws and children, whom
they brought along with them to ſhare our
bounty, and then, the Indians having taken up
their loads, we penetrated into the woods,
along a narrow path ſcarcely diſcernible, owing
to the quantities of withered leaves with which
it was ſtrewed.

After proceeding a few miles, we ſtopped
by the ſide of a little ſtream of clear water to
breakfaſt; on the banks of another ſtream we
eat our dinner; and at a third we ſtopped for
the night. Having laid down their loads, the
Indians immediately began to erect poles, and
cover them with pieces of bark, which they
found lying on the ground, and which had
evidently been left there by ſome travellers who
had taken up their quarters for the night at this
ſame place ſome time before; but we put a
ſtop to their work, by ſhaking out from the
bag in which it was depoſited, our travelling
tent. They perceived now that they muſt
employ themſelves in a different manner, and

knowing perfectly well what was to be done, they at once set to work with their tomahawks in cutting poles and pegs. In less than five minutes, as we all bore a part, the poles and pegs were cut, and the tent pitched.

One of the Indians now made signs to us to lend him a bag, having received which he ran into the woods, and was soon out of sight. We were at a loss to guess what he was in pursuit of; but in a little time he returned with the bag full of the finest cranberries I ever beheld. In the mean time another of them, of his own accord, busied himself in carrying heaps of dried leaves into the tent, which, with our buffalo skins, afforded luxurious beds to men like us, that had slept on nothing better than a board for upwards of a month past. In the upper country it is so customary for travellers to carry their own bedding, that even at our friend Captain E——'s house we had no other accommodation at night than the floor of an empty room, on which we spread our skins. As for themselves, the Indians thought of no covering whatsoever, but simply stretched themselves on the ground beside the fire, where they lay like dogs or cats till morning. At day-break we started, and stopped as on the preceding day beside streams of water to eat our breakfasts and dinners.

From Buffalo Creek to the place where we encamped

encamped on the firſt night, diſtant about twenty-five miles, the country being very flat, and the trees growing ſo cloſely together that it was impoſſible to ſee farther forward in any direction than fifty yards, our journey after a ſhort time became very intereſting. Nothing in its kind, however, could exceed the beauty of the ſcenery that we met with during our ſecond day's journey. We found the country, as we paſſed along, interſperſed with open plains of great magnitude, ſome of them not leſs, I ſhould ſuppoſe, than fifteen or twenty miles in circumference. The trees on the borders of theſe having ample room to ſpread, were luxuriant beyond deſcription, and ſhot forth their branches with all the grandeur and variety which characterizes the Engliſh timber, particularly the oak. The woods round the plains were indented in every direction with bays and promontories, as Mr. Gilpin terms it, whilſt rich clumps of trees, interſperſed here and there, appeared like ſo many cluſters of beautiful iſlands. The varied hues of the woods at this ſeaſon of the year, in America, can hardly be imagined by thoſe who never have had an opportunity of obſerving them; and indeed, as others have often remarked before, were a painter to attempt to colour a picture from them, it would be condemned in Europe as totally different from any thing that ever exiſted in nature.

Theſe

These plains are covered with long coarse grass, which, at a future day, will probably afford feeding to numerous herds of cattle; at present they are totally unfrequented. Throughout the north-western territory of the States, and even beyond the head waters of the Mississippi, the country is interspersed with similar plains; and the farther you proceed to the westward, the more extensive in general are they. Amidst those to the westward are found numerous herds of buffaloes, elks, and other wild graminivorous animals; and formerly animals of the same description were found on these plains in the state of New York, but they have all disappeared long since, owing to their having been so constantly pursued both by the Indians and white people.

Very different opinions have been entertained respecting the deficiency of trees on these extended tracts of land, in the midst of a country that abounds so generally with wood. Some have attributed it to the poverty of the soil; whilst others have maintained, that the plains were formerly covered with trees, as well as other parts of the country, but that the trees have either been destroyed by fire, or by buffaloes, beavers, and other animals.

It is well known that buffaloes, in all those parts of the country where they are found wild, commit great depredations amongst the trees, by by gnawing off the bark; they are alſo very fond of feeding upon the young trees that ſpring up from ſeed, as well as upon the ſuckers of the old ones; it may readily be imagined, therefore, that the entire of the trees, on very extended tracts of land, might be thus killed by them; and as the American timber, when left expoſed to the weather, ſoon decays, at the end of a few years no veſtige of the woods would be found on theſe tracts, any more than if they had been conſumed by fire.

It appears to me, however, that there is more weight in the opinion of thoſe, who aſcribe the deficiency of trees on the plains to the unfriendlineſs of the ſoil; for the earth towards the ſurface is univerſally very light, and of a deep black colour, and on digging but a few inches downwards you come to a cold ſtiff clay. On Long Iſland, in the ſtate of New York, plains are met with nearly ſimilar to theſe in the back country, and the Dutch farmers, who have made repeated trials of the ſoil, find that it will not produce wheat or any other grain, and, in ſhort, nothing that is at all profitable except coarſe graſs. I make no doubt but that whenever a ſimilar trial comes to be made of the ſoil of the plains to the weſtward, it will be found equally incapable of producing any thing but what it does at preſent.

After

After having paffed over a great number of thefe plains of different fizes, we entered once more into the thick woods; but the country here appeared much more diverfified with rifing grounds than it was in any part we had already traverfed. As we were afcending to the top of a fmall eminence in the thickeft part of thefe woods, towards the clofe of our fecond day's journey, our Indian chief, *China-breaft-plate*, who received that name in confequence of his having worn in the American war a thick china difh as an ornament on his breaft, made a fign to us to follow him to the left of the path. We did fo, and having proceeded for a few yards, fuddenly found ourfelves on the margin of a deep extenfive pit, not unlike an exhaufted quarry, that had lain neglected for many years. The area of it contained about two acres, and it approached to a circular form; the fides were extremely fteep, and feemed in no place to be lefs than forty feet high; in fome parts they were confiderably higher. Near the center of the place was a large pond, and round the edges of it, as well as round the bottom of the precipice, grew feveral very lofty pines. The walls of the precipice confifted of a whitifh fubftance not unlike lime-ftone half calcined, and round the margin of the pit, at top, lay feveral heaps of loofe matter refembling lime-rubbifh.

China-breaft-plate, ftanding on the brink of the precipice, began to tell us a long ftory, and pointing to a diftant place beyond it, frequently mentioned the word Niagara. Whether, however, the ftory related to the pit, or whether it related to the Falls of Niagara, the fmoke arifing from which it is by no means improbable might be feen, at times, from the elevated fpot where we ftood, or whether the ftory related to both, we could in no way learn, as we were totally unacquainted with the Seneka language, and he was nearly equally ignorant of the Englifh. I never met with any perfon afterwards who had feen this place, or who knew any thing relating to it. Though we made repeated figns to *China-breaft-plate* that we did not underftand his ftory, he ftill went on with it for near a quarter of an hour; the other Indians liftened to it with great attention, and feemed to take no fmall intereft in what he faid.

I fhould have mentioned to you before, that both the Indians and the white Americans pronounce the word Niagara differently from what we do. The former lay the accent on the fecond fyllable, and pronounce the word full and broad as if written Nee-awg-ara. The Americans likewife lay the accent on the fecond fyllable; but pronounce it fhort, and give the fame found to the letters I and A as

we

we do. Niagara, in the language of the neighbouring Indians, fignifies a mighty rufhing or fall of water.

On the fecond evening of our expedition we encamped on a fmall hill, from whofe top there was a moft pleafing romantic view, along a ftream of confiderable fize which wound round its bafe, and as far as our eyes could reach, appeared tumbling in fmall falls over ledges of rocks. A fire being kindled, and the tent pitched as ufual, the Indians fat down to cook fome fquirrels which we had killed on the borders of the plains. Thefe animals the Indians had obferved, as we came along, on the top of a large hollow tree; they immediately laid down their loads, and each taking out his tomahawk, and fetting to work at a different part of the tree, it was felled down in lefs than five minutes, and fuch of the fquirrels as efcaped their dogs we readily fhot for them.

The Indian dogs, in general, have fhort legs, long backs, large pricked up ears, and long curly tails; they differ from the common Englifh cur dogs in no refpect fo much as in their barking but very feldom. They are extremely fagacious, and feem to underftand even what their mafters fay to them in a low voice, without making any figns, either with the hand or head.

Whilft

Whilſt the ſquirrels were roaſting on a forked ſtick ſtuck in the ground, and bent over the fire, one of the Indians went into the woods, and brought out ſeveral ſmall boughs of a tree, apparently of the willow tribe. Having carefully ſcraped the bark off from theſe, he made a ſort of frame with the twigs, in ſhape ſomewhat like a gridiron, and heaping upon it the ſcraped bark, placed it over the fire to dry. When it was tolerably criſp he rubbed it between his hands, and put it up in his pouch for the purpoſe of ſmoking.

The Indians ſmoke the bark of many different trees, and a great variety of herbs and leaves beſides tobacco. The moſt agreeable of any of the ſubſtances which they ſmoke are the leaves of the ſumach tree, rhus-toxicodendron. This is a graceful ſhrub, which bears leaves ſomewhat ſimilar to thoſe of the aſh. Towards the latter end of autumn they turn of a bright red colour, and when wanted for ſmoking are plucked off and dried in the ſun. Whilſt burning they afford a very agreeable perfume. Theſe leaves are very commonly ſmoked, mixed with tobacco, by the white people of the country; the ſmoke of them by themſelves alone, is ſaid to be prejudicial to the lungs. The ſumach tree bears tufted bunches of crimſon flowers. One of theſe bunches dipped lightly, for a few times, into a bowl of punch,

punch, gives the liquor a very agreeable acid, and in the fouthern ftates it is common to ufe them for that purpofe, but it is a dangerous cuftom, as the acid, though extremely agreeable to the palate, is of a poifonous quality, and never fails to produce a moft alarming effect on the bowels if ufed too freely.

A sharp froft fet in this night, and on the following morning, at day-break, we recommenced our journey with croffing the river already mentioned up to our waifts in water, no very pleafing tafk. Both on this and the fubfequent day we had to wade through feveral other confiderable ftreams.

A few fquirrels were the only wild animals which we met with in our journey through the woods, and the moft folemn filence imaginable reigned throughout, except where a woodpecker was heard now and then tapping with its bill againft a hollow tree. The birds in general flock towards the fettlements, and it is a very rare circumftance to meet with them in the depth of the foreft.

The third evening we encamped as ufual. No fooner had we come to our refting place, than the Indians threw off their clothes, and rolled themfelves on the grafs juft as horfes would do, to refrefh themfelves, the day having proved very hot, notwithftanding the froft the preceding night. We were joined this evening,

evening by another party of the Seneka Indians, who were going to a village fituated on the Genefee River; and in the morning we all fet out together. Early in the day we came to feveral plains fimilar to thofe we had before met with, but not fo extended, on the borders of one of which we faw, for the firft time, a bark hut apparently inhabited. On going up to it, our furprife was not a little to find two men, whofe appearance and manners at once befpoke them not to be Americans. After fome converfation we difcovered them to be two Englifhmen, who had formerly lived in London as *valets de chambre*, and having fcraped together a little money, had fet out for New York, where they expected at once to become great men; however they foon found to their coft, that the expence of living in that city was not fuited to their pockets, and they determined to go and fettle in the back country. They were at no lofs to find perfons who had land to difpofe of, and happening to fall in with a jobber who owned fome of thefe plains, and who painted to them in lively colours the advantage they would derive from fettling on good land already cleared to their hand, they immediately purchafed a confiderable track of this barren ground at a round price, and fet out to fix themfelves upon it. From the neighbouring fettlements, which were

were about ten miles off, they procured the
affiftance of two men, who after having built
for them the bark hut in which we found them
left them with a promife of returning in a fhort
time to erect a log houfe. They had not,
however, been punctual to their word, and unable to wield an axe, or to do any one thing
for themfelves, thefe unfortunate wretches fat
moping in their hut, fupporting themfelves on
fome falt provifions they had brought with
them, but which were now nearly exhaufted.
The people in the fettlements, whom, on arriving there, we afked fome few queftions refpecting thefe poor creatures, turned them into
the greateft ridicule imaginable for being fo
helplefs; and indeed they did prefent a moft
ftriking picture of the folly of any man's attempting to fettle in America without being
well acquainted with the country previoufly,
and competent to do every fort of country
work for himfelf.

It was not without very great vexation that
we perceived, fhortly after leaving this hut,
evident fymptoms of drunkennefs in one of the
Indians, and on examining our brandy cafk it
was but too plain that it had been pillaged.
During the preceding part of our journey we
had kept a watchful eye upon it, but drawing
towards the end of our expedition, and having
had every reafon to be fatisfied with the conduct

duct of the Indians, we had not paid sufficient attention to it this day; and though it could not have been much more than five minutes out of our fight, yet in that fhort fpace of time the fcrew had been forced, and the cafk drained to the laft drop. The Indian, whom we difcovered to be drunk, was advanced a little before the others. He went on for fome time ftaggering about from fide to fide, but at laft, ftopping and laying hold of his fcalping knife, which they always carry with them by their fides, he began to brandifh it with a threatening air. There is but one line of conduct to be purfued when you have to deal with Indians in fuch a fituation, and that is, to act with the moft determined refolution. If you betray the fmalleft fymptoms of fear, or appear at all wavering in your conduct, it only ferves to render them more ungovernable and furious. I accordingly took him by the fhoulder, pufhed him forward, and prefenting my piece, gave him to underftand that I would fhoot him if he did not behave himfelf properly. My companions, whilft I was taking care of him, went back to fee in what ftate the other Indians were. Luckily the liquor, though there was reafon to apprehend they had all had a fhare of it, had not made the fame impreffion upon them. One of them, indeed, was beginning to be refractory, and abfolutely threw

down

down his load, and refused to go farther; but a few words from *China-breaſt-plate* induced him to resume it, and to go on. On coming up to the firſt Indian, and seeing the sad ſtate he was in, they ſhook their heads, and crying, " No good Indian," " No good Indian," endeavoured by signs to inform us that it was he who had pillaged the caſk, and drank all the brandy; but as it was another Indian who carried the caſk, no doubt remained but that they muſt all have had a ſhare of the plunder; that the firſt fellow, however, had drank more than the reſt was apparent; for in a few minutes he dropped down speechleſs under his load; the others haſtened to take it off from his back, and having divided it amongſt themſelves, they drew him aſide from the path, and threw him under ſome buſhes, where he was left to ſleep till he ſhould come again to his senſes.

About noon we reached the Geneſee River, at the oppoſite ſide of which was ſituated the village where we expected to procure horſes. We croſſed the river in canoes, and took up our quarters at a houſe at the uppermoſt end of the village, where we were very glad to find our Indian friends could get no accommodation, for we knew well that the firſt uſe they would make of the money we were going to give them would be to buy liquor, and

intoxicate

intoxicate themselves, in which state they would not fail of becoming very troublesome companions; it was scarcely dark indeed when news was brought us from a house near the river, that they went to after we had discharged them, that they were grown quite outrageous with the quantity of spirits they had drank, and were fighting and cutting each other in a most dreadful manner. They never resent the injuries they receive from any person that is evidently intoxicated, but attribute their wounds entirely to the liquor, on which they vent their execrations for all the mischief it has committed.

Before I dismiss the subject entirely, I must observe to you, that the Indians did not seem to think the carrying of our baggage was in any manner degrading to them; and after having received their due, they shook hands with us, and parted from us, not as from employers who had hired them, but as from friends whom they had been assisting, and were now sorry to leave.

The village where we stopped consisted of about eight or nine straggling houses; the best built one among them was that in which we lodged. It belonged to a family from New England, who about six years before had penetrated to this spot, then covered with woods, and one hundred and fifty miles distant from any other settlement. Settlements are now scattered over the whole of the country, which they had to pass through in coming to it. The house was commodious and well built, and the people decent, civil, and reputable. It is a very rare circumstance to meet with such people amongst the first settlers on the frontiers; in general they are men of a morose and savage disposition, and the very outcasts of society, who bury themselves in the woods, as if desirous to shun the face of their fellow creatures; there they build a rude habitation, and clear perhaps three or four acres of land, just as much as they find sufficient to provide their families with corn: for the greater part of their food they depend on their rifle guns. These people, as the settlements advance, are succeeded in general by a second set of men, less savage than the first, who clear more land, and do not depend so much upon hunting as upon agriculture for their subsistance. A third set succeed these in turn, who build good houses, and bring the land into a more improved state. The first settlers, as soon as they have disposed of their miserable dwellings to advantage, immediately penetrate farther back into the woods, in order to gain a place of abode suited to their rude mode of life. These are the lawless people who encroach, as I have before mentioned, on the

Indian

Indian territory, and are the occasion of the bitter animosities between the whites and the Indians. The second settlers, likewise, when displaced, seek for similar places to what those that they have left were when they first took them. I found, as I proceeded through this part of the country, that there was scarcely a man who had not changed his place of abode seven or eight different times.

As none but very miserable horses were to be procured at this village on the Genesee River, and as our expedition through the woods had given us a relish for walking, we determined to proceed on foot, and merely to hire horses to carry our baggage; accordingly, having engaged a pair, and a boy to conduct them, we set off early on the second morning from that of our arrival at the village, for the town of Bath.

The country between these two places is most agreeably diversified with hill and dale, and as the traveller passes over the hills which overlook the Genesee River and the flats bordering upon it, he is entertained with a variety of noble and picturesque views. We were particularly struck with the prospect from a large, and indeed very handsome house in its kind, belonging to a Major Wadsworth, built on one of these hills. The Genesee River, bordered with the richest woods imaginable, might be seen from it for many miles, meandering through a fertile country; and beyond the flats, on each side of the river, appeared several ranges of blue hills rising up one behind another in a most fanciful manner, the whole together forming a most beautiful landscape. Here, however, in the true American taste, the greatest pains were taking to diminish, and, indeed, to shut out all the beauties of the prospect; every tree in the neighbourhood of the house was felled to the ground; instead of a neat lawn, for which the ground seemed to be singularly well disposed, a wheat field was laid down in front of it; and at the bottom of the slope, at the distance of two hundred yards from the house, a town was building by the major, which, when completed, would effectually screen from the dwelling house every sight of the river and mountains. The Americans, as I before observed, seem to be totally dead to the beauties of nature, and only to admire a spot of ground as it appears to be more or less calculated to enrich the occupier by its produce.

The Genesee River takes its name from a lofty hill in the Indian territory, near to which it passes, called by the Indians Genesee, a word signifying, in their language, a grand extensive prospect.

The

The flats bordering upon the Genefee River are amongſt the richeſt lands that are to be met with in North America, to the eaſt of the Ohio. Wheat, as I told you in a former letter, will not grow upon them; and it is not found that the ſoil is impoveriſhed by the ſucceſſive crops of Indian corn and hemp that are raiſed upon them year after year. The great fertility of theſe flats is to be aſcribed to the regular annual overflowing of the Geneſee River, whoſe waters are extremely muddy, and leave no ſmall quantity of ſlime behind them before they return to their natural channel. That river empties itſelf into Lake Ontario: it is ſomewhat more than one hundred miles in length, but only navigable for the laſt forty miles of its courſe, except at the time of the inundations; and even then the navigation is not uninterrupted the whole way down to the lake, there being three conſiderable falls in the river about ten miles above its mouth: the greateſt of theſe falls is ſaid to be ninety feet in perpendicular height. The high lands in the neighbourhood of the Geneſee River are ſtony, and are not diſtinguiſhed for their fertility, but the valleys are all extremely fruitful, and abound with rich timber.

The ſummers in this part of the country are by no means ſo hot as towards the Atlantic, and the winters are moderate; it is ſeldom, indeed,

indeed, that the snow lies on the ground much longer than six or seven weeks; but notwithstanding this circumstance, and that the face of the country is so much diversified with rising grounds, yet the whole of it is dreadfully unhealthy; scarcely a family escapes the baneful effects of the fevers that rage here during the autumn season. I was informed by the inhabitants, that much fewer persons had been attacked by the fever the last season than during former years, and of these few a very small number died, the fever having proved much less malignant than it was ever known to be before. This circumstance led the inhabitants to hope, that as the country became more cleared it would become much more healthy. It is well known, indeed, that many parts of the country, which were extremely healthy while they remained covered with wood, and which also proved healthy after they had been generally cleared and settled, were very much otherwise when the trees were first cut down: this has been imputed to the vapours arising from the newly cleared lands on their being first exposed to the burning rays of the sun, and which, whilst the newly cleared spots remain surrounded by woods, there is not a sufficient circulation of air to dispel. The unhealthiness of the country at present does not deter numbers of people from coming to settle here

every

every year, and few parts of North America can boaſt of a more rapid improvement than the Geneſee country during the laſt four years.

In our way to Bath we paſſed through ſeveral ſmall towns that had been lately begun, and in theſe the houſes were comfortable and neatly built; but the greater part of thoſe of the farmers were wretched indeed; one at which we ſtopped for the night, in the courſe of our journey, had not even a chimney or window to it; a large hole at the end of the roof ſupplied the deficiency of both; the door was of ſuch a nature, alſo, as to make up in ſome meaſure for the want of a window, as it admitted light on all ſides. A heavy fall of ſnow happened to take place whilſt we were at this houſe, and as we lay ſtretched on our ſkins beſide the fire, at night, the ſnow was blown, in no ſmall quantities, through the crevices of the door, under our very ears.

At ſome of theſe houſes we got plenty of veniſon, and good butter, milk, and bread; but at others we could get nothing whatſoever to eat. At one little village, conſiſting of three or four houſes, the people told us, that they had not even ſufficient bread and milk for themſelves; and, indeed, the ſcantineſs of the meal to which we ſaw them ſitting down confirmed the truth of what they ſaid. We were under the neceſſity of walking on for nine

miles

miles beyond this village before we could get any thing to satisfy our appetites.

The fall of snow, which I have mentioned, interrupted our progress through the woods very considerably the subsequent morning; it all disappeared, however, before the next night, and in the course of the third day from that on which we left the banks of the Genesee River we reached the place of our destination.

LETTER XXXVII.

Account of Bath.—Of the Neighbourhood.— Singular Method taken to improve it.—Speculators.—Description of one, in a Letter from an American Farmer.—Conhorton Creek.—View of the Navigation from Bath downwards.—Leave Bath for Newtown.— Embark in Canoes.—Stranded in the Night. —Seek for Shelter in a neighbouring House. —Difficulty of procuring Provisions.—Resume our Voyage.—Lochartsburgh.—Description of the eastern Branch of the Susquehannah River.—French Town.—French and Americans ill suited to each other.—Wilkesbarré. —Mountains in the Neighbourhood.— Country thinly settled towards Philadelphia.—De-
scription

scription of the Wind-Gap in the Blue Mountains.—Summary Account of the Moravian Settlement at Bethlehem.—Return to Philadelphia.

Philadelphia, November.

BATH is a post town, and the principal town in the western parts of the state of New York. Though laid out only three years ago, yet it already contains about thirty houses, and is increasing very fast. Amongst the houses are several stores or shops well furnished with goods, and a tavern that would not be thought meanly of in any part of America. This town was founded by a gentleman who formerly bore the rank of captain in his Majesty's service; he has likewise been the founder of Williamsburgh and Falkner's Town; and indeed to his exertions, joined to those of a few other individuals, may be ascribed the improvement of the whole of this part of the country, best known in America by the name of the Genesee Country, or the County of the Lakes, from its being watered by that river, and a great number of small lakes.

The landed property of which this gentleman, who founded Bath, &c. has had the active management, is said to have amounted originally to no less than six millions of acres, the greater part of which belonged to an individual

dividual in England. The method he has taken to improve this property has been, by granting land in small portions and on long credits to individuals who would immediately improve it, and in larger portions and on a shorter credit to others who purchased on speculation, the lands in both cases being mortgaged for the payment of the purchase money; thus, should the money not be paid at the appointed time, he could not be a loser, as the lands were to be returned to him, and should they happen to be at all improved, as was most likely to be the case, he would be a considerable gainer even by having them returned on his hands; moreover, if a poor man, willing to settle on his land, had not money sufficient to build a house and to go on with the necessary improvements, he has at once supplied him, having had a large capital himself, with what money he wanted for that purpose, or sent his own workmen, of whom he keeps a prodigious number employed, to build a house for him, at the same time taking the man's note at three, four, or five years, for the cost of the house, &c. with interest. If the man should be unable to pay at the appointed time, the house, mortgaged like the lands, must revert to the original proprietor, and the money arising from its sale, and that of the farm adjoining, partly improved, will in all probability be be found to amount to more than what the poor man had promifed to pay for it: but a man taking up land in America in this manner, at a moderate price, cannot fail, if induftrious, of making money fufficient to pay for it, as well as for a houfe, at the appointed time.

The numbers that have been induced by thefe temptations, not to be met with elfewhere in the States, to fettle in the Genefee County, is aftonifhing; and numbers are ftill flocking to it every year, as not one third of the lands are yet difpofed of. It was currently reported in the county, as I paffed through it, that this gentleman, of whom I have been fpeaking, had, in the notes of the people to whom he had fold land payable at the end of three, or four, or five years, the immenfe fum of two millions of dollars. The original coft of the land was not more than a few pence per acre; what therefore muft be the profits!

It may readily be imagined, that the granting of land on fuch very eafy terms could not fail to draw crowds of fpeculators (a fort of gentry with which America abounds in every quarter) to this part of the country; and indeed we found, as we paffed along, that every little town and village throughout the country abounded with them, and each place, in confequence, exhibited a picture of idlenefs and
diffipation

dissipation. The following letter, supposed to come from a farmer, though somewhat ludicrous, does not give an inaccurate description of one of these young speculators, and of what is going on in this neighbourhood. It appeared in a news-paper published at Wilkesbarré, on the Susquehannah, and I give it to you verbatim, because, being written by an American, it will perhaps carry more weight with it than any thing I could say on the same subject.

" To the Printers of the Wilkesbarré Gazette.

" Gentlemen,

" It is painful to reflect, that speculation has
" raged to such a degree of late, that honest
" industry, and all the humble virtues that
" walk in her train, are discouraged and ren-
" dered unfashionable.

" It is to be lamented too, that dissipation
" is sooner introduced in new settlements than
" industry and economy.

" I have been led to these reflections by
" conversing with my son, who has just re-
" turned from the Lakes or Genesee, though
" he has neither been to the one or the other;
" —in short, he has been to Bath, the ce-
" lebrated Bath, and has returned both a spe-
" culator and a gentleman; having spent his
" money, swopped away my horse, caught the
  " fever

METHOD OF IMPROVING PROPERTY.

"fever and ague, and, what is infinitely worse, that horrid disorder which some call the terra-phobia*.

"We can hear nothing from the poor creature now (in his ravings) but of the captain and Billy—of ranges—townships—numbers—thousands—hundreds—acres—Bath—fairs—races—heats—bets—purses—silk stockings—fortunes—fevers—agues, &c. &c. &c. My son has part of a township for sale, and it is diverting enough to hear him narrate its pedigree, qualities, and situation. In fine, it lies near Bath, and the captain himself once owned, and for a long time reserved it. It cost my son but five dollars per acre; he was offered six in half a minute after his purchase; but he is positively determined to have eight, besides some precious reserves. One thing is very much in my boy's favour—he has six years credit. Another thing is still more so—he is not worth a sous, nor ever will be at this rate. Previous to his late excursion the lad worked well, and was contented at home on my farm; but now work is out of the question with him. There is no managing my boy at home; these golden dreams still beckon him back to Bath, where, as he says, no one need

---

* Our farmer does not seem to have well understood the import of this word, but we may readily guess at his meaning.

"either work or starve; where, though a man
may have the ague nine months in the year,
he may confole himfelf in fpending the other
three fafhionably at the races.

"*A Farmer.*"

"*Hanover, October* 25th, 1796.

The town of Bath ftands on a plain, furrounded on three fides by hills of a moderate height. The plain is almoft wholly divefted of its trees; but the hills are ftill uncleared, and have a very pleafing appearance from the town. At the foot of the hills runs a ftream of pure water, over a bed of gravel, which is called Conhocton Creek. There is a very confiderable fall in this creek juft above the town, which affords one of the fineft feats for mills poffible. Extenfive faw and flour mills have already been erected upon it, the principal faw in the former of which gave, when we vifited the mill, one hundred and twenty ftrokes in a minute, fufficient to cut, in the fame fpace of time, feven fquare feet, fuperficial meafure, of oak timber; yet the miller informed us, that when the water was high it would cut much fafter.

Conhocton Creek, about twenty miles below Bath, falls into Tyoga River, which, after a courfe of about thirty miles, empties itfelf into the eaftern branch of the River Sufquehannah.

During

During floods you may go down in light bateaux along the creek, Tyoga and Sufquehannah rivers, the whole way from Bath to the Chefapeak Bay, without interruption; and in the fall of the year there is generally water fufficient for canoes from Bath downwards; but owing to the great drought that prevailed through every part of the country this year, the depth of water in the creek was found infufficient to float even a canoe of the fmalleft fize. Had it been practicable, it was our intention to have proceeded from Bath by water; but finding that it was not, we once more fet off on foot, and purfued our way along the banks of the river till we came to a fmall village of eight or ten houfes, called Newtown, about thirty miles diftant from Bath. Here we found the ftream tolerably deep, and the people informed us, that excepting at one or two narrow fhoals, they were certain that in every part of it, lower down, there was fufficient water for canoes; accordingly, determined to be our own watermen, being five in number including our fervants, we purchafed a couple of canoes from two farmers, who lived on the banks of the river, and having lafhed them together, in order to render them more fteady and fafe, we put our baggage on board, and boldly embarked.

It was about three o'clock on a remarkably clear

clear though cold afternoon that we left the village, and the current being ſtrong, we hoped to be able to reach before night a tavern, ſituated, as we were told, on the banks of the river, about ſix miles below Newtown. For the firſt two miles we got on extremely well; but beyond this the river proving to be much ſhallower than we had been led to believe, we found it a matter of the utmoſt difficulty to proceed. Our canoes repeatedly ſtruck upon the ſhoals, and ſo much time was conſumed in ſetting them again free, that before we had accompliſhed more than two thirds of our voyage the day cloſed. As night advanced a very ſenſible change was obſervable in the weather; a heavy ſhower of hail came pouring down, and, involved in thick darkneſs, whilſt the moon was obſcured by a cloud, our canoes were drifted by the current, to which, being unable to ſee our way, we had conſigned them, on a bank in the middle of the river. In endeavouring to extricate ourſelves we unfortunately, owing to the darkneſs, took a wrong direction, and at the end of a few minutes found our canoes ſo firmly wedged in the gravel that it was impoſſible to move them. Nothing now remained to be done but for every one of us to jump into the water, and to put his ſhoulder to the canoes. This we accordingly did, and having previouſly un-
laſhed,

lafhed, in order to render them more manageable, we in a fhort time contrived to haul one of them into deep water; here, however, the rapidity of the current was fo great, that notwithftanding all our endeavours to the contrary, the canoe was forcibly fwept away from us, and in the attempt to hold it faft we had the misfortune to fee it nearly filled with water.

Deprived thus of one of our canoes, and of a great part of our baggage in it, which, for ought we knew, was irrecoverably loft, we determined to proceed more cautioufly with the remaining one; having returned, therefore, to the bank, we carried every thing that was in the canoe on our fhoulders to the fhore, which was about forty yards diftant; no very eafy or agreeable tafk, as the water reached up to our waifts, and the current was fo ftrong that it was with the utmoft difficulty we could keep our feet. The canoe being emptied, we brought it, as nearly as we could guefs, to the fpot where the other one had been fwept away from us, and one of the party then getting into it with a paddle, we committed it, purfuant to his defire, to the ftream, hoping that it would be carried down after the other, and that thus we fhould be able to recover both it and the things which it contained. In a few feconds the ftream carried the canoe out of our fight, for the moon fhone but faintly through the clouds, and being all of us totally unacquainted with the river, we could not but feel fome concern for the perfonal fafety of our companion. Before many minutes, however, were elapfed, we had the fatisfaction of hearing his voice at a diftance, and having made the beft of our way along the fhore to the fpot from whence the found proceeded, we had the fatisfaction to find that he had been carried in fafety clofe befide the canoe which had been loft, we were not a little pleafed alfo at finding our portmanteaus at the bottom of the canoe, though well foaked in water; but fuch of our clothes as we had taken off preparatory to going into the water, together with feveral light articles, were all loft.

It froze fo very hard now, that in a few minutes our portmanteaus, and fuch of our garments as had been wetted, were covered with a coat of ice, and our limbs were quite benumbed, in confequence of our having waded fo often through the river. Defirous, however, as we were to get to a houfe, we determined, in the firft inftance, to difpofe of our baggage in a fafe place, left it might be pillaged. A deep hollow that appeared under fome fallen trees feemed well adapted for the purpofe, and having ftowed it there, and covered it with leaves, we advanced forward. There were no traces whatfoever of a path in the

the woods where we landed, and for upwards of a mile we had to force our way through the bufhes along the banks of the river; but at the end of that diftance, we hit upon one, which in a fhort time brought us to a miferable little log houfe. At this houfe no accommodation whatfoever was to be had, but we were told, that if we followed the path through the woods for about a mile farther, we fhould come to a waggon road, upon which we fhould find another houfe, where probably we might gain admittance. We reached this houfe according to the directions we had received; we readily gained admittance into it, and the blaze of an immenfe wood fire, piled half way up the chimney, foon made us amends for what we had fuffered from the inclemency of the weather. The coldnefs of the air, together with the fatigue which we had gone through in the courfe of the day, had by this time given a keen edge to our appetites; no fooner therefore had we warmed ourfelves than we began to make enquiries about what we could get to fatisfy the calls of hunger; but had we afked for a fheep or an ox for fupper at an inn in England, the man of the houfe could not, I verily believe, have been more amazed than was our American landlord at thefe enquiries: " The women were in bed"—" He knew not where " to find the keys"—" He did not believe there "was any thing in the pantry"—"Provisions were very scarce in the country"—"If he gave us any there would not be enough for the family in the morning"—Such were his answers to us. However we plied him so closely, and gave him such a pitiable description of our sufferings, that at length he was moved; the keys were found, the pantry opened, and to satisfy the hunger of five hungry young men, two little flour cakes, scarcely as big as a man's hand each, and about a pint and a half of milk, were brought forth. He vowed he could give us nothing more; his wife would never pardon him if he did not leave enough for their breakfasts in the morning; obliged therefore to remain satisfied, we eat our little pittance, and then laid ourselves down to rest on our skins, which we had brought with us on our shoulders.

In the morning we found that the man had really made an accurate report of the state of his pantry. There was barely enough in it for the family, and unable to get a single morsel to eat, we set out for the little house where we had first stopped the preceding night, which was the only one within two or three miles, there hoping to find the inhabitants better provided for: not a bit of bread however was to be had here; but the woman of the house told us, that she had some Indian corn meal, and

and that if we could wait for an hour or two she would bake a loaf for us. This was moſt grateful intelligence: we only begged of her to make it large enough, and then ſet off to ſearch in the interim for our canoes and baggage. At ſeveral other places, in going down the Suſquehannah, we afterwards found an equal ſcarcity of proviſions with what we did in this neighbourhood. One morning in particular, after having proceeded for about four or five miles in our canoe, we ſtopped to breakfaſt; but nothing eatable was there to be had at the firſt houſe we went to, except a few potatoes that were roaſting before the fire. The people very cheerfully gave us two or three, and told us at the ſame time, that if we went to ſome houſes at the oppoſite ſide of the river we ſhold moſt probably find better fare: we did ſo; but here the inhabitants were ſtill more deſtitute. On aſking them where we ſhould be likely to get any thing to eat, an old woman anſwered, that if we went to a village about four miles lower down the river, we ſhould find a houſe, ſhe believed, where " *they " did keep victuals*," an expreſſion ſo remarkable that I could not help noting it down immediately. We reached this houſe, and finding it well ſtocked with proviſions of every kind, took care to provide ourſelves, not only with what we wanted for immediate uſe, but alſo

also with what we might want on a future occasion, in case we came to any place equally destitute of provisions as those which we had before stopped at; a precaution that was far from proving unnecessary.

But to return. We found our canoes and baggage just as we had left them, and having embarked once more, we made the best of our way down to the house where we had bespoke breakfast, which stood on the banks of the river. The people here were extremely civil; they assisted us in making fresh paddles in lieu of those which we had lost the night before; and for the trifle which we gave them above what they asked us for our breakfasts they were very thankful, a most unusual circumstance in the United States.

After breakfast we pursued our way for about seven miles down the river, but in the course of this distance we were obliged to get into the water more than a dozen different times, I believe, to drag the canoes over the shoals; in short, by the time we arrived at a house in the afternoon, we were so completely disgusted with our water conveyance, that had we not been able to procure two men, as we did in the neighbourhood, to conduct our canoes to the mouth of Tyoga River, where there was reason to imagine that the water would be found deeper, we should certainly have

have left them behind us. The men set out at an early hour in the morning, and we proceeded some time afterwards on foot along the banks, but so difficult was the navigation, that we reached Tyoga Point or Lochartzburg, a small town built at the mouth of the river, several hours before them.

On arriving at this place, we heard to our disappointment, that the Susquehannah, although generally at this season of the year navigable for boats drawing four feet water, was now nearly as low as the Tyoga River, so that in many places, particularly at the rapids, there was scarcely sufficient water to float a canoe over the sharp rocks with which the bed of the river abounds; in fine, we were informed that the channel was now intricate and dangerous, and that no person unacquainted with the river could attempt to proceed down it without great risk; we found no difficulty, however, in hiring from amongst the watermen accustomed to ply on the river, a man that was perfectly well acquainted with it; and having exchanged our two canoes, pursuant to his advice, for one of a very large size, capable of holding us all conveniently, we renewed our voyage.

From Lochartzburgh to Wilkesbarré, or Wyoming, situated on the south-east side of the Susquehannah, the distance is about ninety miles,

miles, and when the river is full, and the current of courfe ftrong, as is ufually the cafe in the fall and fpring of the year, you may go down the whole of this diftance in one day; but owing to the lownefs of the water we were no lefs than four days performing the voyage, though we made the utmoft expedition poffible. In many parts of the river, indeed, we found the current very rapid; at the Falls of Wyalufing, for inftance, we were carried down three or four miles in about a quarter of an hour; but in other places, where the river was deep, fcarcely any current was perceptible in it, and we were obliged to work our way with paddles. The bed of the river abounds with rock and gravel, and the water is fo tranfparent, that in many parts, where it muft have been at leaft twenty feet deep, the fmalleft pebble was diftinguifhable at the bottom. The width of the river varies from fifty to three hundred yards, and fcarcely any ftream in America has a more irregular courfe; in fome places it runs in a direction diametrically oppofite to what it does in others. The country through which this (the eaftern) branch of the Sufquehannah paffes, is extremely uneven and rugged; indeed, from Lochartzburgh till within a fhort diftance of Wilkefbarré, it is bounded the entire way by fteep mountains either on the one fide or the other. The mountains

mountains are never to be met with at both sides of the same part of the river, except it be at places where the river takes a very sudden bend; but wherever you perceive a range of mountains on one side, you are sure to find an extensive plain on the opposite one; scarcely in any part do the mountains extend for more than one mile together on the same side of the river, and in many instances, during the course of one mile, you will perceive more than a dozen different changes of the mountains from one side to the other. It may readily be imagined, from this description of the eastern branch of the Susquehannah, that the scenery along it must be very fine; and, indeed, I think there is no river in America that abounds with such a variety and number of picturesque views. At every bend the prospect varies, and there is scarcely a spot between Lochartzburg and Wilkesbarré where the painter would not find a subject well worthy of his pencil. The mountains, covered with bold rocks and woods, afford the finest foreground imaginable; the plains, adorned with cultivated fields and patches of wood, and watered by the noble river, of which you catch a glimpse here and there, fill up the middle part of the landscape; and the blue hills, peeping up at a distance, terminate the view in the most pleasing manner.

The

The country bordering upon the Sufquehannah abounds with deer, and as we paffed down we met with numberlefs parties of the country people engaged in driving thefe animals. The deer, on being purfued in the neighbouring country, immediately make for the river, where men being concealed in bufhes placed on the ftrand, at the part to which it is expected they will come down, take the opportunity of fhooting them as foon as they enter the water. Should the deer not happen to come near thefe ambufhes, the hunters then follow them in canoes: it feldom happens that they efcape after having once taken to the water.

Very fine fifh are found in every part of the Sufquehannah, and the river is much frequented by wild fowl, particularly by the canvafs back duck.

The whole way between Lochartzburg and Wilkefbarré are fettlements on each fide of the river, at no great diftance from each other; there are alfo feveral fmall towns on the banks of the river. The principal one is French Town, fituated within a fhort diftance of the Falls of Wyalufing, on the weftern fide of the river. This town was laid out at the expence of feveral philanthropic perfons in Pennfylvania, who entered into a fubfcription for the purpofe, as a place of retreat for the unfortunate

nate French emigrants who fled to America. The town contains about fifty log houſes; and for the uſe of the inhabitants a conſiderable track of land has been purchaſed adjoining to it, which has been divided into farms. The French ſettled here ſeem, however, to have no great inclination or ability to cultivate the earth, and the greater part of them have let their lands at a ſmall yearly rent to Americans, and amuſe themſelves with driving deer, fiſhing, and fowling; they live entirely to themſelves; they hate the Americans, and the Americans in the neighbourhood hate, and accuſe them of being an idle diſſipated ſet. The manners of the two people are ſo very different that it is impoſſible they ſhould ever agree.

Wilkeſbarré, formerly Wyoming, is the chief town of Luzerne county. It is ſituated on a plain, bounded on one ſide by the Suſquehannah, and on the other by a range of mountains, and contains about one hundred and fifty wooden dwelling houſes, a church, court houſe, and gaol. It was here that the dreadful maſſacre was committed, during the American war, by the Indians under the command of colonel Butler, which is recorded in' moſt of the hiſtories of the war, and which will for ever remain a blot on the Engliſh annals. Several of the houſes in which the unfortunate victims

victims retired to defend themselves, on being refused all quarter, are still standing, perforated in every part with balls; the remains of others that were set on fire are also still to be seen, and the inhabitants will on no account suffer them to be repaired. The Americans are equally tenacious of the ruins in the neighbourhood of Philadelphia.

It was our intention at first to have proceeded down the river from hence as far as Sunburg, or Harrisburgh; but the weather being now so cold as to render a water conveyance, especially a canoe, where you are always obliged to sit very still, extremely disagreeable, we determined to cross the Blue Mountains to Bethlehem in Pennsylvania, situated about sixty-five miles to the south-east of Wilkesbarré; we accordingly hired horses, as we had done on a former occasion, to carry our baggage, and proceeded ourselves on foot. We set out in the afternoon, the day after that on which we terminated our voyage, and before evening crossed the ridge of mountains which bounds the plain of Wilkesbarré. These mountains, which are extremely rugged and stony, abound with iron ore and coal; for the manufacture of the former several forges have been established, but no use is made of the coal, there being plenty of wood as yet in the country, which is esteemed much more agreeable fuel.

fuel. From the top of them you have a very grand view of the plain below, on which stands the town of Wilkesbarré, and of the river Susquehannah, which may be traced above the town, winding amidst the hills for a great number of miles.

The country beyond the mountains is extremely rough, and but very thinly settled, of course still much wooded. The people, at the few houses scattered through it, appeared to live much better than the inhabitants of any other part of the States which I before passed through. At every house where we stopped we found abundance of good bread, butter, tea, coffee, chocolate, and venison; and indeed we fared sumptuously here, in comparison to what we had done for many weeks preceding.

The woods in many parts of this country consisted almost wholly of hemlock trees, which are of the pine species, and grow only on poor ground. Many of them were of an unusually large size, and their tops so closely matted together, that after having entered into the depth of the woods you could see the sky in but very few places. The brush wood under these trees, different from what I ever saw elsewhere, consisted for the most part of the oleander and of the kalmia laurel, whose deep green served to render the gloom of the woods still more solemn; indeed they seemed completely

pletely to answer the description given by the poets of the sacred groves; and it were impossible to enter them without being struck with awe.

About twenty miles before you come to Bethlehem, in going thither from Wilkesbarré, you cross the ridge of Blue Mountains at what is called the Wind Gap; how it received that name I never could learn. This gap is nearly a mile wide, and it exhibits a tremendously wild and rugged scene. The road does not run at the bottom of the gap, but along the edge of the south mountain, about two thirds of the way up. Above you on the right, nothing is to be seen but broken rocks and trees, and on the left you look down a steep precipice. The rocks at the bottom of the precipice have every appearance, it is said (for we did not descend into it) of having been washed by water for ages; and from hence it has been conjectured that this must have been the original channel of the River Delaware, which now passes through the ridge, at a place about fifteen miles to the north west. Whether this were the case or not it is impossible to determine at this day; but it is certain, from the appearance of the country on each side of the Delaware, that a great change has taken place in this quarter, in consequence of some vast inundation.

On

Moravian settlement.

Beaufort.

On the Atlantic fide of the mountains the country is much lefs rugged than on the oppofite one, and it is more cleared and much more thickly fettled: the inhabitants are for the moft part of German extraction.

Bethlehem is the principal fettlement, in North America, of the Moravians, or United Brethren. It is moft agreeably fituated on a rifing ground, bounded on one fide by the river Leheigh, which falls into the Delaware, and on the other by a creek, which has a very rapid current, and affords excellent feats for a great number of mills. The town is regularly laid out, and contains about eighty ftrong built ftone dwelling houfes and a large church. Three of the dwelling houfes are very fpacious buildings, and are appropriated refpectively to the accommodation of the unmarried young men of the fociety, of the unmarried females, and of the widows. In thefe houfes different manufactures are carried on, and the inmates of each are fubject to a difcipline approaching fomewhat to that of a monaftic inftitution. They eat together in a refectory; they fleep in dormitories; they attend morning and evening prayers in the chapel of the houfe; they work for a certain number of hours in the day; and they have ftated intervals allotted to them for recreation. They are not fubjected, by the rules of the fociety, to perpetual confinement;

but they seldom, notwithstanding, go beyond the bounds of their walks and gardens, except it be occasionally to visit their friends in the town.

The Moravians, though they do not enjoin celibacy, yet think it highly meritorious, and the young persons of different sexes have but very little intercourse with each other; they never enter each other's houses, and at church they are obliged to sit separate; it is only in consequence of his having seen her at a distance, perhaps, that a batchelor is induced to propose for a young woman in marriage, and he is not permitted to offer his proposals in person to the object of his choice, but merely through the medium of the superintendant of the female house. If from the report of the elders and wardens of the society it appears to the superintendant that he is able to maintain a wife, she then acquaints her protegée with the offer, and should she consent, they are married immediately, but if she do not, the superintendant selects another female from the house, whom she imagines would be suitable to the young man, and on his approval of her they are as quickly married. Hasty as these marriages are, they are never known to be attended with unhappiness; for being taught from their earliest infancy to keep those passions under controul, which occasion so much mischief amongst the

mass

mass of mankind; being inured to regular habits of industry, and to a quiet sober life ; and being in their peaceable and retired settlements out of the reach of those temptations which persons are exposed to who launch forth into the busy world, and who mingle with the multitude, the parties meet with nought through life to interrupt their domestic repose.

Attached to the young men's and to the young women's houses there are boarding schools for boys and girls, under the direction of proper teachers, which are also inspected by the elders and wardens of the society. These schools are in great repute, and not only the children of Moravians are sent to them, but also those of many genteel persons of a different persuasion, resident in Philadelphia, New York, and other towns in the neighbouring States. The boys are instructed in the Latin, German, French, and English languages; arithmetic, music, drawing, &c.: the girls are likewise instructed in these different languages and sciences, and, in short, in every thing that is usually taught at a female boarding school, except dancing. When of a sufficient age to provide for themselves, the young women of the society are admitted into the house destined for their accommodation, where embroidery, fine needle-work, carding, spinning, knitting, &c. &c. and other works suitable to females, are carried on. A separate room is allotted for every different business, and a female, somewhat older than the rest, presides in it, to inspect the work, and preserve regularity. Persons are appointed to dispose of the several articles manufactured in the house, and the money which they produce is distributed amongst the individuals engaged in manufacturing them, who, after paying a certain sum towards the maintenance of the house, and a certain sum besides into the public fund of the society, are allowed to keep the remainder for themselves.

After the boys have finished their school education, they are apprenticed to the business which accords most with their inclination. Should this be a business or trade that is carried on in the young men's house, they at once go there to learn it, but if at the house of an individual in the town, they only board and lodge at the young men's house. If they are inclined to agricultural pursuits, they are then put under the care of one of the farmers of the society. The young men subscribe to the support of their house, and to the public fund, just as the young women do; the widows do the same; and every individual in the town likewise contributes a small sum weekly to the general fund of the society.

Situated upon the creek, which skirts the town, there is a flour mill, a saw mill, an oil mill,

mill, a fulling mill, a mill for grinding bark and dye stuff, a tan yard, a currier's yard; and on the Leleigh River an extensive brewery, at which very good malt liquor is manufactured. These mills, &c. belong to the society at large, and the profits arising from them, the persons severally employed in conducting them being first handsomely rewarded for their services, are paid into the public fund. The lands for some miles round the town, which are highly improved, likewise belong to the society, as does also the tavern, and the profits arising from them are disposed of in the same manner as those arising from the mills, the persons employed in managing the farms, and attending to the tavern, being nothing more than stewards or agents of the society. The fund thus raised is employed in relieving the distressed brethren of the society in other parts of the world, in forming new settlements, and in defraying the expence of the missions for the purpose of propagating the gospel amongst the heathens.

The tavern at Bethlehem is very commodious, and it is the neatest and best conducted one, without exception, that I ever met with in any part of America. Having communicated to the landlord, on arriving at it, our wish to see the town and public buildings, he immediately dispatched a messenger for one of the elders, and in less than a quarter of an hour, brother Thomas, a lively fresh coloured little man, of about fifty years of age, entered the room: he was dressed in a plain blue coat and waistcoat, brown corderoy breeches, and a large round hat; there was goodness and innocence in his looks, and his manners were so open and unconstrained, that it was impossible not to become familiar with him at once. When we were ready to sally forth, he placed himself between two of us, and leaning on our arms, and chatting without ceremony, he conducted us first to the young women's house. Here we were shewn into a neat parlour, whilst brother Thomas went to ask permission for us to see the house. In a few minutes the superintendant herself came; brother Thomas introduced her to us, and accompanied by them both we visited the different apartments.

The house is extensive, and the passages and stair-cases are commodious and airy, but the work rooms are small, and to such a pitch were they heated by stoves, that on entering into them at first we could scarcely breathe. The stoves, which they use, are built in the German style. The fire is inclosed in a large box or case formed of glazed tiles, and the warm air is thence conducted, through flues, into similar large cases placed in different parts of the room, by which means every part is rendered equally warm. About a dozen females

males or more, nearly of the same age, were seated at work in each apartment. The entrance of strangers did not interrupt them in the least; they went on with their work, and except the inspectress, who never failed politely to rise and speak to us, they did not even seem to take any notice of our being in the room.

The dress of the sisterhood, though not quite uniform, is very nearly so. They wear plain calico, linen, or stuff gowns, with aprons, and close tight linen caps, made with a peak in front, and tied under the chin with a piece of riband. Pink ribands are said to be worn as a badge by those who are inclined to marry; however, I observed that all the unmarried women wore them, not excepting those whose age and features seemed to have excluded them from every chance of becoming the votaries of Hymen.

The dormitory of the female house is a very spacious apartment in the upper story, which is aired by a large ventilator in the ceiling. It contains about fifty boarded beds without testers, each calculated to hold one person. They sleep here during winter time in the German style, between two feather beds, to which the sheets and blankets are stitched fast; in summer time the heat is too great here to admit even of a single blanket.

After

After having gone through the different apartments of the female house, we were conducted by the superintendant into a sort of shop, where different little articles of fancy work, manufactured by the sisterhood, are laid out to the best advantage. It is always expected that strangers visiting the house will lay out some trifling sum here; and this is the only reward which any member of the society expects for the trouble of conducting a stranger throughout every part of the town.

The house of the sisterhood exhibits a picture of the utmost neatness and regularity, as do likewise the young men's and the widows houses; and indeed the same may be said of every private house throughout the town. The mills, brewery, &c. which are built on the most approved plans, are also kept in the very neatest order.

Brother Thomas, after having shewn us the different public buildings and works, next introduced us into the houses of several of the married men, that were most distinguished for their ingenuity, and in some of them, particularly at the house of a cabinet maker, we were entertained with very curious pieces of workmanship. This cabinet maker brought us a book of Indian ink and tinted drawings, his own performances, which would have been a credit to a person in his situation in any part of the world.

The

The manufactures in general carried on at Bethlehem confift of woollen and linen cloths, hats, cotton and worfted caps and ftockings, gloves, fhoes, carpenters, cabinet makers, and turners work, clocks, and a few other articles of hardware, &c. &c.

The church is a plain building of ftone, adorned with pictures from facred hiftory. It is furnifhed with a tolerable organ, as likewife are the chapels of the young men's and young women's houfes; they accompany their hymns, befides, with violoncellos, violins, flutes, &c. The whole fociety attends the church on a Sunday, and when any one of the fociety dies, all the remaining members attend his funeral, which is conducted with great folemnity, though with little pomp: they never go into mourning for their departed friends.

Every houfe in the town is fupplied with an abundance of excellent water from a fpring, which is forced through pipes by means of an hydraulic machine worked by water, and which is fituated on the banks of the creek. Some of the houfes are fupplied with water in every room. The machine is very fimple, and would eafily raife the water of the fpring, if neceffary, feveral hundred feet.

The fpring from whence the houfes are fupplied with water ftands nearly in the center of the town, and over it, a large ftone houfe with

very

very thick walls, is erected. Houses like this are very common in America; they are called spring houses, and are built for the purpose of preserving meat, milk, butter, &c. during the heats of summer. This spring house in Bethlehem is common to the whole town; a shelf or board in it is allotted to each family, and though there is no watch placed over it, and the door be only secured by a latch, yet every person is certain of finding, when he comes for it, his plate of butter or bowl of milk, &c. exactly in the same state as when he put it in.

The Moravians study to render their conduct strictly conformable to the principles of the Christian religion; but very different notions, notwithstanding, are, and, no doubt, will be entertained respecting some of their tenets. Every unprejudiced person, however, that has visited their settlements must acknowledge, that their moral conduct is truly excellent, and is such as would, if generally adopted, make men happy in the extreme. They live together like members of one large family; the most perfect harmony subsists between them, and they seem to have but one wish at heart, the propagation of the gospel, and the good of mankind. They are in general of a grave turn of mind; but nothing of that stiffness, or of that affected singularity, or pride, as I will call it, it, prevalent amongst the Quakers, is observable in their manners. Wherever their society has extended itself in America, the most happy consequences have resulted from it; good order and regularity have become conspicuous in the behaviour of the people of the neighbourhood, and arts and manufactures have been introduced into the country.

As the whole of the plot of ground, on which Bethlehem stands; belongs to the society, as well as the lands for a considerable way round the town, the Moravians here are not liable to be troubled by intruders, but any person that will conform to their line of conduct will be received into their society with readiness and cordiality. They appeared to take the greatest delight in shewing us their town, and every thing belonging to it, and at parting lamented much that we could not stay longer with them, to see still more of the manners and habits of the society.

They do not seem desirous of adding to the number of houses in Bethlehem; but whenever there is an increase of people, they send them off to another part of the country, there to form a new settlement. Since Bethlehem was founded, they have established two other towns in Pennsylvania, Nazareth and Letitz. The former of these stands at the distance of about ten miles from Bethlehem, and in coming

ing down from the Blue Mountains you pafs through it; it is about half the fize of Bethlehem, and built much on the fame plan. Letitz is fituated at a diftance of about ten miles from Lancafter.

The country for many miles round Bethlehem is moft pleafingly diverfified with rifing grounds; the foil is rich, and better cultivated than any part of America I before faw. Until within a few years paft this neighbourhood has been diftinguifhed for the falubrity of its climate, but fevers, chiefly bilious and intermittent, have increafed to a very great degree of late, and, indeed, not only here, but in many other parts of Pennfylvania, which have been long fettled. During the laft autumn, more people fuffered from ficknefs in the well cultivated parts of the country than had ever been remembered. Various reafons have been affigned for this increafe of fevers in Pennfylvania, but it appears moft probably to be owing to the unequal quantities of rain that have fallen of late years, and to the unprecedented mildnefs of the winters.

Bethlehem is vifited during fummer time by great numbers of people from the neighbouring large towns, who are led thither by curiofity or pleafure; and regularly, twice a week throughout the year, a public ftage waggon runs between it and Philadelphia. We
engaged

engaged this carriage to ourselves, and early on the second day from that on which we quitted Bethlehem, reached the capital, after an absence of, somewhat more than, five months.

LETTER XXXVIII.

Leave Philadelphia.—Arrive at New York.— Visit Long Island.—Dreadful havoc by the Yellow Fever.—Dutch Inhabitants suspicious of Strangers.—Excellent Farmers.—Number of Inhabitants.—Culture of Corn.—Immense Quantities of Grouse and Deer.—Laws to protect them.—Increase of the same.—Decrease of Beavers.—New York agreeable to Strangers.—Conclusion.

MY DEAR SIR,   New York, January 1797.

AFTER having remained a few days at Philadelphia, in order to arrange some matters preparatory to my taking a final leave of that city, I set out once more for New York. The month of December had now arrived; considerable quantities of snow had fallen; and the keen winds from the northwest had already spread a thick crust of ice

over

over the Delaware, whose majestic stream is always the last in this part of the country to feel the chilly touch of the hand of winter. The ice however, was not yet strong enough to sustain the weight of a stage carriage; neither was it very readily to be broken ; so that when we reached the falls of the river, where it is usual to cross in going from Philadelphia to New York, we had to remain for upwards of two hours, shivering before the bitter blasts, until a passage was opened for the boat, which was to convey us and our vehicle to the opposite side. The crossing of the Delaware at this place with a wheel carriage, even when the river is frozen over and the ice sufficiently thick to bear, is generally a matter of considerable inconvenience and trouble to travellers, owing to the large irregular masses of ice formed there, when the frost first sets in, by the impetuosity of the current, which breaking away the slender flakes of ice from the edges of the banks, gradually drifts them up in layers over each other ; it is only at this rugged part, that a wheel carriage can safely pass down the banks of the river.

When the ground is covered with snow, a sleigh or sledge is by far the most commodious sort of carriage to travel in, as neither it nor the passengers it contains are liable to receive any injury whatsoever from an overturn, and
as

as, added to this, you may proceed much fafter and eafier in it than in a carriage on wheels; having faid then that there was fnow on the ground, it will perhaps be a fubject of wonder to you, that we had not one of thefe fafe and agreeable carriages to take us to New York; if fo, I muft inform you, that no experienced traveller in the middle ftates fets out on a long journey in a fleigh at the commencement of winter, as unexpected thaws at this period now take place very commonly, and fo rapid are they, that in the courfe of one morning the fnow fometimes entirely difappears; a ferious object of confideration in this country, where, if you happen to be left in the lurch with your fleigh, other carriages are not to be had at a moment's warning. In the prefent in- ftance, notwithftanding the intenfe feverity of the cold, and the appearances there were of its long continuance, yet I had not been eight and forty hours at New York when every veftige of froft was gone, and the air became as mild as in the month of September.

This fudden change in the weather afforded me an opportunity of feeing, to much greater advantage than might have been expected at this feafon of the year, parts of New York and Long Iflands, which the fhortnefs of my ftay in this neighbourhood had not permitted me to vifit in the fummer. After leaving the im- mediate

mediate vicinage of the city, which ftands at the fouthern extremity of the former of thefe two iflands, but little is to be met with that deferves attention; the foil, indeed, is fertile, and the face of the country is not unpleafingly diverfified with rifing grounds; but there is nothing grand in any of the views which it affords, nor did I obferve one of the numerous feats, with which it is overfpread, that was diftinguifhed either for its elegant neatnefs or the delightfulnefs of its fituation; none of them will bear any comparifon with the charming little villas which adorn the banks of the Schuylkill near Philadelphia.

On Long Ifland much more will be found, in a picturefque point of view, to intereft the traveller. On the weftern fide, in particular, bordering upon the Narrows, or that contracted channel between the iflands, through which veffels pafs in failing to New York from the Atlantic, the country is really romantic. The ground here is very much broken, and numberlefs large maffes of wood ftill remain ftanding, through the viftas in which you occafionally catch the moft delightful profpects of the diftant hills on Staten Ifland and the New Jerfey fhore, and of the water, which is conftantly enlivened by veffels failing to and fro.

To an inhabitant of one of the large towns

on the coaft of America, a country houfe is not merely defirable as a place of retirement from noife and buftle, where the owner may indulge his fancy in the contemplation of rural fcenes, at a feafon when nature is attired in her moft pleafing garb, but alfo as a fafe retreat from the dreadful maladies which of late years have never failed to rage with more or lefs virulence in thefe places during certain months. When at Philadelphia the yellow fever committed fuch dreadful havoc, fparing neither the rich nor the poor, the young nor the aged, who had the confidence to remain in the city, or were unable to quit it, fcarcely a fingle inftance occurred of any one of thofe falling a victim to its baneful influence, who lived but one mile removed from town, where was a free circulation of air, and who at the fame time ftudioufly avoided all communication with the fick, or with thofe who had vifited them; every perfon therefore at Philadelphia, New York, Baltimore, &c. who is fufficiently wealthy to afford it, has his country habitation in the neighbourhood of thefe refpective places, to which he may retire in the hot unhealthy feafon of the year; but this delightful part of Long Ifland, of which I have been fpeaking, though it affords fuch a number of charming fituations for little villas, is unfortunately too far removed from New York to be a convenient place of retreat to men so deeply engaged in commercial pursuits as are the greater number of the inhabitants of that city, and it remains almost destitute of houses; whilst another part of the island, more conveniently situated, is crowded with them, although the face of the country is here flat and sandy, devoid of trees, and wholly uninteresting.

The permanent residents on Long Island are chiefly of Dutch extraction, and they seem to have inherited all the coldness, reserve, and covetousness of their ancestors. It is a common saying in New York, that a Long Island man will conceal himself in his house on the approach of a stranger; and really the numberless instances of shyness I met with in the inhabitants seemed to argue, that there was some truth in the remark. If you do but ask any simple question relative to the neighbouring country, they will eye you with suspicion, and evidently strive to disengage themselves from you; widely different from the Anglo-Americans, whose inquisitiveness in similar circumstances would lead them to a thousand impertinent and troublesome enquiries, in order to discover what your business was in that place, and how they could possibly take any advantage of it. These Dutchmen are in general very excellent farmers; and several of them

them have very extenfive tracks of land under cultivation, for the produce of which there is a convenient and ready market at New York. Amongft them are to be found many very wealthy men; but except a few individuals, they live in a mean, penurious, and moft uncomfortable manner. The population of the ifland is eftimated at about thirty-feven thoufand fouls, of which number near five thoufand are flaves. It is the weftern part of the ifland which is the beft inhabited; a circumftance to be afcribed, not fo much to the fertility of the foil as its contiguity to the city of New York. Here are feveral confiderable towns, as, Flatbufh, Jamaica, Brooklynn, Flufhing, Utrecht; the three firft-mentioned of which contain each upwards of one hundred houfes. Brooklynn, the largeft of them, is fituated juft oppofite to New York, on the bank of the Eaft River, and forms an agreeable object from the city.

The foil of Long Ifland is well adapted to the culture of fmall grain and Indian corn; and the northern part, which is hilly, is faid to be peculiarly favourable to the production of fruit. The celebrated Newtown pippin, though now to be met with in almoft every part of the ftate of New York, and good in its kind, is yet fuppofed by many perfons to attain a higher flavour here than in any other part of America.

Of the peculiar foil of the plains that are fituated towards the center of this ifland, I have before had occafion to fpeak, when defcribing thofe in the weftern parts of the ftate of New York. One plain here, fomewhat different from the reft, is profufely covered with ftunted oaks and pines; but no grain will grow upon it, though it has been cleared, and experiments have been made for that purpofe in many different places. This one goes under the appellation of Brufhy Plain. Immenfe quantities of groufe and deer are found amidft the brufhwood, with which it is covered, and which is fo well calculated to afford fhelter to thefe animals. Laws have been paffed, not long fince, to prevent the wanton deftruction of the deer; in confequence of which they are beginning to increafe moft rapidly, notwithftanding fuch great numbers are annually killed, as well for the New York market, as for the fupport of the inhabitants of the ifland; indeed it is found that they are now increafing in moft of the fettled parts of the ftates of New York, where there is fufficient wood to harbour them; whereas in the Indian territories, the deer, as well as moft other wild animals, are becoming fcarcer every year, notwithftanding that the number of Indian hunters is alfo decreafing; but thefe people purfue the fame deftructive fyftem of hunting,

formerly

formerly practifed on Long Ifland, killing every animal they meet, whether young or full grown. Notwithftanding the ftrong injunctions laid upon them by the Canadian traders, to fpare fome few beavers at each dam, in order to perpetuate the breed, they ftill continue to kill thefe animals wherever they find them, fo that they are now entirely banifhed from places which ufed to abound with, and which are ftill in a ftate to harbour them, being far removed from the cultivated parts of the country. An annual deficiency of fifteen thoufand has been obferved in the number of beaver fkins brought down to Montreal, for the laft few years.

From Long Ifland I returned to this city; which the hofpitality and friendly civilities I have experienced, in common with other ftrangers, from its inhabitants, induce me to rank as the moft agreeable place I have vifited in the United States: nor am I fingular in this opinion, there being fcarcely any traveller I have converfed with, but what gives it the fame preference. Whilft I continue in America it fhall be my place of refidence: but my thoughts are folely bent upon returning to my native land, now dearer to me than ever; and provided that the ice, which threatens at prefent to block up the harbour, does not cut off our communication with the Atlantic, I fhall
speedily

speedily take my departure from this Continent, well pleased at having seen as much of it as I have done; but I shall leave it without a sigh, and without entertaining the slightest wish to revisit it.

FINIS.

www.ingramcontent.com/pod-product-compliance
Lightning Source LLC
Chambersburg PA
CBHW030426300426
44112CB00009B/868